Ontology Alignment
Bridging the Semantic Gap

SEMANTIC WEB AND BEYOND
Computing for Human Experience

Series Editors:

Ramesh Jain
University of California, Irvine
http://ngs.ics.uci.edu/

Amit Sheth
University of Georgia
http://lsdis.cs.uga.edu/~amit

As computing becomes ubiquitous and pervasive, computing is increasingly becoming an extension of human, modifying or enhancing human experience. Today's car reacts to human perception of danger with a series of computers participating in how to handle the vehicle for human command and environmental conditions. Proliferating sensors help with observations, decision making as well as sensory modifications. The emergent semantic web will lead to machine understanding of data and help exploit heterogeneous, multi-source digital media. Emerging applications in situation monitoring and entertainment applications are resulting in development of experiential environments.

SEMANTIC WEB AND BEYOND
Computing for Human Experience
addresses the following goals:

➢ brings together forward looking research and technology that will shape our world more intimately than ever before as computing becomes an extension of human experience;
➢ covers all aspects of computing that is very closely tied to human perception, understanding and experience;
➢ brings together computing that deal with semantics, perception and experience;
➢ serves as the platform for exchange of both practical technologies and far reaching research.

Additional information about this series can be obtained from
http://www.springer.com

Ontology Alignment
Bridging the Semantic Gap

by

Marc Ehrig
University of Karlsruhe
Germany

Springer

Marc Ehrig
University of Karlsruhe
76139 Karlsruhe
Germany

Ontology Alignment: Bridging the Semantic Gap
by Marc Ehrig

ISBN 978-1-4419-4104-6

e-ISBN-10: 0-387-36501-X
e-ISBN-13: 978-0-387-36501-5

Printed on acid-free paper.

Dissertation, genehmigt von der Fakultät für Wirtschaftswissenschaften der Universität Fridericiana zu Karlsruhe, 2005. Referent: Prof. Dr. Rudi Studer, Korreferenten: Prof. Dr. Kuno Egle, Dr. (habil) Jérôme Euzenat

9 8 7 6 5 4 3 2 1

springer.com

Contents

Part III Implementation and Application

Part IV Towards Next Generation Semantic Alignment

Part V Appendix

List of Figures

List of Tables

Preface

In today's knowledge society, a large number of information systems use many different individual schemas to represent data. Ontologies are one promising approach for representing knowledge in a formal way. Many such ontologies have been developed in recent years. Semantically linking these ontologies is a necessary precondition to establish interoperability between agents or services, or simply humans working with them. Consequently, ontology alignment becomes a central issue, when building a world-wide Semantic Web. Integrating data per se is a billion dollar industry. As one can easily imagine, this cannot be done manually beyond a certain complexity, size, or number of, here, ontologies. Automatic or at least semi-automatic techniques have to be developed to reduce the burden of manual creation and maintenance of alignments.

The purpose of this book is to foster understanding in new semantic technologies, data integration, and the interaction between the two fields. In this application-driven work, the reader is presented a methodology and advice for a concrete tool for aligning ontologies. This is going to be done on theoretical and practical level for both research-focused audiences and developers. Goal is not to align ontologies by only integrating the syntax, but actually bringing together entities which have the same meaning, thus bridging the semantic gap.

The book begins with a short motivation, followed by a thorough investigation of the foundations including up-to-date related work on ontology alignment and application scenarios with their respective requirements. The six-step ontology alignment process consists of determining relevant features of individual entities, selection of promising alignment candidates, similarity assessment and aggregation, interpretation of the similarities for alignment, and, if applicable, several iterations thereof. As result one receives those pairs of entities which correspond to each other. Complex similarity considerations are claimed the key for identifying these alignments. The basic approach is extended through novel methods focusing on efficiency, machine learning optimization, active user inclusion, scenario-adaptive alignment, and an integrated strategy. The implementation and evaluation shows that both the (semi-) automatic ontology alignment process itself and its output improve significantly. Examples of running applications using the new strategies including one commercial product prove the practical value. Further pointers for next steps in ontology alignment are given including a generalization for other structures and schemas before a summary closes this work.

Using semantic features can help to reach levels of alignment which have never been possible before. The exploitation and application of these advantages is just starting. Methods in this work are basic elements of this development and are expected to be continuously enhanced. In this sense, they will lastingly affect future research and implementation. Therefore, the topic of ontology alignment coupled with the application-focused methodology is appropriate to excite interest of a broad readership.

Karlsruhe, April 2006
Marc Ehrig

Acknowledgements

This book would not have been possible without the invaluable support of many persons. Each of them guided me further towards the goal of creating a comprehensive work on ontology alignment, for which I thank every single one very much.

In first place, it was my advisor Prof. Dr. Rudi Studer, who gave me the challenge and the chance to do this research. He granted me the freedom, the trust, and the help I needed.

I also thank the reviewers comprising Prof. Dr. Kuno Egle, Dr. habil. Jérôme Euzenat, Prof. Dr. Hartmut Schmeck, and Prof. Dr. Ute Werner, who through their objective reflection provided valuable feedback. Further, I am grateful to Susan Lagerstrom-Fife and Sharon Palleschi from Springer for the successful and smooth collaboration on publishing this book.

My friends from Karlsruhe, Peter Haase, Jens Hartmann, Prof. Dr. Steffen Staab, Dr. York Sure, and Christoph Tempich were the closest co-workers, but especially main contributors and critics when I was developing new ideas. This list needs to be extended to all the great friends and colleagues at LS3WIM in Karlsruhe. The nice atmosphere was indeed an essential basis resulting in many professional and social events, which make my time in Karlsruhe unforgettable. Numerous people around the world continuously improved this work through helpful and detailed discussions.

I would like to acknowledge that this research would not have been possible without the funding of the European Union through the projects SWAP, SEKT, and Knowledge Web.

Finally, I thank my family: Aline, Helga, and Volker, who since the very beginning have always been reliable partners at my side motivating me to continue on my path.

1

Introduction and Overview

1.1 Motivation

"The basic economic resource – the means of production – is no longer capital, not natural resource, nor labor. It is and will be knowledge." (Drucker, 1993). Society is rapidly changing into a knowledge society. With knowledge being the core economic resource, the capability of managing it has become a critical factor (Probst et al., 1998). Knowledge which is not applied neither has a value for a company, nor in a macro-economical sense for the prosperity of a society. Applying it nowadays typically involves information technology. While IT might not matter (Carr, 2003), the knowledge in information systems does, probably more than ever before.

In computer science knowledge is represented in a variety of ways: Databases or collections of documents and emails exist in large numbers; There are explicit schemas and structures, such as internet links, folder hierarchies, or descriptions of business processes. Additionally, with computational resources still becoming cheaper every year the flood of information increases. People are desperately looking for means to grasp this different knowledge altogether, and not only individual elements of information. Since the beginning of computer systems, information integration has always been a topic and one can expect this challenge to continuously trigger research and development. As one important step, physical exchange of data is not an issue any longer; being part of the global internet is a commodity for most enterprises. However, most existing knowledge representations are still not compatible with each other. In recent years, agreements on syntax have been made, e.g., the Extensible Markup Language (XML) (Bray et al., 2004). Many companies are already exchanging data based on XML, but it requires a lot of human effort to understand and integrate the meanings (the semantics). The next step towards a better understanding is an explicit and semantically rich representation through ontologies (Gruber, 1995), which consist of entities, relations in between, and axioms restricting or enhancing the representations. The Semantic Web community (Berners-Lee et al., 2001) relying on such ontologies faces a different, but related, heterogeneity problem. Many individual ontologies have emerged recently, some of them representing the same contents. Despite using the same syntax, the Web Ontology Language OWL (Smith et al., 2004), they may still differ considerably in naming or structure. Understanding the common meaning of the different representations stays difficult for humans interpreting them, yet almost impossible for machine-based approaches.

Ontology alignment in the sense of identifying relations between individual elements of multiple ontologies is a necessary precondition to establish interoperability between agents or services using different individual ontologies. Moreover, human users want to access the knowledge represented in numerous ontologies in a transparent way to ease their tasks of searching or browsing. The gain are new insights which can then be inferred by combining the information contained in the various ontologies. Thus, ontology alignment and mapping are crucial and essential issues to resolve when building an integrated corporate knowledge web or even a world-wide Semantic Web. Generally, there are two approaches for integrating ontologies. Ontology engineers discuss, negotiate, and vote, to directly come up with a shared ontology, which normally is a very tedious and long process. Alternatively, alignment is performed afterwards, thus aligning ontologies and schemas, which already exist. For this, correspondences between the objects in the ontologies need to be identified. The book will focus on the latter scenario. As one can easily imagine, such aligning cannot be done manually beyond a certain complexity, size, or number of ontologies any longer. Automatic or at least semi-automatic techniques have to be developed to reduce the burden of manual creation and maintenance of alignments. In recent years we have already seen a range of research work on approaches proposing such alignments (Agrawal and Srikant, 2001; Noy and Musen, 2003; Doan et al., 2003). When we tried to apply these methods to the scenarios addressed in some of our project contributions (Ehrig et al., 2003b; de Bruijn and Feier, 2005), we found that existing alignment approaches were not suitable for the ontology integration tasks at hand, as they all ignored different important practical aspects of ontology alignment, such as an adequate high quality, efficiency, or user interaction. New approaches were required to overcome these short-comings. A focus on application is a necessary step to enable a breakthrough of the novel semantic technologies.

Efforts on solving the alignment issue now gain momentum – with the valid hope that knowledge integration can be achieved to a much higher degree than it has ever been possible before. For the first time representations are self-explanatory. They include the information required to be semantically aligned with each other. Aligning ontologies based on their explicitly encoded semantics and an with an application focused perspective will be topic of this book.

1.2 Contribution

Our overall goal will be to provide a concise methodology and implementation for aligning ontologies with each other. Ontologies are supplied to the ontology alignment system and alignments are returned, as graphically depicted in Figure 1.1. This work will show that by adhering to a novel stepwise process with innovative individual methods one can significantly improve both the (semi-) automatic ontology alignment process itself and its results. Such methods will make extensive use of the encoded semantics and rely on the similarity of individual elements. For the end-user, this work will additionally provide an easy-to-use tool for ontology alignment.

Fig. 1.1. Ontology Alignment

1.2.1 Problem Outline

By elaborating on some underlying issues the introduced goal is specified more precisely. These issues also give clear indicators to distinguish the efforts in this book from related work. They will continuously imply decisions on the method design later in this work.

- An IT application has to deal with a *scenario* of heterogeneous and distributed knowledge in which *collaboration* is required. The knowledge has to be integrated (or aligned) not only syntactically on representation format level but also semantically. Of course, there may be many different scenarios, each with specific aspects, which all have to be respected for the ontology *alignment* approach. We will create such semantic alignments for collaboration.
- Knowledge is encoded in semantically rich structures: Namely, these are *ontologies*. *"Logic supplies the form, consisting of framework and inferencing capabilities, whereas ontology supplies the content, consisting of the entities, relations, and constraints in the application domain."* (Kent, 2000). Aligning only taxonomies or topic maps is addressed as a sub-problem, but as pointed out in the motivation the new chance for integration lies in the advanced semantic representations. We will focus on creating alignments for full-fledged ontologies.

- We want the considerations of this work to have practical impact. In other words, we are dealing with the *real world* with specific application requirements. This also means data is of varying size and adheres to different terminologies. Moreover, the semantic representation will not be complete; it will only contain the information which seemed reasonable to the original creator, including a restricted set of logical axioms. Most probably the representation will not be perfect either, thus have errors and mistakes in it. Finally, one has to deal with typical hard- and software environments. Our methods will address these real world issues of alignment.

- Alignment methods need to be *flexible* enough to be transferred to other applications, domains, and even types of semantic structures. The goal is not to create solely a tool fitting exactly one defined ontology alignment problem. We will provide such open methods.

- Even though the objective of this work is to be *theoretically* well-founded and give many pointers to existing work thereon, the focus will be on solving specific problems thus addressing their *practical* difficulties with new theoretic methods and evaluating the new approaches, rather than creating a new complete theory of ontology alignment. We will address theory and practice.

1.2.2 Solution Pathway

These paragraphs will briefly outline how the goal with the underlying issues is going to be met. In an early stage of research on this topic, we could already see that many existing alignment methods may be mapped onto a generic alignment process. We will make this process explicit. We will also demonstrate the validity of our idea that *entities are the same, if their features are similar*. Here we give an overview of the six major process steps in a typical order.

1. Feature Engineering, i.e., select excerpts of the overall ontology specification to describe a specific entity (e.g., the label or its relation to other entities).
2. Search Step Selection, i.e., choose two entities from the ontologies to actually compare for an alignment.
3. Similarity Assessment, i.e., indicate a similarity for a given description (feature) of two entities (e.g., a string comparison of the labels, or a comparison of the instances of two concepts).
4. Similarity Aggregation, i.e., aggregate the multiple similarity assessments for one entity pair into a single measure.
5. Interpretation, i.e., use all aggregated numbers, a threshold, and an interpretation strategy to propose whether two entities should eventually be aligned or not.
6. Iteration, i.e., as the similarity of one entity pair influences the similarity of other entity pairs which are structurally connected to the first one, the

equality needs to be propagated through the ontologies and similarities have to be recalculated.

Numerous additional novel methods will extend the alignment process to meet the claims made on the previous pages and the requirements of different applications. These extensions address the semantics in ontologies and respond to the needs of users dealing with them:

- Very efficient calculation of alignments can be achieved by using the ontology structure to select the most promising alignment candidates for comparison.
- Many existing approaches require humans to select weights or interpretation schemes on top of the determined similarities, which is possible only with great difficulty. Quality may therefore be boosted using up-to-date machine learning techniques.
- In fact, human input can be very beneficial for some cases. Most effective and for the user least intrusive interaction will therefore be investigated and implemented.
- Methods are going to be developed that explicitly adapt to the application-specific requirements. This allows to reuse one ontology alignment implementation for many scenarios.
- Most of the presented methods require semantic structures to function. We will show that this is neither necessarily restricted to ontologies nor to one-to-one alignments only.

The details on how these ambitious goals are going to be reached and their implementation and evaluation will follow in twelve chapters.

1.3 Overview

Before starting, this section will give the reader an overview on the contents of this book and help with guidelines on reading it.

1.3.1 Structure

This first Chapter 1 constitutes the introduction and motivation to the following work. It clearly defines the goal and demarcates it against existing work. The composition of this book is presented in this section together with a reader's guide.

Part I (Chapters 2 to 4) will describe the basis for ontology alignment. In specific, it will define the two keywords *ontology* and *alignment*. It will then shift to considerations that are more practical by explaining similarity and its usage for ontologies. Further, it will examine the underlying use cases for ontology alignment resulting in core requirements to create a well-founded process in later chapters. Before creating a new approach, it is essential to understand related work. This will include both theoretic work and existing approaches for alignment of ontologies or other well-defined structures, mostly database schemas.

Part II (Chapters 5 and 6) will then present the core of the research contribution. A general process for ontology alignment will be introduced. Each step of the process is then going to be described in detail showing different possible methods. These will be evaluated thereafter. For this a detailed description on how the evaluation is going to be performed will also be given in this part. The requirements from the preceding foundations are going to be solved by individual specific approaches: efficiency considerations, machine learning aid, active user interaction, adaptive strategies based on underlying use cases, and an overall integrated strategy. All these methods will also be thoroughly evaluated.

The work to be presented has been implemented in the tool FOAM (framework for ontology alignment and mapping). Other implementation approaches will also be mentioned in Part III (Chapters 7 to 9). Afterwards, we will show how the implementations are applied in five case studies: Bibster, Xarop, a Legal Case Study, a Digital Library, and for Heterogeneous Groups in Consulting. These case studies have been or are still performed within the context of European Union projects tightly interconnected to industry application, the ideal setting for a proof in practice.

Part IV (Chapters 10 and 11) will be directed to the future of semantic alignment. The alignment approach is going to be generalized for other semantic structures apart from ontologies. Often real world use requires complex alignments. Thus, this topic will be addressed. Considerations on the theoretical possibilities of alignment will also be presented. A general outlook will close this part.

To finalize the work a conclusion will be given in Chapter 12. Once more the results will be summarized and reflected onto the predetermined goals. Final statements will conclude the work.

The Appendix in Part V (Chapters A to C) will have additional information such as an extended description of the used ontologies with statistics and graphical representations. The complete evaluation results will follow. Finally, more documentation on the FOAM tool is going to be provided.

1.3.2 Reader's Guide

Even though this book has been written to be read as an integrated piece of work, there are possible shortcuts suiting different readerships: people generally interested in ontologies and Semantic Web; persons willing to learn about integrating schemas and data structures; tool developers; individual researchers looking out for new ideas in this area; or ontology alignment experts interested in the novel methods.

All are encouraged to read this introduction (Chapter 1). Readers already familiar with ontologies and the Semantic Web or the basics of integration, may skip the corresponding chapters in Part I. The chapter on similarity should not be missed though. Scenarios and their requirements extend the previous motivation. Related work may be skipped if the reader is mainly interested in the novel approaches. The core ontology alignment process of Part II is the basis for the following approaches and it is recommended to closely read this chapter. From the following chapters the readers may choose those that apply best to their interests: efficiency considerations, machine learning, user interaction, or adaptive strategies. The three implementations and the five application scenarios (Part III) are widely independent, allowing to be read separately. If the readers are planning to use the methodology, for example, through the open source FOAM framework, they are advised to read this chapter. Part IV is directed towards the future and gives pointers, which go beyond this work with new ideas for extended fields. The conclusion (Chapter 12) again summarizes this work.

With the right motivation and a brief overview of what to expect in mind, we can now directly address the topic of ontology alignment.

Part I

Foundations

2

Definitions

Any good research needs a strong foundation. This chapter lays these foundations for the book. One characteristic of original research is the lack of a standardized vocabulary. Therefore, we will first explain the terminology of ontology and alignment. Then the concept of similarity and its meaning for ontologies will be described, on both an abstract and a concrete level with examples. Only with a thorough understanding of the main expressions, it is possible to follow the ideas of the succeeding chapters.

2.1 Ontology

In the last years, ontologies have increasingly been used in computer science, but also in biology and medicine, or knowledge management. Accompanying this development, the definitions of ontology have varied considerably. As *ontology* is one of the key terms, this section will define its further usage here.

2.1.1 Ontology Definition

In philosophy, ontology is the theory of *"the nature of being or the kinds of existents"* (mer, 2006). The Greek philosophers Socrates and Aristotle were the first developing the foundations of ontology. Socrates introduced the notion of abstract ideas, a hierarchy among them, and class-instance relations. Aristotle added logical associations. The result is a well-structured model, which is capable of describing the real world. Still, it is not trivial to include all the extensive and complex relations of our environment. Looking at ontology from a different point of view, from mathematics, we perceive a complex directed graph, which represents knowledge about the world. This model is extended with logical axioms to allow for inferencing. In modern history, first papers resuming the philosophical discipline ontology were published around 1960 (Strawson and Bubner, 1975).

Artificial Intelligence and web researchers have adopted the term *"ontology"* for their own needs. Currently there are different definitions in the literature of what an ontology should be. Some of them are discussed in Guarino (1997), the most prominent, focused on here, being *"An ontology is an explicit specification of a conceptualization."* (Gruber, 1995). A conceptualization refers to an abstract model of some phenomenon in the world by identifying the relevant concept of that phenomenon (Studer et al., 1998). Explicit means that the types of concepts used and the constraints on their use are explicitly defined. This definition is often extended by three additional conditions: *"An ontology is an explicit,* formal *specification of a* shared *conceptualization* of a domain of interest.*"* where formal refers to the fact that the ontology should be machine-readable (which excludes, for instance, natural language). Shared reflects the notion that an ontology captures consensual knowledge, i.e., it is not private to an individual. Shared does not necessarily mean globally shared, but accepted by a group. Thus, the integration problem addressed in this work therefore stays unsolved by this definition. Ontology alignment remains necessary. Finally, the reference to a domain of interest indicates that for domain ontologies one is not interested in modeling the whole world, but rather in modeling just those parts of a certain domain relevant to the task.

Common to all these definitions is their high level of generalization, which is far from a precise mathematical definition. The reason for this is that the definition should cover all different kinds of ontologies, and should not be related to a particular method of knowledge representation (van Heijst et al., 1997). However, to study structural aspects, we have to commit ourselves to one specific ontology model and to a precise, detailed definition. This section presents the definition of this key term ontology that has been developed in the knowledge management group at the Institute AIFB at the University of Karlsruhe. The definition adheres to the Karlsruhe Ontology Model as expressed in Stumme et al. (2003).

Definition 2.1 (Core Ontology). *A core ontology is a structure*

$$S := (C, \leq_C, R, \sigma, \leq_R)$$

consisting of

- *two disjoint sets C and R whose elements are called concept identifiers and relation identifiers (or concepts and relations for short),*
- *a partial order $\leq_C$ on C, called concept hierarchy or taxonomy,*
- *a function $\sigma\colon R \to C \times C$ called signature,[1] where $\sigma(r) = \langle dom(r), ran(r) \rangle$ with $r \in R$, domain $dom(r)$, and range $ran(r)$,*
- *a partial order $\leq_R$ on R, called relation hierarchy, where $r_1 \leq_R r_2$ iff $dom(r_1) \leq_C dom(r_2)$ and $ran(r_1) \leq_C ran(r_2)$.*

---

[1] In contrast to some other definitions, we here actually restrict the model to binary relations.

For simplification, datatypes such as integers or strings are treated as special kinds of concepts, $D \subset C$. Further, we say, if $c_1 <_C c_2$, for $c_1, c_2 \in C$, then c_1 is a *subconcept of* c_2, and c_2 is a *superconcept of* c_1. If $c_1 <_C c_2$ and there is no $c_3 \in C$ with $c_1 <_C c_3 <_C c_2$, then c_1 is a *direct subconcept of* c_2, and c_2 is a *direct superconcept of* c_1. We denote this by $c_1 \prec c_2$. *Super-* and *subrelations* as well as their direct counterparts are defined analogously. The core ontology is often also referenced to as schema.

Relationships between concepts and/or relations as well as constraints can be expressed within a logical language such as first-order logic or Horn-logic. We here provide a generic definition, which allows the use of different languages and logics.

Definition 2.2 (Axioms). *Let L be a logical language. An L-axiom system for a core ontology is a pair*

$$A := (AI, \alpha)$$

where

- *AI is a set whose elements are called axiom identifiers and*
- *$\alpha \colon AI \to L$ is a mapping.*

The elements of $A := \alpha(AI)$ are called axioms. *S is considered to be part of the language L.*

The core ontologies formalize the intentional aspects of a domain. The extensional aspects are provided by knowledge bases, which contain assertions about instances of the concepts and relations.

Definition 2.3 (Knowledge Base). *A knowledge base is a structure*

$$KB := (C, R, I, \iota_C, \iota_R)$$

consisting of

- *two disjoint sets C and R as defined before,*
- *a set I whose elements are called instance identifiers (or instances for short),*
- *a function $\iota_C \colon C \to \mathfrak{P}(I)$ called concept instantiation,*
- *a function $\iota_R \colon R \to \mathfrak{P}(I^2)$ with $\iota_R(r) \subseteq \iota_C(dom(r)) \times \iota_C(ran(r))$, for all $r \in R$. The function ι_R is called relation instantiation.*

With datatypes being concepts as stated for core ontologies, concrete values are analogously treated as instances, $V \subset I$.

We provide names for the concepts (and relations). Instead of name, we call them sign to allow for more generality.

Definition 2.4 (Lexicon). *A lexicon for an ontology is a structure*

$$Lex := (G_C, G_R, G_I, Ref_C, Ref_R, Ref_I)$$

consisting of

- *three sets G_C, G_R and G_I whose elements are called signs for concepts, relations, and instances, resp.,*
- *a relation $Ref_C \subseteq G_C \times C$ called lexical reference for concepts, Ref_R and Ref_I analogously.*

In this work, an ontology consists of a core ontology, axioms, instantiating data in the knowledge base, as well as a corresponding lexicon.

Definition 2.5 (Ontology). *An ontology O is therefore defined through the following tuple:*

$$O := (S, A, KB, Lex)$$

consisting of

- *the core ontology S,*
- *the L-axiom system A,*
- *the knowledge base KB, and*
- *the lexicon Lex.*

In this book we will often refer to a set of entities E. An entity $e \in E$ interpreted in an ontology O is either a concept, a relation, or an instance, i.e., $e_{|O} \in C \cup R \cup I$. We usually write e instead of $e_{|O}$ when the ontology O is clear from the context of the writing.

By enhancing these definitions with an actual ontology language, such as OWL in the next section, ontologies are given a well-defined semantics. Through axioms, it is possible to formalize a wide range of correlations. Especially the expressive semantics distinguishes ontologies from other schema such as topic maps,[2] XML trees (Bray et al., 2004),[3] database schemas, or classification schemas, e.g., modeled through UML.[4] The semantics of ontologies allows inferring additional knowledge. In our case, we will extensively use the defined semantics to derive alignments.

2.1.2 Semantic Web and Web Ontology Language (OWL)

The internet is a large platform for information. After its impressive development in the past decade, an incredible amount of data is now available. World knowledge seems easily reachable. Still, we are far away from the point where we can access knowledge just as easily as browsing through the web. Unfortunately, most of the information provided is meant to be human-readable only. It is in a non-standardized form and unstructured in the relation it uses. The main problem of sharing knowledge with people via computer rises from the missing capabilities of the machine to recognize the meaning of the processed information. Solving this dilemma will be a goal for the next years.

---

[2] http://www.topicmaps.org/xtm/1.0/
[3] http://www.w3.org/XML/
[4] http://www.uml.org/

The vision of a Semantic Web was first brought up by Berners-Lee et al. (2001). *"The Semantic Web will bring structure to the meaningful content of Web pages, creating an environment where software agents roaming from page to page can readily carry out sophisticated tasks for users."* The web will become machine-readable and processable based on ontologies improving its effectiveness by magnitudes. In a more recent interview (Berners-Lee, 2005), he added: *"The Semantic Web is designed to smoothly interconnect personal information management, enterprise application integration, and the global sharing of commercial, scientific, and cultural data. We are talking about data here, not human documents."* As the prospective killer application he sees company intranets where sharing with semantics begins in a smaller controlled environment. Just as the internet started in closed environments, the Semantic Web is also expected to take this path.

An approach to overcome the barrier of machines not recognizing meaning is the application of ontologies to formalize knowledge in a machine and human readable form. This enables the user to search for information based on meaning rather than syntax. A key issue is therefore the definition of standards to represent the underlying structures, the ontologies. Each language offers different modeling primitives. RDF-Schema (Brickley and Guha, 2004),[5] a schema language built on top of the Resource Description Framework (RDF), allows to define taxonomies and relations between concepts. The Web Ontology Language (OWL) (Smith et al., 2004; Patel-Schneider et al., 2004)[6] is more expressive. OWL was developed keeping the primitives of description logics (Baader et al., 2003) in mind. As in this work ontology alignment is supposed to make use of expressive semantics, it will rely on OWL. Apart from RDF(S) and OWL, one should mention F-Logic as a logic-based ontology representation (Kifer et al., 1995).

OWL is currently recommended by the World Wide Web Consortium (W3C) as language for modeling ontologies for the Semantic Web. Historically, it evolved from the DAML+OIL[7] language, which was developed by joining the European standard OIL (Ontology Inference Layer) with its American counterpart DAML (DARPA Agent Markup Language) into a unified framework. OWL is an expressive language, allowing many ontology-modeling paradigms, such as specifying hierarchical relationships between classes and restrictions and for modeling attributes and associations under a well-defined semantics. The latter allows inferring information that is not explicitly present in the ontology. Furthermore, OWL provides for the description of the state of the world by asserting information about individuals and relationships between them. There exist three sublanguages of OWL, here arranged according to their complexity: OWL Lite presents a subset that allows for easy inferencing; OWL DL includes many constructs from description logics; OWL Full

---

[5] http://www.w3.org/RDF/
[6] http://www.w3.org/TR/owl-features/
[7] http://www.w3.org/TR/daml+oil-reference/

finally allows any use of RDF statements, thus problems with inferencing may arise. In specific, we will focus on OWL DL. It has the following predefined constructs on concepts, relations, and instances:

- subsumption of concepts and relations;
- domains and ranges of relations;
- (in)equality definitions;
- symmetry, transitivity, reflexivity of relations;
- restrictions on relations;
- cardinality constraints;
- boolean combinations of concept expressions: union, intersection, complement;
- enumeration of instances to define a concept;
- inverse relations;
- lexical annotations such as labels or comments;
- and ontology information such as version numbers or import requests for other ontologies.

Whereas some constructs are directly reflected in the ontology definition of the previous section, others correspond to additional axioms. Currently, efforts are made to extend the ontology model with a rule language. SWRL, the Semantic Web Rule Language (Horrocks and Patel-Schneider, 2004),[8] offers possibilities for representing complex axioms and first implementations have been provided.

2.1.3 Ontology Example

To clarify the term ontology as used here, this section contains an ontology example. We will repeatedly refer to this example throughout the work to illustrate the approaches for ontology alignment. The ontology describes the domain of automobiles as a car dealer who has modeled his stock and customer relations might have. It is a simple example, but noticeably helps to explain the basic ontology constructs.

The ontology is graphically shown in Figure 2.1. Concepts are depicted as rectangular boxes, relations as hexagons, and instances as rounded boxes. Subsumption relations are drawn as solid arrows. A relation has an incoming arrow from its domain and an outgoing arrow to its range. The instantiations of concepts and relations are depicted as dotted, arrowed lines. The example contains the six concepts object, vehicle, owner, boat, car, and speed, the two relations of belonging to somebody and speed, and the three instances Marc, Porsche KA-123, and 300 km/h. There is a subsumption relation between object, vehicle, and boat, resp. car; a vehicle is an object, a boat is a vehicle, etc. Each vehicle belongs to an owner and each car has a specific speed. On instance level, the Porsche KA-123 belongs to Marc and has the speed 300

---

[8] http://www.daml.org/rules/proposal/

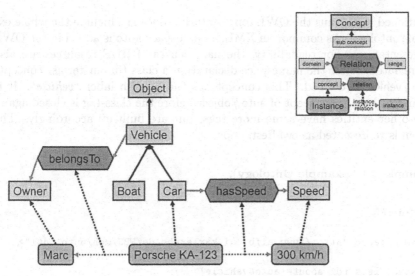

Fig. 2.1. Ontology Example

km/h. Further, the axiom that every car needs to have at least one owner is defined. Axioms are not depicted in the graph, but represented in the next paragraphs. The example is fictitious and any concurrences with the real world are purely by chance.

Formally, this ontology is defined according to $O := (S, A, KB, Lex)$. To keep the representation as short and illustrating as possible, it does not contain all constructs of the above example.

- schema $S = (C, \leq_C, R, \sigma, \leq_R) = (\{object, vehicle, owner, \ldots\},$
  $\{(vehicle, object), (boat, vehicle), \ldots\}, \{belongsTo, hasSpeed\},$
  $\{belongsTo \rightarrow (vehicle, owner), hasSpeed \rightarrow (car, speed)\}, \{\})$
- axioms[9] $A = \{\forall x\ car(x) \Rightarrow \exists y\ belongsTo(x, y)\}$
- knowledge base $KB = (C_{KB}, R_{KB}, I, \iota_C, \iota_R) =$
  $(\{object, vehicle, owner, \ldots\}, \{belongsTo, hasSpeed\},$
  $\{Marc, PorscheKA123, 300km/h\},$
  $\{owner \rightarrow \{Marc\}, car \rightarrow \{PorscheKA123\}, speed \rightarrow \{300km/h\}\},$
  $\{belongsTo \rightarrow \{(PorscheKA123, Marc)\},$
  $hasSpeed \rightarrow \{(PorscheKA123, 300km/h)\})$
- In the example the lexicon only contains the identifiers as lexical entries, i.e., $Lex = (\{$ *"object"*, *"vehicle"*, $\ldots\}, \ldots, \{($ *"object"*, $object),$ $($ *"vehicle"*, $vehicle), \ldots\}, \ldots)$.

Finally, this ontology is expressed in OWL (Example 2.1), or more precisely the RDF/XML representation of OWL. Again each construct is only

---

[9] The notation here is according to first-order logic.

mentioned once, thus the OWL representation does not include the whole example ontology. As common in XML, a namespace auto is added in the OWL representation. For readability, the namespaces of RDF resources are also abbreviated. After the namespace declaration a class (in our terms: concept) auto#vehicle is defined. This concept has the English label *"vehicle"*. It is defined to be a subconcept of auto#object before the class-tag is closed again. The other entities have some more tags, but are built-up accordingly. The axiom is represented as owl:Restriction.

Example 2.1 (Example Ontology).

```
<rdf:RDF
...
xmlns:auto="http://www.aifb.uni-karlsruhe.de/WBS/meh/auto1.owl">

<owl:Class rdf:about='auto#vehicle'>
 <rdfs:label xml:lang='en'>vehicle</rdfs:label>
 <rdfs:subClassOf rdf:resource='auto#object'/>
</owl:Class>
<owl:Class rdf:about='auto#car'>
 <rdfs:label xml:lang='en'>car</rdfs:label>
 <rdfs:subClassOf rdf:resource='auto#vehicle'/>
 <rdfs:subClassOf>
  <owl:Restriction>
    <owl:onProperty rdf:resource='auto#belongsTo'/>
    <owl:minCardinality>1</owl:minCardinality>
  </owl:Restriction>
 </rdfs:subClassOf>
</owl:Class>
...
<owl:ObjectProperty rdf:about='auto#belongsTo'>
 <rdfs:label xml:lang='en'>belongs to</rdfs:label>
 <rdfs:domain rdf:resource ='auto#vehicle'/>
 <rdfs:range rdf:resource='auto#owner'/>
</owl:ObjectProperty>
...
<auto:Owner rdf:about='auto#Marc'/>
...
<auto:Car rdf:about='auto#Porsche KA-123'>
 <rdfs:label xml:lang='en'>Porsche KA-123</rdfs:label>
 <auto:belongsTo rdf:resource='auto#Marc'/>
 <auto:hasSpeed rdf:resource='auto#300 km/h'/>
</auto:Car>
</rdf:RDF>
```

This example concludes the definition of ontologies, our basic semantically rich structures. They will ease the task of alignment by allowing exploiting their semantics.

2.2 Ontology Alignment

The considered research field of ontology alignment and integration features a big number of terms such as alignment, mapping, mediation, merging, etc. Unfortunately, the definitions from different authors are confusing, partially inconsistent, and at times even contradicting. The goal of this section is therefore to adhere to one definition for each term. Especially *alignment*, the second key term in the title of this work, will be explained.

2.2.1 Ontology Alignment Definition

The dictionary (mer, 2006) again gives a general comprehensible sense for alignment. To align something means, *"to bring into line"*. This very brief definition already emphasizes that aligning is an activity after which the involved objects are in some mutual relation.

We here define our use of the term ontology alignment similarly to Klein (2001). Given two ontologies, aligning one ontology with another one means that for each entity (concept, relation, or instance) in the first ontology, we try to find a corresponding entity, which has the same intended meaning, in the second ontology. An alignment therefore is a one-to-one equality relation. Obviously, for some entities no corresponding entity might exist.

Definition 2.6 (Ontology Alignment). *An ontology alignment function, align, based on the set E of all entities $e \in E$ and based on the set of possible ontologies O is a partial function*

$$align : E \times O \times O \rightharpoonup E$$

We write $align_{O_1,O_2}(e)$ for $align(e, O_1, O_2)$. We leave out O_1, O_2 when they are evident from the context and write $align(e)$ instead. Once a (partial) alignment, $align$, between two ontologies O_1 and O_2 is established, we say entity e is aligned with entity f when $align(e) = f$. A pair of entities (e, f) that is not yet in $align$ and for which appropriate alignment criteria still need to be tested is called a candidate alignment. In this work, if not explicitly mentioned otherwise, alignment is an equality alignment.

Apart from one-to-one equality alignments, as mainly investigated here and most of the related existing work, in real world one entity often has to be aligned not only to equal entities, but based on another relation (e.g., subsumption). Further, there are complex composites such as a concatenation of terms (e.g., name equals first plus last name) or an entity with restrictions (e.g., a sports car is a car going faster than 250 km/h). Do and Rahm (2002) and Dhamankar et al. (2004) propose approaches for identifying such alignments. As many complex alignments consist of elementary alignments, our work may be seen as basis for this. Our elementary alignments are not restricted to equality relations. We therefore extend the above basic definition of alignment by introducing a set of alignment relations M. M includes but is not restricted to identity, subsumption, instantiation, and orthogonality. A set of alignments based on taxonomical relations is presented in Giunchiglia et al. (2004). In fact, towards the end of this book in Section 10.2, we will show how our approach also fits this problem of general ontology alignment.

Definition 2.7 (General Ontology Alignment). *A general ontology alignment function, genalign, based on the vocabulary, E, of all terms $e \in E$, based on the set of possible ontologies, O, and based on possible alignment relations, M, is a partial function*

$$genalign : E \times O \times O \rightharpoonup E \times M$$

This last understanding is part of the alignment definition researchers have agreed on in the context of Knowledge Web (Euzenat et al., 2004),[10] a European network of excellence of leading institutions on semantic technologies. Supporting the transition process of ontology technology from academia to industry is the major goal of Knowledge Web. This will be achieved through standardization, education, and integrating research. Responding to the integration task, the partners defined an alignment as a set of correspondences (i.e., quadruples): $\langle e, f, r, l \rangle$ with e and f being the two aligned entities, r representing the relation holding between them, and l (additionally) expressing the level of confidence $[0, 1]$ in the alignment statement.

2.2.2 Ontology Alignment Representation

Currently there is no generally agreed standardized format for saving ontology alignments. In this section we therefore propose the two possible representation formats that are most accepted and used in the alignment community.

The first possibility is to adhere to existing constructs, e.g., in OWL. OWL provides equality axioms for concepts, relations, and instances: owl:equivalentClass, owl:equivalentProperty, and owl:sameAs. It is also possible to express inequality through owl:differentFrom. The advantage of this representation is that OWL inference engines will automatically interpret the alignment and reason across several ontologies. The downside is the very strict equality. A confidence value cannot be interpreted accordingly. Complex alignments as mentioned before are not possible.

The second possibility is based on work of Euzenat (2004). The representation uses RDF/XML to formalize ontology alignments. After the general

---

[10] http://knowledgeweb.semanticweb.org/

definition of the involved ontologies, the individual alignments are represented in cells with each cell having the attributes entity 1, entity 2, measure (the confidence), and the relation (normally '='). This representation corresponds to the Knowledge Web definition of alignment (Definition 2.7). Due to its different parameters, it can easily be used for many alignment applications. Unfortunately, it is not directly in an ontology format. Therefore, an explicit import is required to transform the alignments into a suitable format for inferencing. For this importer one also needs to define how to handle confidence values of an alignment.

Alternative representations are the MAFRA semantic bridging ontology (SBO), Contextualized OWL, the rule language SWRL, the OMWG mapping language (OML), and SKOS. An overview thereof is found in Euzenat et al. (2006).

In the later chapters of this work we will not provide alignments in either of the just introduced formats to keep the representation of alignments simple. Alignments are presented in tables with each row containing the tuple of entities and confidence $\langle e, f, l \rangle$. This tuple can be easily translated into either of the two previous formats.

2.2.3 Ontology Alignment Example

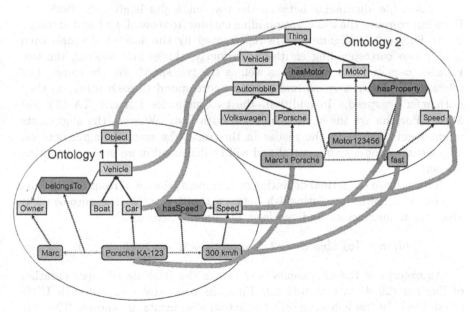

Fig. 2.2. Ontology Alignment Example

Table 2.1. Alignment Table

Ontology O_1	Ontology O_2	Confidence
object	thing	1.0
vehicle	vehicle	1.0
car	automobile	1.0
speed	speed	1.0
hasSpeed	hasProperty	1.0
Porsche KA-123	Marc's Porsche	1.0
300 km/h	fast	0.9

The following example illustrates alignments. The example consists of two simple ontologies that are to be aligned. The two ontologies O_1 and O_2 describing the domain of cars are given in Figure 2.2. The meanings of shapes, colors, and lines are the same as in the previous ontology example of Section 2.1.3. The first ontology has already been described in the ontology section; it is our running example. The second ontology covers the same domain but is modeled slightly differently. Beneath an overall thing concept, there exists a vehicle, which in turn has the subclasses automobile, Volkswagen, and Porsche. Further, there is a motor and speed. The automobile has a Motor which in turn has a property speed. A specific Porsche, Marc's Porsche, with the fast Motor123456 is also represented.

Reasonable alignments between the two ontologies is given in Table 2.1. Each line contains the two corresponding entities from ontology 1 and ontology 2. In Figure 2.2, alignments are represented by the shaded channels each linking two corresponding entities. Obviously, things and objects, the two vehicles, cars and automobiles, as well as the two speeds are the same. The relations of having a speed and property correspond to each other, as they both refer to speed. In addition, the two instances Porsche KA-123 and Marc's Porsche are the same, which are both fast. Whereas the alignments might seem obvious to the reader in this case, the common agreement on alignments is not easy in general and will be discussed more in the evaluation Section 5.4.

Returning to the formal definition of alignment, the set of result alignments is given as follows. To distinguish between the two ontologies, ontology 1 is given the namespace o1 and ontology 2 the namespace o2.

$$align = \{o1\text{:object} \rightarrow o2\text{:thing}, o1\text{:vehicle} \rightarrow o2\text{:vehicle}, \ldots\}$$

An excerpt of the alignments is shown in the RDF-based representation of Euzenat (2004) in Example 2.2. First the two ontologies and their URIs are defined. In the following cells the actual alignments are shown. The first one aligns o1:object with o2:thing. The confidence measure is very high with a value of 1.0, and the semantic relation between the two entities is equality (in contrast to subsumption or part of).

Example 2.2 (Example Alignment Representation in RDF(S)).

```
<rdf:RDF>
<Alignment>
  <xml>yes</xml>
  <level>0</level>
  <type>11</type>
  <onto1>ontology1.owl</onto1>
  <onto2>ontology2.owl</onto2>
  <uri1>http://aifb.uni-karlsruhe.de/ontology1.owl</uri1>
  <uri2>http://aifb.uni-karlsruhe.de/ontology2.owl</uri2>
  <map>
    <Cell>
      <entity1 rdf:resource='ontology1.owl#object'/>
      <entity2 rdf:resource='ontology2.owl#thing'/>
      <measure rdf:datatype='XMLSchema#float'>1.0</measure>
      <relation>=</relation>
    </Cell>
    <Cell>
      <entity1 rdf:resource='ontology1.owl#vehicle'/>
      <entity2 rdf:resource='ontology2.owl#vehicle'/>
      <measure rdf:datatype='XMLSchema#float'>1.0</measure>
      <relation>=</relation>
    </Cell>
    ...
  </map>
</Alignment>
</rdf:RDF>
```

2.3 Related Terms

The focus of this work will be alignment of ontologies. Apart from alignment, there are many related terms, which will be defined and differentiated. The definitions are taken from Klein (2001), Ding et al. (2002), as well as de Bruijn et al. (2005). Unfortunately, the usage of the terms differs considerably.

Combining:

Two or more different ontologies are used for a task in which their mutual relation is relevant. The combining relation may be of any kind, not only identity. Therefore, no information on how the relation is established can be given at this point.

Integration:

For integration, one or more ontologies are reused for a new ontology. The original concepts are adopted unchanged, possibly, they are extended, but their origin stays clear, e.g., through the namespace. The ontologies are merely integrated rather than completely merged. This approach is especially interesting, if given ontologies differ in their domain. Through integration, the new ontology can cover a bigger domain in the end. Ontology alignment may be seen as a prestep for detecting where the involved ontologies overlap and can be connect with each other. The most prominent integration approaches are union and intersection (Wiederhold, 1994), where either all entities of both ontologies are taken or only those which have correspondences in both ontologies.

Matching:

For matching, one tries to find two corresponding entities. These do not necessarily have to be the same. A correspondence can also be, e.g., in terms of a lock and the fitting key. A certain degree of similarity along some specific dimension is sufficient, e.g., the pattern of the lock/key. Whereas combining allows many different relations at the same time, matching implies one specific kind of relation. A typical scenario for matching is web service composition, where the output of one service has to match the corresponding input of the next service. Any schema matching or ontology matching algorithm may be used to implement the Match operator. Matching corresponds to our definition of general alignment, however, where a fixed relation between the aligned entities expresses the kind of match.

Mapping:

Ontology mapping is used for querying of different ontologies. An ontology mapping represents a function between ontologies. The original ontologies are not changed, but the additional mapping axioms describe how to express concepts, relations, or instances in terms of the second ontology. They are stored separately from the ontologies themselves. Often mappings can only be applied in one direction, e.g., the instances of a concept in ontology 1 may all be instances of a concept in ontology 2, but not vice versa. This is the case, if the mappings have only restricted expressiveness and the complete theoretical mapping relation cannot be found for the actual representation. A typical use case for mapping is a query in one ontology representation, which is then rewritten and handed on to another ontology. The answers are then mapped back again. Whereas alignment merely identifies the relation between ontologies, mappings focus on the representation and the execution of the relations for a certain task.

Mediation:

Ontology mediation is the upper-level process of reconciling differences between heterogeneous ontologies in order to achieve interoperation between data sources annotated with and applications using these ontologies. This includes the discovery and specification of ontology alignments, as well as the actual usage of these alignments for certain tasks, such as mapping for query rewriting and instance transformation. Furthermore, the term ontology mediation also subsumes merging of ontologies.

Merging:

For merging, one new ontology is created from two or more ontologies. In this case, the new ontology will unify and replace the original ontologies. This often requires considerable adaptation and extension. Individual elements of the original ontologies are present within the new ontology, but cannot be traced back to their source. Alignment again is a prestep to detect the overlap of entities.

Transformation:

When transforming ontologies, their semantics is changed (possibly also changing the representation) to make them suitable for purposes other than the original one. This definition is so general that it is difficult to relate alignment to it.

Translation:

We here define translation as an operation restricted to data translation (Popa et al., 2002), which may also include the syntax, e.g., translating an ontology from RDF(S) to OWL. The representation format of an ontology is changed while the semantics is preserved. As we are talking about semantic alignments, translation is an underlying requirement when the formats differ, but we do not address translation itself.

This list consolidated common definitions, as they are used in this work.

2.4 Ontology Similarity

Similarity plays a central role for ontology alignment in this work. Here, the meaning of similarity needs to be explained. Thereafter, similarity for ontologies is given a general framework (Ehrig et al., 2005a) followed by specific assigned similarities.

2.4.1 Ontology Similarity Definition

Ontology similarity, as used in this work, refers to the comparison of whole ontologies or subelements thereof. This comparison returns a numerical value indicating whether the two elements have a high or low degree of similarity. This can be formally laid down through the following definition.

Definition 2.8 (Ontology Similarity). *A similarity function*

$$sim : \mathfrak{P}(E) \times \mathfrak{P}(E) \times O \times O \rightarrow [0,1]$$

is a function that maps a pair of entity sets (expressed through the power set $\mathfrak{P}(E)$ of entities) and their corresponding ontologies O to a real number expressing the similarity between two sets such that

- *$\forall e, f \in \mathfrak{P}(E), O_1, O_2 \in O, sim(e, f, O_1, O_2) \geq 0$ (positiveness)*
- *$\forall e, f, g \in \mathfrak{P}(E), O_1, O_2 \in O, sim(e, e, O_1, O_2) \geq sim(f, g)$ (maximality)*
- *$\forall e, f \in \mathfrak{P}(E), O_1, O_2 \in O, sim(e, f, O_1, O_2) = sim(f, e, O_2, O_1)$ (symmetry)*
- *$\forall e, f \in \mathfrak{P}(E), O_1, O_2 \in O, sim(e, f, O_1, O_2) = 1 \Leftrightarrow e = f$: Two entity sets are identical.*
- *$\forall e, f \in \mathfrak{P}(E), O_1, O_2 \in O, 0 < sim(e, f, O_1, O_2) < 1$: Two entity sets are similar/different to a certain degree.*
- *$\forall e, f \in \mathfrak{P}(E), O_1, O_2 \in O, sim(e, f, O_1, O_2) = 0 \Leftrightarrow e \neq f$: Two entity sets are different and have no common characteristics.*

Different similarity measures $sim_k(e, f, O_1, O_2)$ are indexed through a label k. As before, we leave out O_1, O_2 when they are evident from the context and write $sim_k(e, f)$ instead. e and f may be sets of concepts, relation, or instances. This includes subtrees or even whole ontologies. A set may also consist of only one entity, thus in the extreme case reducing the similarity to a similarity between two individual elements.

As our goal alignment relation is equality, and equality is a symmetric relation, we adhere to a symmetric similarity, although we are aware that it is controversially discussed (Mitra and Wiederhold, 2001). Humans tend not to follow the symmetry rule when they decide on similarity between two objects (Bernstein et al., 2005a). Normally, the similarity between object 1 and object 2 is rated in the context of object 1, whereas for similarity between object 2 and object 1 the context is object 2.

2.4.2 Similarity Layers

Since an ontology represents a conceptualization of a domain, comparing two ontology entities goes far beyond the representation of these entities only (syntax level). Rather, it should take into account their relation to the real world entities they are referencing, i.e., their meaning, as well as their purpose in the real world, i.e., their usage. In order to achieve such a comprehensive comparison, we use a semiotic view (theory of signs) on ontologies and define our framework for similarity in three layers, as shown in Figure 2.3: Data-, Ontology-, and Context Layer (Ehrig et al., 2005a). The arrangement of these layers already indicates that they build upon each other. We enhance these by an additional orthogonal dimension representing specific domain knowledge. Initial blueprints for such a division in layers are found in the semiotics (theory of signs) for example in Maedche and Staab (2002), where they are called symbolic, semantic, and pragmatic layer, respectively. Other classifications focused on matching, but clearly related to the notion of similarity, are presented in Rahm and Bernstein (2001) and Shvaiko and Euzenat (2005).

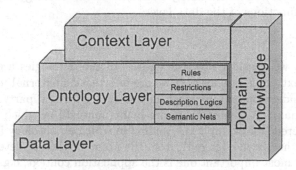

Fig. 2.3. Similarity Layers

Data Layer:

On this first layer, we compare entities by only considering data values of simple or complex datatypes, such as integers and strings. To compare data values, we may use generic similarity functions such as the edit distance for strings. For integers, we determine a relative distance between them. Complex datatypes made up of simple datatypes also require more complex measures, but which are effectively compiled of simple measures.

Ontology Layer:

For the second layer, the ontology layer, we consider semantic relations between the entities. In fact, one may split this layer again along the semantic complexity, which is derived from the layer cake of Berners-Lee (2000). On the lowest level, we just treat the ontology as a graph with concepts and relations. These Semantic Nets were introduced by Quillan (1967). This level is enhanced by description logics like semantics (Baader et al., 2003), e.g., a taxonomy is created over concepts, in which a concept inherits all the relations of its superconcepts. For example, if certain edges are interpreted as a subsumption hierarchy, it is possible to determine the taxonomic similarity based on the number of is-a edges separating two concepts. Besides intensional features, we also rely on the extensional dimension, i.e., assess concepts to be the same, if their instances are similar. For restrictions, e.g., in the ontology language OWL, we again use different heuristics. Higher levels of the ontology layer cake also become interesting for similarity considerations. Especially if similar rules between entities exist, these entities will be regarded as similar.

For this type of similarity, one has to process higher order relationships. Unfortunately, there has not been sufficient research and practical support for the rule layer in the Semantic Web in general, even less for similarity considerations. However, first work has been done in this direction through Fürst and Trichet (2005). The similarity functions of the ontology layer fall back on similarity functions of the data layer.

Context Layer:

On this layer, we consider how the entities of the ontologies are used in an external context. This implies that we use information external to the ontologies. We consider contexts as local models that encode a party's subjective view of a domain. Although there are many contexts in which an ontology can be considered (for example the context in which an ontology is developed, or in which it has been changed), from the point of view of determining the similarity, the most important one is the application context, e.g., how a specific entity of an ontology has been used in the context of a given application. An example for this is the Amazon portal[11] in which, given information about which people buy which books, one may decide if two books are similar or not. Therefore, the similarity between two ontology entities is easily determined by comparing their usage in an ontology-based application. A naïve explanation is such that similar entities have similar patterns of usage. The main problem remains how to define these usage patterns (Stojanovic, 2005) in order to discover the similarity in the most efficient way. To generalize the description of such patterns, we reuse the similarity principle in the terms of usage: Similar entities are used in similar context. We use both directions of the implication in discovering similarity: If two entities are used in the same (related) context, then these entities are similar and vice versa; if in two contexts the same (related) entities are used then these contexts are similar.

Domain Knowledge:

Special shared ontology domains have their own additional vocabulary, e.g., the bibliographic domain often relies on the Dublin Core (Caplan, 1995) constructs dc:author or dc:title. This domain specific vocabulary is treated in a special way, thus returning own similarities, i.e., an author similarity or title similarity instead of a general attribute similarity. The right part of Figure 2.3 shows the domain-specific aspects. As this domain-specific knowledge may be situated at any level of ontological complexity, it is presented as a vertical box across all of them.

2.4.3 Specific Similarity Measures

After having presented the general similarity layers, we now show specific measures, which fit the framework. The list of measures is by no means

---

[11] http://www.amazon.com/

complete, but shall give an overview of important individual similarities. They will be reused later on in this work for identifying ontology alignments. An extensive work, not necessarily focused on ontology similarity only, has been provided by Bernstein et al. (2005b).

Data Layer

In the ontology definition section we have defined datatypes to be concepts, and their concrete values being instances $V \subset I$. These value instances allow special operators for comparison based on the individual letters of a string or the numerical value of an integer. The lexical signs (typically strings) for concepts, relations, and instances ($G = G_C \cup G_R \cup G_I$), are also compared based on data layer similarities. In this section we will not distinguish between V and G, thus $v \in (V \cup G)$.

Equality:

For some datatypes and scenarios, it is appropriate to require equality of data values for entities to be similar. An example where this is necessary would be data values that are used as identifiers. v_1 and v_2 are respective data values.

$$sim_{equality}(v_1, v_2) := \begin{cases} 1, & \text{if } v_1 = v_2, \\ 0, & \text{otherwise} \end{cases} \quad (2.1)$$

Syntactic Similarity:

Levenshtein (1965) introduced a widely-used measure to compare two strings, the so-called edit distance. The idea behind this measure is to take two strings and determine how many atomic actions are required to transform one string into the other one. Atomic actions are addition, deletion, and replacement of characters, but also shifting their position. The number of operations are expressed in *ed*. For our purposes, we rely on the syntactic similarity of Maedche and Staab (2002), which is inverse to the edit distance measure.

$$sim_{syntactic}(v_1, v_2) := \max(0, \frac{\min(|v_1|, |v_2|) - ed(v_1, v_2)}{\min(|v_1|, |v_2|)}) \quad (2.2)$$

Names are a prominent example, which require syntactic similarity. Small variations such as different cases or typing errors still lead to a high similarity. Many other possibilities to compare strings exist, e.g., Stoilos et al. (2005). Often it will also be necessary to use bag-of-words approaches when the label does not only contain one word but a whole description. Chaves (2003) for instance uses stemming (Porter, 1980) and the sequence of words instead of characters to determine the similarity.

Distance-Based Similarity for Numeric Values:

For numeric datatypes with a limited range (e.g., subsets of integer or double) it is advisable to dispose of a similarity measure that assigns the similarity between two numerical values based on their arithmetical difference (Bergmann, 2002). A generic example of such a distance-based similarity measure is

$$sim_{diff}(v_1, v_2) := 1 - \left(\frac{|v_1 - v_2|}{maxdiff}\right)^{\gamma} \tag{2.3}$$

where $v_1, v_2 \in [\min_{v \in V}(V), \max_{v \in V}(V)]$ and $maxdiff = \max_{v \in V}(V) - \min_{v \in V}(V)$ for a numeric datatype V. The parameter $\gamma \in \mathbb{R}^+$ may be used to lessen or amplify the influence of increasing differences on the similarity assessment.

Objects

Whereas on the data layer we simply compare data values with each other, we now define how to actually compare objects, without respecting their semantic type yet. In our similarity framework objects only exist on the upper layers making object similarities part of the ontology layer.

Object Equality:

Object equality of ontology objects is based on existing logical assertions. This assertion may be explicitly included in the ontology definition, e.g., owl:sameAs, or have been identified at an earlier point in time either manually or by an automatic approach.

$$sim_{object}(e, f) := \begin{cases} 1 & align(e) = f, \\ 0 & \text{otherwise} \end{cases} \tag{2.4}$$

Dice Coefficient:

Often it is necessary to compare not only two entities but also two sets of entities E and F. Two sets of entities may be compared based on the overlap of the sets' individuals ($e \in E, f \in F$) (Castano et al., 1998):

$$sim_{dice}(E, F) := \frac{2 \cdot |E \cap F|}{|E| + |F|} \tag{2.5}$$

Unfortunately, the dice coefficient only returns results if the individuals are marked with a unique identifier where equal individuals have the same identifier, even across several ontologies. Only then, it is possible to exactly determine whether an individual is in only one or both of the sets.

Jacquard Coefficient:

This coefficient is related to the previous set similarity. It calculates the fraction of overlapping elements compared to the number of all existing elements in the two sets.

$$sim_{jacquard}(E, F) := \frac{|E \cap F|}{|E \cup F|} \tag{2.6}$$

Single Linkage:

The maximum similarity between two sets is a basic operator for comparisons. Linkage measures are typically used for measuring distances of sets for data mining, e.g., for clustering. Here we apply them for similarities instead. In contrast to the coefficient similarities, single linkage also deals with similarities of individual entities. In specific, it determines the maximum. For this, we rely on other measures that already did the calculation of similarity values $[0, 1]$ between single entities.

$$sim_{single}(E, F) = \max_{(e,f)|e \in E, f \in F}(sim(e, f)) \tag{2.7}$$

Average Linkage:

Many other related similarities, e.g., based on average similarities between the sets' individuals are also possible.

$$sim_{complete}(E, F) = \frac{\sum_{\forall(e,f)|e \in E, f \in F} sim(e, f)}{|E| \cdot |F|} \tag{2.8}$$

Multi Similarity:

This measure compares sets by representing them through an average element each. As the individual entities have various different features, it is difficult to create a feature vector representing the whole sets. Therefore, we use a technique known as a prestep to multidimensional scaling. We describe each entity through a vector representing the similarity to any other entity contained in the two sets. For both sets, a representative vector can be created by calculating an average vector over all individuals. Please note, that this averaging means that we cannot distinguish any longer, if one entity pair of the sets was very similar or many entity pairs were only slightly similar. Finally, we determine the cosine between the two set vectors through the scalar product as the similarity value.

$$sim_{multi}(E, F) = \frac{\sum_{e \in E} e}{|\sum_{e \in E} e|} \cdot \frac{\sum_{f \in F} f}{|\sum_{f \in F} f|} \tag{2.9}$$

with $\mathbf{e} = (sim(e, e_1), sim(e, e_2), \ldots, sim(e, f_1), sim(e, f_2), \ldots)$, $\mathbf{f}$ analogously.

This measure has several advantages. In contrast to any similarity based on maximum considerations, multi similarity is monotonic and thus more suited for optimization. A differing number of elements in the sets does not distort the similarity, e.g., when only one element needs to be aligned with many elements, still the whole range of [0,1] for similarity may occur. Vice versa, the equality of only two elements in the sets does not lead to an overall high similarity.

For more set similarities we refer to Valtchev (1999); Brinkhoff (2004); Bernstein et al. (2005a).

Ontology Layer

We continue with specific similarity measures derived from the ontology structure. As for the other layers, these measures are examples; many others are also possible.

Label Similarity:

One basic feature of entities in ontologies is their label. Labels are human identifiers (names) for entities, normally shared by a community of people speaking a common language. We rely on string similarity to compare the labels, in our case syntactic similarity.

$$sim_{label}(e, f) := sim_{syntactic}(label(e), label(f)) \qquad (2.10)$$

Dictionaries (WordNet (Fellbaum, 1998)) may further be used for comparisons even across languages. Two strings representing synonyms return 1, otherwise 0. Please note that homonyms would erroneously also return high similarities.

Taxonomic Similarity for Concepts:

One possible generic measure to determine the semantic similarity of concepts C within one ontology, in one concept hierarchy $\leq_C$, has been presented in Rada et al. (1989):

$$sim_{taxonomic}(c_1, c_2) := \begin{cases} e^{-\alpha l} \cdot \frac{e^{\beta h} - e^{-\beta h}}{e^{\beta h} + e^{-\beta h}}, & \text{if } c_1 \neq c_2, \\ 1, & \text{otherwise} \end{cases} \qquad (2.11)$$

$\alpha \geq 0$ and $\beta \geq 0$ are parameters scaling the contribution of shortest path length l and depth h in the concept hierarchy, respectively. The shortest path length is a metric for measuring the conceptual distance of c_1 and c_2. The intuition behind using the depth of the direct common subsumer in the calculation is that concepts at upper layers of the concept hierarchy are more general and are semantically less similar than concepts at lower levels. This measure is easily used analogously for relation R comparisons through $\leq_R$.

Extensional Concept Similarity:

Besides describing a concept $c \in C$ through its features (intension), using the extension is also feasible. Two concepts are similar, if they have similar instances I. We use a set similarity for comparing the sets of instances, e.g., multi similarity.

$$sim_{extension}(c_1, c_2) := sim_{multi}(\iota_C(c_1), \iota_C(c_2)) \tag{2.12}$$

Domain and Range Similarity:

We define a similarity measure for relations $r \in R$ based on their domain and range definitions given by σ_R:

$$sim_{domRan}(r_1, r_2) := 0.5 \cdot (sim_{object}(ran(r_1), ran(r_2))$$
$$+sim_{object}(dom(r_1), dom(r_2))) \tag{2.13}$$

Concept Similarity of Instances:

Instances I have a certain similarity if they are assigned to the same parent class through ι_C.

$$sim_{parent}(i_1, i_2) = sim_{object}(c_1, c_2) \ with \ i_1 \in \iota_C(c_1), i_2 \in \iota_C(c_2) \tag{2.14}$$

As there are many more ontological structures, which are used to determine the similarity of entities, this list can easily be extended. In fact, the general approach for ontology alignment in this book will refer to some additional ones later on.

Context Layer

The similarity of two objects on the contextual level is defined as:

$$sim_{use}(e, f) := sim_{diff}(\text{Usage}(e, con), \text{Usage}(f, con)), \tag{2.15}$$

where $e, f \in E$ are entities from the ontology model (e.g., two concepts or two instances) and Usage(e, con) corresponds to the frequency of the usage of e in the context con. As we already mentioned, the context could be a portal application in which the given entities are used. Note that this formula can be easily extended in order to compare the usage of some selected characteristics of two entities, instead of the entities themselves. It enables several levels of abstractions in which the similarity can be discovered. For example, two books are similar if their authors (that are different persons) have many coauthored publications.

Especially the two areas of context similarity and domain knowledge will not be extended here as a reasonable description cannot be given in general, but requires a fixed application scenario. Section 8.2 will present such similarities for one specific case, the Bibster application.

2.4.4 Similarity in Related Work

Similarity measures for ontological structures have been widely researched, e.g., in cognitive science, databases, software engineering and artificial intelligence. Rodríguez and Egenhofer (2000) give a general overview of similarity. In Bisson (1995) we find measures that deal both with the local structure of the objects and the relational structure that exist between the objects thus approaching some of the issues of our ontology layer. In Bisson (1992) the attention is restricted to the comparison of concepts. Furthermore, Bisson does not distinguish relations into taxonomic relations and other ones, thus ignoring the semantics of inheritance. Weinstein and Birmingham (1999) compute description compatibility in order to answer queries that are formulated with a conceptual structure that is different from the one of the information system. Their measures depend largely on a shared ontology that mediates between locally extended ontologies. This is related to our domain-specific measures, which make use of a shared ontology. Their algorithm also seems less suited to evaluate similarities of sets of lexical entries, taxonomies, and other relations.

Bernstein et al. (2005a) presented interesting results on how humans interpret similarity. They assembled a catalogue of ontology-based similarity measures, which have experimentally been compared with a similarity gold standard obtained by surveying 50 human subjects. Results show that similarity predictions among humans and among algorithms varied substantially, but can be grouped into cohesive clusters. It will be interesting to apply these findings for alignment in future.

2.4.5 Heuristic Definition

The main operator for comparisons is similarity. Moreover, the listed concrete similarities are sufficient for most cases of ontology alignment as considered here. However, it is also possible to use other more general operators, which are here summarized through the term heuristics. In the end, they are a generalization of similarity as required for general or complex ontology alignment (Section 10.2).

Definition 2.9 (Heuristic). *A heuristic for a relation ρ is a function*

$$heur_\rho : \mathfrak{P}(E) \times \mathfrak{P}(E) \times O \times O \to [0, 1]$$

- $\forall e, f \in \mathfrak{P}(E), heur(e, f, O_1, O_2) \geq 0$ *(positiveness)*
- $heur_\rho(e, f, O_1, O_2) = 1$: *The relation ρ holds between the two objects.*
- $0 < heur_\rho(e, f, O_1, O_2) < 1$: *The relation ρ holds to a certain degree.*
- $heur_\rho(e, f, O_1, O_2) = 0$: *The relation ρ does not hold.*

Heuristics measure to which degree a relation such as inclusion (on sets, strings, or numbers), overlap, or also dissimilarity is met. A complete list of heuristics and their concrete implementation for ontologies is beyond the focus of this work, as they are only required for few methods of identity ontology alignment. The corresponding implementations will be defined in the respective sections when they are required.

An example for a heuristic on numerical values is the *smaller than* relation. In this case, we adhere to a fuzzy notion of the relation *smaller than*. Comparing two prices might result in:

$$smallerThan(price(e), price(f)) = smallerThan(9, 10) = 0.8 \qquad (2.16)$$

In contrast to existing work, the similarity layers present a concise structure for different similarity measures and help users to find the ones suiting their need best. We will make use of it for our ontology alignment.

3

Scenarios

In this book, ontology alignment is supposed to suit specific practical scenarios and not only a high-level theory. This was one of the basic claims presented in the beginning. For this reason, the next sections will examine concrete use cases and derive requirements for ontology alignment from them. As they make clear in which direction the research needs to head, these requirements are another important part of the foundations. Based on these findings, new approaches for ontology alignment will then be possible.

3.1 Use Cases

In many research projects such as *Semantic Web and Peer-to-Peer* (SWAP) (Ehrig et al., 2003b),[1] *Semantically enabled Knowledge Technologies* (SEKT) (de Bruijn and Feier, 2005),[2] the network of excellence *Knowledge Web* (Euzenat et al., 2004),[3] or *Data, Information and Process Integration with Semantic Web Services* (DIP) (Cimpian et al., 2004),[4] semantic integration is an issue, which needs to be addressed. The projects SWAP and SEKT will be elaborated on again for the concrete application of ontology alignment in Chapters 8 and 9. In these projects, the case study partners (the users) provided their needs. Here, we abstract from the actual needs and derive a set of more general use cases that need ontology alignment. The use cases have been carefully selected to depict a wide range of scenarios. They are orthogonal as far as possible. The cases show many facets of ontology alignment and therefore are capable of covering different user views. Real world applications typically are a combination of these extreme cases rather than being represented by exactly one of them. For each use case, we will mention its origin,

---

[1] http://swap.semanticweb.org/
[2] http://www.sekt-project.com/
[3] http://knowledgeweb.semanticweb.org/
[4] http://dip.semanticweb.org/

the necessary procedure, the requirements on an alignment approach therein, and an illustrative example.

3.1.1 Alignment Discovery

The use case of alignment discovery typically applies, if the future use of the results is not completely clear at the time of aligning. It is also the standard case when the focus lies on the process of aligning itself, which is the task in some research work packages or evaluation initiatives, rather than in an alignment application.

Alignment discovery is not a goal for mediation itself, but a prestep. For two ontologies, the alignments are merely identified (discovered). They comprise both schema and instance information. These alignments are then stored. The actual applications will make use of the predefined alignments at a later step in time.

Unfortunately, such a use case is only of limited value, as by keeping the actual application open, the alignment strategy cannot focus towards it and therefore only provide an average or default alignment. Defining fixed requirements is therefore relatively difficult. Automation level and quality are dependent of future use. Alignments should therefore be saved with additional metadata, such as the confidence level, that an alignment is correct. No statement about the quality requirements of the alignments can be made at the time of discovery. Time is not critical, as the actual application is decoupled from the time-consuming alignment process. User interaction may also be possible. At application runtime, predefined alignments only have to be loaded and processed.

We here show an example where plain alignment discovery is needed for. In SEKT the case studies require different mediation activities. However, mediation is mainly handled by one component, namely the OntoMap tool and its reasoning engine. Whether the alignment information is used for query answering or merging, is not clear at the time the alignment request is sent to the approach. Therefore, it needs to return alignments enhanced with as much information as possible. An internal filtering of too low quality results, is then performed within the OntoMap tool for the respective mediation action – ontology mapping.

3.1.2 Agent Negotiation / Web Service Composition

Often agents use different representations of the world, thus resulting in different expressions on their goals, their possible input or output. The descriptions of web services differ as well, even if they are modeled through ontologies. The goal of agents or services is to collaborate despite the heterogeneous representations, and solve the tasks they were built for. One way to solve this problem is to refer to standard upper-level ontologies. In all other cases ontology alignment is required.

Ontology alignment is needed to match several agents or services. Only if the meanings of different ontologies are understood, a matcher may decide, if the agents or services fit allowing an execution afterwards.

This alignment needs to be fast, reliable, and correct. Especially if several web services are concatenated the last point becomes increasingly important. Otherwise, wrong results are handed through. Often agents or services are envisioned to be businesses, connected to costs. Users will not tolerate wrong results if they are billed for them. At times, it might be possible to have a user check whether the found compositions are correct, in other cases the process will have to be fully automatic.

For example, in the DIP project, services are modeled within the WSMO framework (Fensel and Bussler, 2002). One of the core elements of this framework is the mediation component. Only if composition works, the web services can actually collaborate. To find out whether input and output of the services match, they have to be aligned, and as this information is encoded in ontologies, one requires ontology alignment (Burstein and McDermott, 2005). For example, it is possible to integrate the booking services of an air carrier and a hotel reservation network for traveling.

3.1.3 Data Integration

Relational databases are currently the most popular data storage paradigm in enterprises. As was shown in Volz et al. (2004), a large amount of the information currently available over the web is actually stored in relational databases. Through a lifting step (Volz et al., 2003) the schemas may be translated into ontologies. Yet the problem of integrating the data remains. For (ontology-based) applications, equal instances should not be distinguishable, even if they originate from different underlying repositories. The original repositories should be transparent.

The data from different sources needs to be integrated and presented to the user in a unified way, if they are the same. Alignment is a prestep for this.

The actual data integration is assumed an action only performed once. Most times this can be done in the background without strict time requirements. However, due to an assumed high amount of instance information it will have to be done mostly automatically. Only in exceptional cases, a human intervenes to resolve conflicts. Depending on the application, quality requirements for data integration differ. Generally, one may assume that for this use case alignments have to be correct. Missing alignments will not be as critical. Correct data integration is based on an already (partially) integrated schema such as resulting from the use case of ontology merging.

Data integration is a requirement within SWAP. In specific, for the Bibster application users adhere to one shared ontology scheme, but multiple instances, often containing the same bibliographic information, are returned upon a query in the peer-to-peer network. These instances then need to be integrated automatically. Ontology alignment helps to fulfill this task.

3.1.4 Ontology Evolution / Versioning

Ontologies are not static objects, they evolve, they develop over time. A method to keep track of the relations between newly created ontologies and the existing ones, and the data that conforms to them consistently is called versioning (Stojanovic, 2004). Business processes should seamlessly continue with new versions (Stojanovic et al., 2002). Ontology alignment can provide the necessary linking information between different versions of evolving ontologies.

With an existing alignment between the different ontology versions actions performed on the old version can be directly transferred to its new representation, and if necessary vice versa as well. Often such alignments are not enough. Representations linking to the old structure have to be adjusted according to the alignment. This means, that the new schema needs to replace the old schema. This also implies that the classification of instances has to be changed; further attributes may also have to be altered.

Quality of ontology alignment for evolution should generally be high. Fortunately, one can assume that different sequential versions of ontologies will have a high overlap. Identifying corresponding objects should be considerably easier than for the other use cases. A human helps to ensure the quality. Time is not a critical factor in the first place, but as evolution occurs to already existing ontologies, these might already have big amounts of data that then would have to be checked for alignments as well. This last statement implies a fast ontology alignment approach after all.

Experiences in the database field have shown that despite existing evolution strategies the change information is often lost. A frequent request is therefore to detect the links between different versions in schemas. This is also the case for the ontologies from different schema versions in the SEKT use cases. Ontology alignment is necessary for this.

3.1.5 Ontology Merging

Ontology merging is a use case for various applications. Ontologies of business departments or individual persons are merged to create a larger potentially company wide understanding. This is one promising approach for actually engineering ontologies in a distributed manner (Pinto et al., 2004a; Casanovas et al., 2005). In this scenario, ontologies are merely schema information. The merged ontology is the basis for succeeding integration steps such as data integration.

Source ontologies are merged into one target ontology. In general, the original ontologies disappear and only the merged ontology remains. Before two entities can be merged, they need to be identified through an alignment step.

The final ontology has to be correct in the sense of soundness and completeness. If only a lower level of completeness can be reached, the inferencing capabilities of the merged ontology decrease, which might be tolerable, but generally not wished. Ontology alignment for merging will therefore normally include a human in the loop, who checks the merged ontologies for correctness. For unclear alignments an explanation of the machine's recommendations is helpful. The human post-processing allows lowering the absolute quality requirements on the automatic alignment process. However, poor suggestions will leave the user unsatisfied. Time resources tend to be less critical, as the merging process may be run in the background in a batch mode. In the end, i.e., after the human post-processing, quality requirements have to be high.

For ontology merging, we refer to SEKT and in particular its case study in the legal domain. Knowledge is extracted from existing databases. From their schemas, ontologies are derived. To receive an integrated view, e.g., for extending the ontology model or simply querying, these multiple ontologies need to be merged. This action is additionally supervised by an ontology engineer to ensure the quality standards of the application are met.

3.1.6 Query and Answer Rewriting / Mapping

An operation occurring frequently in knowledge management applications is querying of information sources. For this task users formulate a query in a query language based on one ontology, normally the individual's or community's ontology. This query is sent to a query engine. Possibly, it is also passed across the network to other computers (Tempich et al., 2004). The query engine then returns an answer fitting the query. We want to allow an application to query different heterogeneous information sources without actually caring about all the different ontological representations.

In order to achieve this, a query written in terms of the source, needs to be rewritten using the terms of the target. Rewriting means to map the schema information as well as the instance information included in the query from the source to the target ontology. After execution of the query and before presented to the user again, the results have to be again transformed back to the original representation, following the same process as for the query transformation.

This rewriting may be complex, so that not only one-to-one alignments have to be identified. Additionally the rewriting has to be performed during runtime, thus quickly, and finally this normally will have to be provided fully automatically. Fortunately, a user being used to internet search engines will presumably be tolerant towards wrong results, as long as the correct results are also returned.

Within the SWAP project query and answer rewriting was a main use case. The SWAP system is peer-to-peer based where every individual has an ontology extracted from his personal data. Nevertheless, to allow exchanging information the ontologies of the underlying data need to be aligned. Queries and answers are mapped when they are sent around in the network. Only this way collaboration on the semantic level becomes possible.

3.1.7 Reasoning

The final use case also heavily dependent on ontology alignment is reasoning in a big or even global setting such as envisioned for the Semantic Web. New information is inferred from distributed and heterogeneous ontologies. Unfortunately, in a distributed web of ontologies errors and inconsistencies cannot be completely eliminated. This will also have effects on the alignment of different ontologies.

Inferencing uses both schema and instance data. Information does not have to be explicitly integrated as long as a mapping across ontology borders is possible.

The probably biggest task are requirements on quality. The alignments have to be correct. Otherwise, inferencing, especially in a global setting, quickly results in wrong results, which again trigger additional wrong results in a cascading manner. First approaches to handle conflicting inconsistent information in reasoners are discussed Huang et al. (2005). Inferencing runs in the background making time a lesser problem. The same holds for the process of ontology alignment required for this. Obviously, the alignment process has to be completed without user interaction, as the user might not even be aware of an inferencing process running somewhere using his ontology.

The value of a future Semantic Web is also justified through its expected reasoning capabilities, which integrates information from all over the web. As this global setting does not assume any fixed ontologies, the information needs to be aligned first. Only then it is possible to infer that, e.g., a small hotel with seaview (modeled in the hotel's ontology) may be reached with a specific air carrier (modeled in the air carrier's ontology), as location of the first and destination of the latter actually overlap.

3.2 Requirements

For this work, we will now extract the most important requirements for ontology alignment from the previous use case descriptions. As they are based on the actual needs of various users, we expect the list of requirements to be rather complete from this perspective. Depending on the final application, these requirements will vary with respect to importance. An ontology alignment approach has to be able to deal with all of them. At least, it has to make clear which requirements have actually been addressed and which will not be solved.

The following requirements for ontology alignment have been identified from the use cases:

- *Quality* is a main issue when trying to create an ontology alignment approach. Quality has to be high in terms of both accuracy and completeness. Depending on the use case, the actual focus may shift more towards either one.

- At least for some use cases *efficiency* may not be neglected. Resources for time and memory are restricted. An ontology alignment approach has to deal with these restrictions.
- Different levels of *user interaction* with the ontology alignment system are another requirement. Fully automatic approaches are needed for some use cases. Semi-automatic approaches for others. Further, it is desirable to have an *explanation* on why two entities are aligned or not.
- From the previous requirements, one already sees that they differ depending on the underlying *use case*. A system should be flexible enough to react to these differing requirements. As requirements might be extended or additional use cases show up, the system has to be easily *parameterizable* and adaptable.
- Simple one-to-one alignments are only a first step and not sufficient for many applications. New approaches for *complex alignments* need to be investigated.
- Finally, as already mentioned in the introduction, the work should not be generally restricted to ontologies. *Other structures* and schemas also need to be aligned.

Whereas the introduction has given a general overview of the problems and a goal description, this section has provided detailed requirements, which are going to be addressed when developing and ontology alignment approach in the remainder of this work.

4

Related Work

Ontology alignment touches many related fields. Data integration but also ontology integration are not new topics. To ensure the reuse of existing ideas an extensive investigation on related work is necessary before an own innovative approach is developed. This chapter starts with theoretic considerations on alignment. It will then focus on other actual approaches for ontology alignment. We will reach out to related fields, in specific the integration efforts of the database community, which has been approaching this issue for many years. A good overview of related work is also given in de Bruijn et al. (2006).

4.1 Theory of Alignment

A very comprehensive survey on existing work for ontology alignment is given in Kalfoglou and Schorlemmer (2003). As the authors have a strong theoretical background, we here refer to their discussions. They classify the theoretical frameworks into three groups: algebraic approaches, information-flow-based approaches, and translation frameworks. These frameworks represent the mathematical foundations for any alignment approach.

4.1.1 Algebraic Approach

In Bench-Capon and Malcolm (1999) the authors extend the concept of abstract data type to formalize ontologies and their relations building upon a universal algebra. Besides the definitions of ontology, signature, and data domains, they more importantly define the notion of morphisms in this context. Morphisms are structure-preserving transformations and are the core of the algebraic approach. In this framework aligning two ontologies O_1 and O_2 means to search for a pair of ontology morphisms p_1 and p_2 from an unknown ontology O_X to the two ontologies, which need to be aligned as depicted in Figure 4.1. For the next step of ontology merging one can then rely on the construction of categorical pushouts (Hitzler et al., 2005) based on these morphisms.

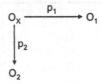

Fig. 4.1. Morphisms on Ontologies

Jannink et al. (1998) propose a different algebraic approach. Their algebra is based on category-theoretic constructions, through which the contexts from knowledge sources are extracted and combined. See also Mitra and Wiederhold (2002) for the discussion of such an algebra. The approach is less formal than the previous one. Categories are defined as the union of concept specifications and their instances. Again, pushouts are applied to these categories. *"Morphisms allow translation from one specification to another when there is no semantic mismatch. Therefore, they are applicable when intensions and extension are not distinguishable, such as in mathematical structure."* In the end, their approach is used to identify semantic mismatches between the intensions and extensions of concepts, or alternatively, if no mismatch occurs, to align the elements.

4.1.2 Information-Flow-based Approach

Kent (2000) demonstrates how ontology sharing is formalizable within the conceptual knowledge model of Information Flow (IF) (Barwise and Seligman, 1997). He assumes that there exists a common generic ontology specified as a logical theory. This common generic ontology consists of the terminology and semantics shared by diverse communities. Participating communities extend this generic ontology in their own ontologies. Specification links connect the community ontologies with the generic ontology. The yet open task is to align the community ontologies. The author proposes two steps for this. In a first lifting step from theories to logics, instances (the semantic elements) are added. The author assumes that there is a natural set of connections between instances. An instance of one community is connected to an instance of another community, when they agree on common inherited types (in our terminology: the concepts, relations, and axioms). Based on these instances it is possible to align the concepts. The second step, the fusion step, then creates a core ontology of community connections (virtual logic). *"Instance connections and identifier types comprise a natural quotient construction on the participating community ontologies. The virtual ontology of community connections is computable as this quotient."* The fusion of participating ontologies is done by creating a virtual ontology of community connections, i.e., the linkage of instances. Through the new ontology, the logics of the involved community ontologies are therefore now interlinked.

Kalfoglou and Schorlemmer (2002) propose the IF-Map methodology. They extended the approach of Kent, but also use algebraic considerations. In their approach, they have community ontologies linked to a reference ontology. They then look for logic infomorphisms from which they derive the alignments.

4.1.3 Translation Framework

A translation framework has been provided by Ciocoiu et al. (2001), a logic-based approach. Ontologies can be translated, if it is possible to express all statements of one ontology in the other ontology. The statements have to be equivalent with respect to their foundational theories – for this, the foundational theories have to be the same. Besides this strong translation, the authors also propose a partial translation where only sub-ontologies have to be completely translated or the ontologies can be extended with additional definitions. Finally, they introduce weak translations, where the theory only has to be interpreted in the other one. To actually set up this framework the authors propose an interchange ontology library. In this interchange library, all participating ontologies are modeled soundly and completely. From these axiomatizations it will then be easy to determine and construct the translation between any of the involved ontologies.

All the presented theories deliver valuable input of ideas on how to set up an ontology alignment approach. However, they cannot be applied directly, as they require complete intensional or extensional modeling of the involved ontologies. As one of the goals of this work is to be robust against possible missing or wrong information, we will extend the theories with considerations on similarity rather than logical equivalence. This will lead to new approaches for ontology alignment.

4.2 Existing Alignment Approaches

This section will show which alignment approaches already exist and what their specific characteristics are. This gives us a solid grounding for developing an own approach respecting the requirements we had identified.

4.2.1 Classification Guidelines for Alignment Approaches

Before describing the approaches, we will create classification guidelines for alignment approaches. This makes it easier to identify the methods that are specific for each individual approach. We will now explain the four main dimensions: input schema, alignment process, output schema, and use case. The dimensions are inspired by Rahm and Bernstein (2001) and Shvaiko and Euzenat (2005).

Input schemas:

Generally, this work focuses on aligning whole ontologies. However, for related work we look beyond ontologies. There are many input schemas, which need to be aligned.

- Apart from ontologies, there are structures with less semantic structure such as directed acyclic graphs, trees, or classification schemas. For integration, database schemas may also be the input. Specific schemas such as XML Schema or Entity-Relationship-Models (ERM) have other special semantics.
- The syntactic representations, which various approaches handle, are another dimension of input, though XML makes a grounding.
- In general one also distinguishes between schemas with instances and without instances.

Process:

The main dimension is the process of aligning. In fact, the processes of ontology alignment approaches differ most, as there exist a large number of parameters and methods.

- The process may be based on a strict logic and infer alignments. Or it may rely on heuristics and collect evidence for alignments.
- Some approaches focus on the syntax whereas others include the whole semantics of the model. In addition, the degree of incorporated semantics differs. Are only linguistic properties taken into account? Does the approach rely on explicitly modeled constraints?
- The approaches may focus on the individuals (instances) or the structure (schema).
- In most cases one has more than one type of evidence pointing towards alignment. The question remains how they are combined, with automatic aggregation being one possibility and manual checking being another one. Automatic aggregation may be based on rules or learned classifiers, as presented in Doan and Halevy (2005). Multiple rules or learned classifiers may be also be combined.
- Additional external sources help to improve results. Some approaches make extensive use of this, e.g., by consulting dictionaries (such as Word-Net) or relying on additional instance bases.
- Finally, alignment approaches vary in the degree of automation, ranging from fully manual through automatic recommendations to fully automatic.

Output:

Likewise the output differs considerably for different approaches.

- Depending on the input schema, different elements are aligned: concepts, relations, and instances; nodes and vertices; classes, objects, and attributes; individual elements or whole structures.
- The simplest cases are one-to-one alignments. In real world, one will often encounter n-to-m alignments instead. The question what kind of relation is finally identified has to be answered as well: Equivalence of entities is most common, but subsumption, overlap, or complete orthogonality are other options. Most alignments are simple, but first steps towards complex alignment are made.
- In most of today's algorithms, alignments are not only provided per se any longer. A confidence value for the alignments is provided by most approaches. Often one can refer to confidence as probability, making it possible to reason with the inexact information.

Use Case:

In many surveys on ontology alignment, the use cases are not considered a dimension for distinction. Even though they might not directly be reflected in input, process, or output, they definitely influence the complete setting of the alignment process.

- Typical use cases are data integration, ontology (or schema) merging, and creation of mappings for translation between different schemas.

In fact, the use cases are the reason why different approaches cannot be directly compared.

4.2.2 Ontology Alignment Approaches

The subsequent concrete existing ontology alignment approaches will be described along the dimensions just introduced. A summarizing table will be presented in the end.

ONION

In their tool ONION (ONtology compositION system), Mitra et al. (2000) provide an approach for resolving heterogeneity between different ontologies. Their basic assumption is that merging of whole ontologies is too costly and inefficient. Therefore, they focus on creating so called *articulation rules*, which link corresponding concepts. As manual creation of these rules is not very efficient either, they use a semi-automatic approach, which takes into account heuristics on several simple relations, such as labels, subsumption hierarchies and attribute values. Dictionary information is also used for the alignment process. From these relations a match is presented to the user who then has to decide whether the alignment is valid or not. The articulation rules' linking can be applied when an application inquires information from two ontologies. The work is based on their theory on composition algebras (Mitra and Wiederhold, 2001).

SMART, PROMPT, Anchor-PROMPT, PromptDiff

SMART was the first step towards a number of tools created by Noy and Musen (1999). The tools are available as plug-ins for the Protégé ontology environment (Noy et al., 2001).[1] SMART is an algorithm that is mainly linguistic-based. It checks concept names for similarity and then matches relations and attributes. SMART provides one-to-one alignments of ontology entities.

PROMPT (Noy and Musen, 2000) is a tool that provides a semi-automatic approach to ontology merging. It is based on the SMART algorithm. After having identified alignments by matching of labels, the user is prompted to mark the entity pairs that should actually be merged. During merging, PROMPT presents possible inconsistencies such as name conflicts or relations not pointing anywhere any longer. The user then decides on how to react and resolve the issues manually.

Anchor-PROMPT (Noy and Musen, 2001) represents an advanced version of PROMPT that includes similarity measures based on ontology structures. So-called anchor points, alignment pairs in the ontologies, are identified first, normally through string-based comparisons of the entities or by directly having them assigned by the user. Based on these known anchor points the structures of the ontologies are traversed resulting in propositions of additional alignments of entities between the known anchor points. Specifically, paths are traversed along hierarchies as well as along other relations. Afterwards the results are again presented to the user, including an explanation, and the user decides whether to merge the proposed entities or not. This process is continued in several iterations.

PromptDiff (Noy and Musen, 2002) is a tool to compare different ontology versions. Different heuristic matchers are used to determine the similar entities. The matchers are combined in a fixed-point manner until no further changes occur. PromptDiff makes use of the fact that two versions of one ontology have considerable overlap.

The PROMPT-Suite (Noy and Musen, 2003) thus consists of different approaches tackling different questions around ontology alignment. PROMPT is one of the most used tools for ontology merging, also due to its easy use within the Protégé environment.

---

[1] http://protege.stanford.edu/

Chimaera

Chimaera (McGuinness et al., 2000) is an interactive tool for ontology merging. Its basic ontology format is OKBC,[2] but it can also handle other languages. After executing a linguistic matcher, Chimaera uses the results for triggering the merging operation. During this process, the human has to decide whether to merge or not. Chimaera also provides proposals on reorganizing the taxonomy once a merge has been processed. Overall, Chimaera allows diagnosing and manual editing for ontology merging. The actual alignment of entities however is based on simple measures.

FCA-Merge

The FCA-Merge approach has been presented by Stumme and Maedche (2001). As the name already suggests, its goal is to merge ontologies. It is based on formal concept analysis as described in Ganter and Wille (1999). Given two ontologies in a first step FCA-Merge populates them with instances that are extracted from a set of documents. This step is necessary, as most ontologies do not have sufficient instances, but these are required for formal concept analysis. Based on these instances the ontologies are represented as concept lattices, i.e., concepts are seen as sets of instances. At this point lexical information is used to retrieve domain specific information. Using formal concept analysis the two contexts are integrated and a new lattice is created thereof. Pruning steps are applied to keep the size of the lattices small. In a last step, the lattice has to be transformed back into an ontology. This step has to be done manually. To solve conflicts, such as duplicates, FCA-Merge has an automatic support to guide the user through the process. One should mention that FCA-Merge deals only with concept hierarchies and underlying instances – alignment of relations is not supported.

LSD, GLUE

The LSD (Learning Source Descriptions) system uses machine learning techniques to match an unknown data source against a previously determined global schema (Doan et al., 2001). Given a user-supplied alignment from a data source to the global schema, the preprocessing step examines instances from that data source to train the learner, thereby discovering characteristic instance patterns and matching rules. If the concept instances in the second schema match the first classifier, the concepts are regarded as identical. The individual matchers' results are then again used to train an overall *"global"* matcher. Applying this matcher, it is now possible to determine alignments between the global data source and new sources.

LSD was later extended to GLUE (Doan et al., 2003). GLUE is more oriented towards ontologies. As for LSD, it searches for the most similar

---

[2] http://www.ksl.stanford.edu/software/OKBC/

concepts in two ontologies using several matchers. Their learning component determines concept classifiers (matchers) for instances based on instance descriptions, i.e., the textual content of webpages, or their naming. In fact, GLUE uses a multi-learning strategy because there are many different types of information the concept classifiers can rely on. They range from instance names to word frequency in documents, or the value formats. From these learned concept classifiers they derive whether concepts in two schemas correspond to each other. In recent work of the authors (Sayyadian et al., 2005), they investigated how to increase the basis of training data by creating them automatically. They showed that for database schema alignment results improve.

Concepts and relations are further compared using *relaxation labeling*. The intuition of relaxation labeling is that the label of a node (in our terminology: alignment assigned to an entity) is typically influenced by the features of the node's neighborhood in the graph. The authors explicitly mention subsumption, frequency, and nearby nodes. A local optimal alignment for each entity is determined using the similarity results of neighboring entity pairs from a previous round. The individual constraint similarities are summed for the final alignment probability. The additional relaxation labeling, which considers the ontological structures, is again based solely on manually encoded predefined rules. Normally one needs to check all possible labeling configurations, which includes the alignments of all other entities. The developers are well aware of the problem arising in complexity, so they set up sensible partitions, i.e., labeling sets with the same features are grouped and processed only once. The probabilities for the partitions are determined. One assumption is that features are independent, which the authors admit does not necessarily hold true. Through multiplication of the probabilities one finally receives the probability of a label fitting the node, i.e., of one entity being aligned with another one. The pair with the maximal probability is the final alignment result.

The GLUE machine learning approach is suitable for a scenario with extensive textual instance descriptions, but may not suit a scenario focused more onto ontology schema. Relations or instances cannot be directly aligned with GLUE. The authors have successfully tested their approach on ontologies of two websites.

OLA

The OWL Lite Aligner (OLA) was introduced by Euzenat and Valtchev (2004). It uses different components of the involved ontologies to determine similarity. The base similarities are calculated from labels. Iteratively the base similarities influence each other until the similarities are well-balanced between all pairs of the two ontologies. In each iteration the similarities are recalculated taking into account the similarity of neighboring nodes, whereas neighboring means that there is a relation to them. This makes OLA an approach using both element information and structural information. The flowing similarities are weighted differently according to the relation (subsumption, instantiation, ...). The user sets these weights according to his preferences. Finding the correct alignments is an optimization problem with maximal similarities. It is closely related to the similarity flooding approach of Melnik et al. (2002) (Section 4.2.3). The OWL Lite Aligner returns one-to-one alignments of concepts, relations, and instances.

We give a final overview of the ontology alignment approaches in Table 4.1. The discussion of the approaches PROMPT, GLUE, and OLA is resumed in Section 5.3 with a direct link to the to-be-introduced general ontology alignment process.

4.2.3 Schema Alignment Approaches

Schema alignment is tightly related to ontology alignment. Therefore, a number of these approaches are now presented.

SemInt

SemInt (Li and Clifton, 1994) creates alignments between individual attributes of two schemas. Unlike most other approaches, it does not provide name-based or graph-based matching. It bases its analysis on the information available from the schema of a relational database management system and the instance data. Value distributions and averages consequently are converted to signatures. For these signatures, SemInt applies two similarity operators. It uses either the Euclidian distance or a trained neural network to determine the match candidates. The authors express that both approaches have advantages and disadvantages, which differ according to the application. The neural network faces some efficiency problems (Clifton et al., 1997). The contribution of SemInt was to provide one of the first approaches not opting for a hard-wired combination of individual rule-based similarities, but using a machine-learning-based approach.

DIKE

DIKE (Palopoli et al., 2000) is an approach to automatically determine synonym and inclusion (is-a, hypernym) relationships. The input are entity-relationship schemas. To the end, different similarity values between two objects are calculated based on their related objects such as attributes. These may also only be related indirectly through relation paths. The more distant related objects are, the less important they are for determining the similarity. The goal is to find similar, but not necessarily identical objects. It also identifies other kinds of relations. A relation holds if the similarity value is above a fixed threshold.

Table 4.1. Ontology Alignment Approaches

	ONION	PROMPT	Anchor-PROMPT
Input	ontologies	RDF(S) ontologies	RDF(S) ontologies
Process	semi-automatic approach based on labels, hierarchies, and attribute values; users validate proposals	semi-automatic approach based on label equality	semi-automatic approach using the structure (anchor-points)
Output	articulation rules	proposals for user	proposals for user
Use Case		ontology merging	ontology merging

	Chimaera	FCA-Merge	GLUE
Input	OKBC ontologies	ontologies	schemas/ontologies
Process	interactive tool using linguistic matcher; diagnosis tools	semi-automatic approach based on FCA, i.e., instances	multi-strategy approach using learned matchers for instances and relaxation labeling to include structure
Output		new lattice for ontology	alignments
Use Case	ontology merging	ontology merging	alignment discovery

	OLA
Input	OWL-Lite ontologies
Process	automatic approach; base similarity from labels fix-point computation for structure different relation weights
Output	alignments
Use Case	alignment discovery

ARTEMIS

ARTEMIS (Analysis of Requirements: Tool Environment for Multiple Information Systems) (Castano et al., 2001) is a component of the MOMIS heterogeneous database mediator (Bergamaschi et al., 2001). Individually developed schemas are to be integrated into a virtual global one. ARTEMIS is based on different similarities (which the authors refer to as affinity), that is to say name similarity (using WordNet), datatype similarity, and structural similarity of the involved entities. These similarities are then summed with appropriate weights. Based on the overall similarity and a hierarchical clustering technique ARTEMIS categorizes classes into groups where each group presents a more general class with a set of global attributes. Through a mapping table, the original source schemas are linked to the virtual global schema.

Cupid

Cupid (Madhavan et al., 2001) is a hybrid matcher based on element- and structure-level matching. In terms of input data, it is very generic and has been applied to XML and different relational data models. The algorithm comprises three steps. In the first step, elements (nodes of the schema) are compared by linguistic means, also including external information on synonyms. Secondly, for the structural matching the data model has to be transformed into a tree. Pairs are then compared by examining their leaf sets. A similarity is calculated through a weighted mean of linguistic and structural similarity. In the third phase, a threshold is applied to eventually decide on an alignment or not. The authors emphasize that setting the threshold is application dependent and cannot be done in general.

Similarity Flooding, Rondo

Melnik et al. (2002) presented an approach for integration based on the concept of similarity flooding. It was later implemented in Rondo (Melnik et al., 2003). The input schemas are directed acyclic graphs. Basic element level similarity is determined using string-based comparisons. Through a fixed-point computation, this initial similarity is spread throughout the graphs from similar nodes to the adjacent neighbors based on propagation coefficients. However, as the edges are not labeled, no semantic interpretation of them is exploited. After a few iterations the similarity converges to a maximum, the fix-point is reached. It is the solution of a clearly stated optimization problem. Very close to this approach is the Falcon system of Hu et al. (2005). They use two graphs influencing each other: the actual objects and the RDF statements. This allows to include labeled edges, i.e., relations. Similarities are then calculated on these two graphs.

COMA

COMA (COmbination of MAtching algorithms) (Do and Rahm, 2002) is a schema matching system, which aims at combining multiple individual matchers in a flexible way. The goal is to match real world schemas. Prior to starting the alignment, the schemas are transformed into a directed acyclic graph. The alignment process then consists of three phases, which are repeated iteratively. The first phase is an optional user feedback phase. Here the user sets the parameters of the algorithm, e.g., choose among the matchers and accept or reject proposed matches. Thereafter, the individual matchers are calculated. These are based mainly on linguistic information, also using background dictionaries, and structural elements as children or leaves. In the third phase, the matchers are combined either using a maximum, weighted, average, or minimum strategy. Different approaches for threshold determination are given. It is also possible to run the approach in a fully automatic mode.

CTXMatch, S-Match

Giunchiglia et al. (2004) present an approach to derive semantic relations between classes of two classification schemas, which are extracted from databases or ontologies. Based on the labels the system identifies equivalent entities. For this, it also makes use of synonyms defined in WordNet. Other element level matchers are also included. Through a SAT-solver the system identifies additional relations between the two schemas. The SAT-solver takes the structure of the schemas into account, especially the taxonomy and its inferred implications, e.g., the fact that any object in a class is also an element of all the superclasses thereof. As result, the system returns equivalence, subsumption, or mismatch between two classes. In a recent version S-Match also provides explanations of the alignments (Shvaiko et al., 2005). Their argumentation presents numerous individual reasons for this.

As in the previous section, we summarize the different approaches along the four dimensions input, process, output, and use case in Table 4.2.

4.2.4 Global as View / Local as View

Some widespread approaches in data-integration systems are shortly introduced: Global-as-View (GAV), Local-as-View (LAV), and more recently Global-Local-as-View (GLAV) (Ullman, 1997). Depending on the underlying view paradigm querying the structures has to be handled differently.

Global-as-View:

In this view, for each entity in the global schema, we write a query over the local data source entities. It is assumed that the data corresponding to a

Table 4.2. Schema Alignment Approaches

	SemInt	DIKE	ARTEMIS
Input	schemas	entity-relationship-schemas	database schemas
Process	automatic approach based on database catalog and instances; distances or neural network for matcher	automatic approach; objects are similar, if related (also indirectly) attributes are similar	database mediator based on name, datatype, and structural similarity; virtual global schema
Output	attribute alignments	synonyms and inclusion	class alignment
Use Case			schema mediation

	Cupid	Similarity Flooding	COMA
Input	relational schemas (incl. XML)	direct acyclic graphs	schemas
Process	hybrid matcher based on element- (labels) and structure-level matching; application dependent threshold	automatic approach basic string comparison, fixed-point computation for structure	combination of multiple matchers; linguistic information, dictionaries; simple structural elements; different combination strategies
Output	alignments	alignments	alignments
Use Case			

	S-Match
Input	classification schemas
Process	SAT-solver; linguistic similarity, dictionaries; solver respects structural elements
Output	relations between classes; explanations
Use Case	alignment

concept of the global view can actually be retrieved from the local data sources through a specific query. The local data sources have to be at least as detailed as the global schema. This view on integration makes querying easy, as each global entity in the query simply has to be replaced by its query/view on the local schemas. However, every time a change occurs in the local sources, the global schema views need to be replaced. High dynamicity is difficult to handle.

Local-as-View:

For the second view, local-as-view describes the local data source in the opposite direction. Contents of data sources are described as a query over the global schema, i.e, the global schema has to be more detailed than the local ones. The global information content is described in terms of those entities the users are familiar with, their local terms. Query processing is more difficult, as the system is not told explicitly how to reformulate the global entities for local source queries. Changes in the sources are less critical, as they are only changed locally and do not affect the global schema.

Global-Local-as-View:

Friedman et al. (1999) proposed a Global-Local-as-View approach, which combines both Global-as-View and Local-as-View. The restrictions on the direction of the view are overcome. Data is retrieved by using views over the source relations and conjunctions thereof on global level. The overall expressivity is therefore higher than in either of the previous two mentioned views. Complete transformations are only possible if local and global schemas have the same representation granularity.

These three notions are very important when mapping objects onto each other and their consequences for queries and corresponding answers. This book addresses an issue which is situated before the actual mapping. GAV, LAV, and GLAV therefore do not directly effect our considerations on ontology alignment.

Despite the diversity of existing approaches both on theoretical and application level, none of them sufficiently suit our purposes, as they all neglect some of the important requirements identified in the previous chapter. Keeping all this related work in mind and making use of their findings, we are now ready to develop our novel approach for ontology alignment.

Part II

Ontology Alignment Approach

5

Process

After the foundations, the next step in research methodology is the actual creative and innovative one. This central chapter of the book will now develop a new approach for ontology alignment based on the previous findings. In fact, this will be achieved through several elements. First, we will shape a general underlying process for alignment. Specific methods for each process step are then going to lead to a concise basic approach (Ehrig and Sure, 2004a). The modular composition makes it easy to follow the new ideas in this work. We will show that already existing approaches also fit this process very well. Furthermore, in later chapters different methods in the process are going to be substituted to better meet the previously identified requirements. An additional important section for proving the value of this work is a thorough evaluation. After we will have introduced the fundamentals of ontology alignment evaluation, we will directly evaluate the novel approach and show its strengths and weaknesses.

5.1 General Process

The introduction mentioned that this work would focus on real world ontologies. These are not necessarily correct and complete and may contain contradictions. Pure theories for ontology alignment, which derive identity logically as presented in the previous chapter, therefore may not suit the case. This work follows a more robust approach based on comparisons, namely similarity considerations among other heuristics to identify objects to align. In a way, human ontology alignment is imitated in an artificial intelligent way. *Entities are the same, if their features are similar enough.* Features in ontologies represent a certain meaning, certain semantics the ontology modeler and user has in mind. Nevertheless, even two equal objects might be modeled slightly differently, resulting therein that the features will not be exactly the same, but they will be similar. Whereas low similarities do not give us any support regarding alignments, high similarity values are a strong evidence for alignments. Goldstone (2001) discusses this tight relation between similarity and alignment. He also points out that not every similarity is equally important, thus some kind of weighting is necessary. Through the upcoming process, our procedure is to collect evidence for alignments – expressed through different high similarity values. This is a core hypothesis of this work. In fact, many related approaches have the same hypothesis as we have seen in the previous chapter. Similarity (or proximity) has also been used for semantic mapping of databases (Kashyap and Sheth, 1996).

Most existing alignment approaches (Do and Rahm, 2002; Doan et al., 2003; Noy and Musen, 2003) are subsumed by a general canonical process. For some approaches certain process steps are merged or their order is changed, but they all have the same elements. An exception are the reasoning-based approaches such as presented in Ciocoiu et al. (2001) or Giunchiglia et al. (2004), which only partially follow it. An overview of our general alignment process will be given here. The individual process steps will then be explained in detail in the next section. Figure 5.1 illustrates input, output, and the six main steps in between of the now following general process.

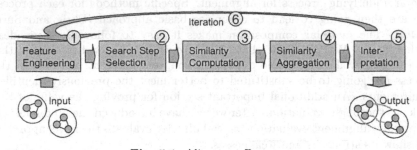

Fig. 5.1. Alignment Process

Input:

Input for the process are two or more ontologies, which need to be aligned with one another. Additionally, it is often possible to enter preknown (manual) alignments. They can help to improve the search for alignments.

1. Feature engineering:

Small excerpts of the overall ontology definition are selected to describe a specific entity. These excerpts are not arbitrary constructs, but have a specific meaning within the ontology – they represent a certain semantics. In a later step these features are then used for comparison. For instance, the alignment process may only rely on a subset of OWL primitives, possibly only the taxonomy, or even just the linguistic descriptions of entities (e.g., the label "car" to describe the concept o1:car).

2. Search Step Selection:

The derivation of ontology alignments takes place in a search space of candidate alignments. This step may choose to compute the similarity of certain candidate concepts pairs $\{(e, f)|e \in O_1, f \in O_2\}$ and to ignore others (e.g., only compare o1:car with o2:automobile and not with o2:hasMotor).

3. Similarity Computation:

For a given description of two entities from the candidate alignments this step indicates a similarity (e.g., sim_{label}(o1:car,o2:automobile) = $sim_{syntactic}$("car", "automobile") = 0). In some related work this step does not only return a similarity, but actually a value of either 0 or 1; these are then called individual matchers based on a certain feature.

4. Similarity Aggregation:

In general, there may be several similarity values for a candidate pair of entities, e.g., one for the similarity of their labels and one for the similarity of their relationship to other entities. These different similarity values for one candidate pair have to be aggregated into a single aggregated similarity value (e.g., (sim_{label}(o1:car,o2:automobile) + $sim_{subconcepts}$(o1:car,o2:automobile) + $sim_{instances}$(o1:car,o2:automobile))/3=0.5).

5. Interpretation:

The interpretation finally uses individual or aggregated similarity values to derive alignments between entities. The similarities need to be interpreted. Common mechanisms are to use thresholds (Do and Rahm, 2002; Noy and Musen, 2003) or to combine structural and similarity criteria (Doan et al., 2003). In the end, a proposition of alignment (or not) for the selected entity pairs is returned (e.g., $align$(o1:car) ='$\perp$').[1]

6. Iteration:

The similarity of one entity pair influences the similarity of neighboring entity pairs, for example, if the instances are equal this affects the similarity of the concepts and vice versa. Therefore, the similarity is propagated through the ontologies by following the links in the ontology. Several algorithms perform an iteration over the whole process in order to bootstrap the amount of structural knowledge. In each iteration, the similarities of a candidate alignment are recalculated based on the similarities of neighboring entity pairs. Eventually, it may lead to a new similarity (e.g., sim(o1:car,o2:automobile) = 0.85), subsequently resulting in a new alignment

---

[1] '$\perp$' indicates that no valid alignment was found.

(e.g., *align*(o1:car) = o2:automobile). Iteration terminates when no new alignments are proposed. Note that in a subsequent iteration, one or several of steps 1 through 5 may be skipped, because all features might already be available in the appropriate format or because similarity computation might only be required in the first round.

Output:

The output is a representation of alignments, e.g., an alignment table indicating the relation $align_{O_1,O_2}$ and possibly with additional confidence values.

Each of the presented steps has specific methods with corresponding parameters, which have to be set. We therefore refer to the process as a *parameterizable alignment method* (PAM) (Ehrig et al., 2005b). Instantiations of these parameters are presented in the next section. The quality of the process and its results will be subsequently evaluated. Please bear in mind that even though we are referring to ontologies, similarity, and equivalence, these three terms may be replaced by any structure, heuristic, and binary relation. In Section 10.1 this extension will be conducted.

5.2 Alignment Approach

We will now expand our general process by explaining its individual steps in detail and show concrete instantiations thereof. To provide a toolbox of methods and their parameters common to many approaches that align ontologies is the principal idea of these sections. This detailed stepwise approach for ontology alignment is novel and one core contribution. The explanations will not be restricted to the theoretical level only. The last paragraph of each section will provide an actual practical alignment approach for implementation. This alignment approach, which we refer to as Naïve Ontology alignMent (NOM) (Ehrig and Sure, 2004a), gives us a least common denominator, on the basis of which different approaches can be compared more easily.

5.2.0 Input

Input for the alignment approach are the two ontologies O_1 and O_2, such as represented in Figure 5.2.

Definition 5.1 (Input). *Given a set of ontologies O,*

$$input : O \to \mathfrak{P}(O)$$

selects two or more ontologies thereof.

If more than two ontologies are taken, all ontologies are compared pairwise. A higher expressivity of the ontologies, such as OWL constructs provide, would be favorable. More semantic information allows for more actions to identify alignments. Preknown alignments may be introduced, thus giving the alignment algorithm good starting points especially for the elements of structural alignment.

5.2.1 Feature Engineering

To compare two entities from two different ontologies O_1 and O_2, one considers their characteristics, their features F.

Definition 5.2 (Feature Engineering). *From two ontologies a list of features F is determined through*

$$feat: O \times O \to \mathfrak{P}(F)$$

The selected features are specific for an alignment generation algorithm. In any case, the features of ontological entities (of concepts C, relations R, and instances I) need to be extracted from intensional and extensional ontology definitions. We do not interpret the ontologies as graphs only, but, in fact, want to exploit the semantics of each individual feature for our purposes. See also Euzenat and Valtchev (2003) and Ehrig and Sure (2004a) for an overview of possible features and a classification of them:

- *Identifiers* comprise strings with dedicated formats, such as unified resource identifiers (URIs) or labels defined in the lexicon *Lex* of the ontology. Labels are the most common feature used when considering related work approaches.
- The *primitives of RDF-Schema* yet provide a wide range of features, for example, properties or the defined subclass/subproperty relations ($\leq_C, \leq_R$). These also include inferred subclass/subproperty relations.
- *OWL primitives* further extend these features. One entity may, e.g., be declared being equal to another entity or a union of others. Basically, each OWL-DL primitive (Section 2.1) can be used as a feature for alignment.
- *Derived features* constrain or extend simple primitives (e.g., most-specific-class-of-instance). These are not directly modeled in the ontology, but are inferred from it.
- For *aggregated features*, we need to compare more than one simple primitive, e.g., a sibling is every instance of the parent concept of the original instance. These are also not directly modeled in the ontology.
- Also a more *complex axiom A* may be the basis for identifying alignments. If in one ontology we know that a fast car has a fast motor and belongs to the group of street vehicles, and in the other, we know there is a sports car, which runs on roads and has a fast motor, we infer that sports car is a fast car. To achieve such comparisons, the individual variables (typically

entities) and operators of the logical axioms in both ontologies need to be compared. The handling of axioms for alignment has indeed been addressed in Fürst and Trichet (2005).

- Often ontology alignment has to be performed for a specific application of one domain, which is expressed within the ontology definition O. For these scenarios, *domain-specific features* provide excess value to the alignment process. Returning to our example, the speed relation is not a general ontology feature, but a feature that is defined in the automobile domain ontology. Thus it will be important for correctly and only aligning representations of concrete vehicles. As one may imagine in this context, the domain ontology-specific feature-value pair (speed, fast) is more exact than a generic (some relation, some range) pair.

- *External features* are any kind of information not directly encoded in the ontology, such as a bag-of-words from a document describing an instance. In fact, if the ontologies are weak in expressivity, examining the external features may be the only way to find alignment results.

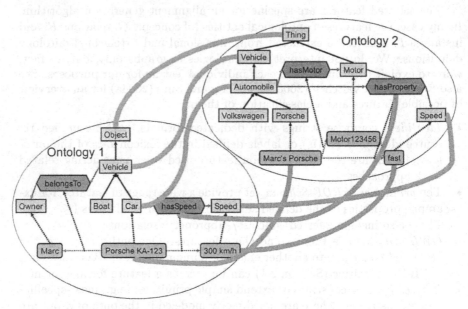

Fig. 5.2. Ontology Alignment Example

We refer to our running example. The actual features consist of a juxtaposition of relation name and entity name. The car concept in ontology 1 is characterized through its label *"car"*, the subconcept vehicle that it is linked to, its concept sibling boat, and the has speed relation. Car is also described by its instances, here only Porsche KA-123. The relation has speed in turn is described through the domain car and the range speed. An instance is Porsche KA-123, which is characterized through the instantiated property instance of belonging to Marc and having a speed of 300 km/h. The actual comparison of these features will follow on the next pages.

NOM:

For the Naïve Ontology Alignment approach (NOM) we rely on identifiers, RDF(S) primitives, and derived features only. The complete list of used features is presented in Table 5.1. The first column indicates which types of entities are compared. For concepts, e.g., we examine eleven features such as the labels, relations, super-, and subconcepts as mentioned in the third column. The first line in the table essentially means that concepts are compared by their labels applying the syntactic similarity measure. For comparison the same features are taken in both ontologies. An exception are number 8 and 9, where the direct subconcepts of one ontology are compared with the direct superconcepts of the other one. We will refer to this special case at a later point in the process.

5.2.2 Search Step Selection

Before the comparison of entities can be initiated, it is necessary to choose which entity pairs (e, f) from the ontologies actually to consider.

Definition 5.3 (Search Step Selection). *Given two ontologies for alignment, we define*

$$sele : O \times O \rightarrow \mathfrak{P}(E \times E)$$

resulting in a set of entity pairs where E are the entities as previously defined.

The most common methods for candidate alignments are to compare:

- all entities of the first ontology O_1 with all entities of the second ontology O_2: $(e, f) \in E_1 \times E_2$;
- or only those entities of the same type (concepts, relations, and instances): $(e, f) \in (C_1 \times C_2) \cup (R_1 \times R_2) \cup (I_1 \times I_2)$.

To the best of our knowledge, all related work approaches use either of these strategies for the search step selection. We refer to them as *complete agendas*.

NOM:

Applying the second strategy, which we also use in NOM, to the example ontologies (Figure 5.2), we receive 42 (6x7) concept, four (2x2) relation, and nine (3x3) instance pairs. For instance, we compare the relations o1:belongsTo and o1:hasSpeed with o2:hasMotor and o2:hasProperty. Any of these pairs will then be treated as a candidate alignment.

Table 5.1. Features and Similarity Measures in NOM. The corresponding ontology is indicated through an index.

Comparing	No.	Feature	Similarity Measure
Concepts	1	(label,X_1)	syntactic(X_1, X_2)
	2	(identifier,X_1)	equality(X_1, X_2)
	3	(X_1,sameAs,X_2) relation	object(X_1, X_2)
	4	(direct relations,Y_1)	multi(Y_1, Y_2)
	5	all (inherited relations,Y_1)	multi(Y_1, Y_2)
	6	all (superconcepts,Y_1)	multi(Y_1, Y_2)
	7	all (subconcepts,Y_1)	multi(Y_1, Y_2)
	8	(subconc.,Y_1) / (superconc., Y_2)	multi(Y_1, Y_2)
	9	(superconc.,Y_1) / (subconc., Y_2)	multi(Y_1, Y_2)
	10	(concept siblings,Y_1)	multi(Y_1, Y_2)
	11	(instances,Y_1)	multi(Y_1, Y_2)
Relations	1	(label,X_1)	syntactic(X_1, X_2)
	2	(identifier,X_1)	equality(X_1, X_2)
	3	(X_1,sameAs,X_2) relation	object(X_1, X_2)
	4	(domain,X_{d1}) and (range,X_{r1})	object(X_{d1}, X_{d2}), (X_{r1}, X_{r2})
	5	all (superrelations,Y_1)	multi(Y_1, Y_2)
	6	all (subrelations,Y_1)	multi(Y_1, Y_2)
	7	(relation siblings,Y_1)	multi(Y_1, Y_2)
	8	(relation instances,Y_1)	multi(Y_1, Y_2)
Instances	1	(label,X_1)	syntactic(X_1, X_2)
	2	(identifier,X_1)	equality(X_1, X_2)
	3	(X_1,sameAs,X_2) relation	object(X_1, X_2)
	4	all (parent-concepts,Y_1)	multi(Y_1, Y_2)
	5	(relation instances,Y_1)	multi(Y_1, Y_2)
Relation-Instances	1	(domain,X_d1) and (range,X_r1)	object(X_{d1}, X_{d2}), (X_{r1}, X_{r2})
	2	(parent relation,Y_1)	multi(Y_1, Y_2)

5.2.3 Similarity Computation

Similarities actually represent evidence that two entities are the same, thus can be aligned. The similarity computation between an entity e and an entity f is done by using a wide range of similarity functions. Each similarity function is composed of the introduced feature (F) existing in both ontologies and a corresponding similarity measure.

Definition 5.4 (Similarity Computation). *For each entity pair and corresponding feature, similarities are defined as*

$$sim : E \times E \times F \to [0,1]^k$$

Table 5.1 shows possible feature/similarity combinations. The similarity measures have been extensively defined and explained in a previous chapter. To compare strings, e.g., as from the labels, one can rely on $sim_{syntactic}$, to determine the similarity of two entity sets one may use sim_{multi}. Of course, this table will never be complete: There are many more features to be considered as well as more similarity measures to compare these features. More expressive ontologies or domain knowledge will extend this table. Doan and Halevy (2005) refer to the explicit combination of semantic features and similarity as rule-based approaches, in contrast to instance-based learned approaches.

Let us consider the example. We will examine the candidate alignment (o1:car, o2:automobile). For every feature a similarity is computed. We only present three of them here:

sim_{label}(o1:car,o2:automobile) = $sim_{syntactic}$("car","automobile") = 0.0

$sim_{superconcept}$(o1:car,o2:automobile)

   = sim_{multi}({o1:vehicle{,{o2:vehicle}) = 1.0

$sim_{relation}$(o1:car,o2:automobile)

   = sim_{multi}({o1:hasSpeed},{o2:hasProperty,o2:hasMotor}) = 0.5^2

NOM:

Our practical alignment approach relies on exactly the features and similarities as shown in Table 5.1.

5.2.4 Similarity Aggregation

According to our hypothesis, we align entities by comparing their similarity. We assume that a combination of the so far presented features and similarity measures leads to better alignment results than using only one at a time. Clearly not all introduced similarity values have to be used for each aggregation, especially as some have a high correlation.

Definition 5.5 (Similarity Aggregation). *Multiple similarity values are aggregated to one value:*

$$agg : [0,1]^k \rightarrow [0,1]$$

Even though several approaches for alignment exist, no research paper especially focused on the combination and integration of these methods for ontologies. Do and Rahm (2002) address this problem for database structures, but leave the combination decision to the user in the end.

Generally, similarity aggregation can be expressed through:

$$sim_{agg}(e,f) = agg(sim_1(e,f),\dots sim_k(e,f)) \tag{5.1}$$

with (e,f) being a candidate alignment and agg a function over the individual similarity measures sim_1 to sim_k. Often this function leads to a simpler equation of

$$sim_{aggs}(e,f) = \frac{\sum_{k=1\dots n} w_k \cdot adj_k(sim_k(e,f))}{\sum_{k=1\dots n} w_k} \tag{5.2}$$

---

[2] In fact, entities are not only compared by their name, but also through other features such as the range, which leads to 0.5 here.

with w_k being the weight for each individual similarity measure and adj_k being an adjustment function to transform the original similarity value (adj : $[0,1] \to [0,1]$). An explanation of the usage of these variables will follow. We here present four approaches for aggregation.

Averaging:

All the individual weights are equally set to 1, the adjustment function adj_k is set to be the identity function id, the value is not changed. The result is a simple average over all individual similarities:

$$w_k = 1, \; adj_k(x) = id(x) \tag{5.3}$$

Linear Summation:

The adjustment function is again set to be the identity function.

$$adj_k(x) = id(x) \tag{5.4}$$

For this aggregation, the weights w_k have to be determined. The weights are assigned manually or learned, e.g., using machine learning on a training set. Berkovsky et al. (2005) have thoroughly investigated the effects of different weights on the alignment results. In our approach, we are only looking for similarity values supporting the claim that two entities are equal. A missing similarity is not necessarily treated as negative evidence. This consideration is derived from the open world assumption, which the ontologies, e.g., in OWL-DL, adhere to. One characteristic of this linear summation is that one can prove that eventually the alignments converge over the iterations (Valtchev, 1999). It is a fix-point optimization problem. Linear summation is most widely used in related work approaches. In most approaches, the user himself decides on the weights.

Linear Summation with Negative Evidence:

Often it is clearer to determine that two entities should *not* be aligned than the positive counterpart. A negative value for w_k may be applied, if the individual similarity is not evidence of an alignment, but contrariwise actually indicates that two entities should not be aligned. Typical examples of such a case are superconcepts of the first entity having a high similarity with subconcepts of the second entity. Such a case has been included in Table 5.1 as the similarity functions 8 and 9 for concepts.

Sigmoid Function:

A more sophisticated approach emphasizes high individual similarities and de-emphasizes low individual similarities. In the given case, a promising function is the sigmoid function sig, which has to be shifted to fit our input range of $[0,1]$ (see Figure 5.3).

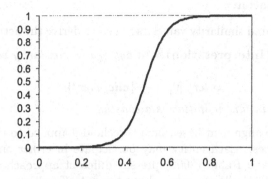

Fig. 5.3. Sigmoid Function

$$adj_k(x) = sig_k(x - 0.5) \qquad (5.5)$$

with $sig_k(x) = \frac{1}{1+e^{-a_k x}}$ and a_k being a parameter for the slope.

The rational behind using a sigmoid function is explained best using an example. When comparing two labels, the chance of having the same entity, if only one or two letters differ, is very high; these might just be because of type errors or different grammatical forms. Whereas, if only three or four letters match, there is no information in this similarity at all; an aggregation of several of these low values should not lead to an alignment. High values are therefore further increased, low values decreased. The parameters of the sigmoid function can be regarded as an extension of the similarity methods, as they have to be adjusted according to the method sim_k they are applied to. Afterwards, the modified values are summed with specific weights w_k attached to them.

For the running example, we use the simple linear aggregation. We assume ten individual similarities when comparing two concepts of which only the first are shown in the following formula:
$sim_{agg}(\text{o1:car,o2:automobile}) = (1.0 \cdot sim_{label}(\text{o1:car,o2:automobile}) + 1.0 \cdot sim_{superconcept}(\text{o1:car,o2:automobile}) + 1.0 \cdot sim_{relation}(\text{o1:car,o2:automobile}) + 1.0 \cdot sim_{instance}(\text{o1:car,o2:automobile}) + \ldots)/10 = 0.5$

NOM:

Besides the standard weighted aggregation, NOM uses the sigmoid function for weighting its similarity measures as a second alternative. The weights have been manually set by an ontology engineer understanding the constructs of ontologies and their implication on similarity and alignment. Further, it makes use of the negative evidence by allowing weights to be negative.

5.2.5 Interpretation

From the aggregated similarity values, we need to derive the actual alignment.

Definition 5.6 (Interpretation). *An aggregated similarity value may lead to an alignment.*

$$inter : [0, 1] \dashrightarrow \{alignment\}$$

where alignment in this definition is a constant.

We assign the alignment based on a threshold θ applied to the aggregated similarity measures. Each entity may participate in either one or multiple alignments. Do and Rahm (2002) present different approaches to calculate a threshold. Every similarity value above the cut-off indicates an alignment; every value below the cut-off is dismissed.

Constant Similarity Value:

For this method, a fixed constant represents the threshold.

$$\theta = const. \tag{5.6}$$

The constant threshold seems reasonable as we are collecting evidence for alignments. If too little evidence is extracted from the ontologies, it is simply not possible to reliably present alignments from this. This is in line with the results presented in Ehrig and Sure (2004a). However, it is difficult to determine this value. One possibility is an average that maximizes the quality in several test runs. Alternatively, it might make sense to let experts determine the value. The latter only works if experts can actually interpret the similarity value and therefore the whole process up to this point.

Delta Method:

For this method, the threshold for similarity is defined by taking the highest similarity value of all and subtracting a fixed value from it.

$$\theta = \max_{e \in O_1, f \in O_2} (sim_{agg}(e, f)) - const. \tag{5.7}$$

N Percent:

This method is closely related to the former one. Here we choose the highest found similarity value and subtract a fixed percentage p from it.

$$\theta = \max_{e \in O_1, f \in O_2} (sim_{agg}(e, f))(1 - p) \tag{5.8}$$

The latter two approaches are motivated through the idea that similarity is also dependent on the types of ontologies or the domain. The calculated maximum similarity is an indicator for this and is fed back into the algorithm. Unfortunately, if two ontologies do not have any overlap, the maximum function does not return reasonable results.

Next one has to decide in how many alignments an entity may be involved.

One Alignment Link:

The goal of this method is to attain a single alignment between two entities from the best similarity values. As there is only one *best* match, every other match is a potential mistake, which should be dropped. Practically we remove alignment table entries that include already aligned entities. From the set of candidate alignments $(U \times V)$ a greedy strategy determines the pair with the largest aggregated similarity value first $(arg\max)$. Ties are broken arbitrarily, but with a deterministic strategy. This pair is stored as alignment $(align(e, f))$. Every other alignment that involves one of the just aligned entities (e or f) is removed from the remaining candidates. The process is repeated until no further non-aligned entity pairs exist. It is also possible to use other methods for cleansing of the alignment table. In the end, this is a search problem that tries to maximize the aggregated similarity of all found alignments.[3]

$$align(e, f) \leftarrow (\mathrm{sim}_{\mathrm{agg}}(e, f) > \theta) \wedge ((e, f) = argmax_{(g,h) \in U \times V} sim_{agg}(g, h)).$$
$$(5.9)$$

with U and V only containing entities not aligned so far

Multiple Alignment Links:

Often it makes sense to keep multiple alignments. In this case, the interpretation is expressed more easily through the following formula.

$$align(e, f) \leftarrow \mathrm{sim}(e, f) > \theta. \qquad (5.10)$$

In the example, the two entities car and automobile resulted in an overall similarity of 0.5. Applying a fixed threshold of $\theta = 0.7$, the two entities are not aligned due to the too low similarity.

$align(\text{o1:car}) = `\bot` \leftarrow sim_{agg}(\text{o1:car,o2:automobile}) = 0.5$

NOM:

NOM interprets similarity results by two means. First, it applies a fixed threshold to discard spurious evidence of similarity (constant similarity value). Second, NOM enforces the one alignment link strategy by ignoring candidate alignments that violate this constraint and by favoring candidate alignments with highest aggregated similarity scores.

---

[3] Strictly spoken, the described greedy strategy does not return the maximum, but therefore is easy processable.

5.2.6 Iteration

Entities are considered similar, if their position in the structure is similar. And the structure similarity is expressed through the similarity of the other entities in the structure. Thus, for calculating the similarity for one entity pair, many of the described methods rely on the similarity input of other neighboring entity pairs. A first round uses only basic comparison methods based on labels and string similarity to compute the similarity between entities or alternatively rely on manually pre-given alignments. By doing the computation in several rounds, one can then access the already computed pairs and use more sophisticated structural similarity measures as well. This is related to the similarity flooding algorithm of Melnik et al. (2002), which in contrast to the iteration step in ontology alignment does not interpret the edges through which the similarity is spread.

Several possibilities when to stop the calculations have been described in the literature: a fixed number of iterations; a fixed time constraint; or changes of alignments below a certain threshold. Depending on the application scenario, these parameters are assigned different values, because some applications have a focus on very exact results leading to a high number of iterations, whereas others need results fast at the cost of losing some quality.

In his work Valtchev (1999) proved that an approach converges when certain characteristics apply to the similarity spreading algorithm. In specific, the weighting and aggregation function is critical in this context. Convergence can only be guaranteed if the overall similarity, i.e., the sum of all individual similarities (not just the similarities of actual alignments) rises monotonically with decreasing gradient for each iteration. If the limit of the future sequence of estimated overall similarity changes is lower than the distance of any candidate alignment to the threshold, one can conclude that this gap will never be closed, thus the alignments will not change. The iterations are discontinued.

When having more than one round of calculation, the question arises whether the results of each round should be converted/adjusted before they are fed back for the next round. One approach is to reuse only the similarity of the best alignments found. A possible way is to give the best match a weight of 1, the second best of $\frac{1}{2}$, and the third of $\frac{1}{3}$. Potentially correct alignments are kept with a high probability, but it is possible for second best alignments to replace them. The danger of having the system being diverted by low similarity values is minimized. On the other hand, this way the overall similarity may potentially drop (by a complete drop-out of one entity for alignment), and the guarantee for convergence is lost.

For an example we refer to Figure 5.2. In a first iteration for comparing o1:car and o2:automobile one can only rely on the evidence of labels, as there is no other information on whether the structural elements are similar yet. This leads to a very low similarity $sim_{agg}($o1:car, o2:automobile$) = 0.1$. In a second iteration we can now use the identified alignments of the first iteration. The two vehicles have been aligned, the Porsche instances as well. Thus, the structural similarity of car and automobile is higher now: $sim_{agg}(\text{o1:car}, \text{o2:automobile}) = 0.85$. Subsequently $align(\text{o1:car}) = \text{o2:automobile}$ results after all.

NOM:

For the first round, NOM uses only a basic comparison method (label and syntactic similarity) to compute the similarity between entities. In the second round and thereafter NOM relies on all the structural similarity functions listed in Table 5.1. As we also include negative evidence in our considerations, we cannot guarantee the monotonic increase of similarity and thus convergence. However, in all our tests we have found that after ten rounds hardly any additional changes occur in the alignment table. This is independent from the actual size of the involved ontologies. NOM therefore restricts the number of runs to a fixed number of ten.

5.2.7 Output

The output of the process is a list of alignments as represented in Table 5.2.

Definition 5.7 (Output). *Given two ontologies an output of alignments is created through*

$$output : O \times O \to E \times E \times [0..1] \times \{alignment\}$$

As the alignment has been computed based on similarity, we also added the aggregated similarity value in this table – if necessary also the individual similarities of each feature may be stored. Further, it makes sense to prolong the result table by unclear or doubtful alignments, which the user then can manually add or drop. For this representation, it is necessary to mark the pairs that actually represent valid alignments and which do not.

NOM:

NOM follows this strategy and returns the extended list of alignments. This representation can be easily transformed into an RDF serialization as shown in Section 2.2.

We have finally developed a complete approach for ontology alignment. All entities from the two ontologies of one type are treated as candidate alignments. They are compared using a wide range of ontology features from RDF(S) with corresponding similarities. The similarities are aggregated using a sigmoid function and manually assigned weights. For the interpretation step, NOM enforces the one alignment link strategy with a fixed threshold. Ten iterations are performed. The result of our running example is shown in Table 5.2. The two aligned entities are represented in columns one and two. The overall aggregated similarity between them and whether this is interpreted as an alignment or not follow in columns three and four. Object (in

Table 5.2. Alignment Table with Similarity

Ontology O_1	Ontology O_2	Similarity	Alignment
object	thing	0.95	yes
vehicle	vehicle	0.9	yes
car	automobile	0.85	yes
speed	speed	0.8	yes
hasSpeed	hasProperty	0.75	yes
Porsche KA-123	Marc's Porsche	0.75	yes
300 km/h	fast	0.6	no
motor	owner	0.3	no

ontology 1) and thing (in ontology 2) are similar to a degree of 0.95, which indeed means an alignment. The similarity of motor and owner with 0.3 is too low to trigger an alignment.

5.3 Process Description of Related Approaches

To illustrate the generality of our alignment process, we here present four of the mentioned related ontology alignment approaches, this time described along the process. In specific, we elaborate on current up-to-date approaches: PROMPT, Anchor-PROMPT, GLUE, and OLA.

5.3.1 PROMPT, Anchor-PROMPT

The PROMPT-Suite (Noy and Musen, 2003) consists of different approaches tackling different questions around ontology alignment, mainly for ontology merging.

1. Feature Engineering:

The original PROMPT only uses labels. The labels could be taken, e.g., from an RDF(S) ontology. Anchor-PROMPT uses several different relations of an ontology as shown in Table 5.4.

2. Search Step Selection:

PROMPT relies on a complete comparison. Each pair of entities from the ontologies is checked for similarity.

3. Similarity Computation:

On the one hand, PROMPT determines alignment based on whether entities have similar labels. It checks for identical labels as shown in Table 5.3. On the other hand, Anchor-PROMPT traverses paths between anchor points. The anchor points are entity pairs already identified as being equal, e.g., based on their identical labels. Along these paths, new alignment candidates are suggested. Paths are traversed along hierarchies as well as along other relations (see Table 5.4). This corresponds to our similarity functions based on super- and subconcepts no. 6 and 7 and direct relations no. 4 in Table 5.1. However, the comparison uses other similarity measures, as the path is respected rather than just the entities in the set.

4. Similarity Aggregation:

As PROMPT uses only one similarity measure, aggregation is not necessary. Anchor-PROMPT however needs to aggregate, which unfortunately is not explained in detail, but points to an average calculation.

5. Interpretation:

PROMPT presents the entity pairs that have identical labels to the user. Anchor-PROMPT applies a threshold before doing so. For these pairs, chances are high that they are actually the same. The user manually selects the ones he deems to be correct, which are then merged. PROMPT and Anchor-PROMPT are therefore semi-automatic tools for ontology alignment.

6. Iteration:

The similarity computation does not rely on any previously computed entity alignments. One round is therefore sufficient in PROMPT. In Anchor-PROMPT, iteration is done to allow manual refinement. After the user has acknowledged the proposition, the system recalculates the corresponding similarities and presents new merging suggestions.

In the running example of Figure 5.2 PROMPT/Label only identifies the two vehicles and the two speed concepts as alignment, as they are the only ones with identical labels. Anchor-PROMPT performs better. Assuming that the two Porsches are given as an anchor-alignment Anchor-PROMPT will follow the paths between the Porsches and the vehicles. This way, it is able to also identify car and automobile as equal concepts.

PROMPT and its derivatives have shown to perform very well on aligning. In this book we provide methods that can help to improve these approaches. In specific, by treating the different structure elements with different weights (possibly learned) performance should rise. Furthermore, efficiency has not been an issue in PROMPT so far. Finally, the different PROMPT versions

Table 5.3. Features and Similarity Measures in PROMPT/Label

Comparing	No.	Feature	Similarity Measure
Entities	1	$(label, X_1)$	$equality(X_1, X_2)$

Table 5.4. Features and Similarity Measures in Anchor-PROMPT

Comparing	No.	Feature	Similarity Measure
Concepts	1	(label,X_1)	equality(X_1, X_2)
	4	(direct relations,Y_1)	path(Y_1, Y_2)
	6	all (superconcepts,Y_1)	path(Y_1, Y_2)
	7	all (subconcepts,Y_1)	path(Y_1, Y_2)
Other Entities	1	(label,X_1)	equality(X_1, X_2)

are designed for specific use cases such as ontology merging or versioning. Integrating these techniques into one powerful tool has yet to be done.

5.3.2 GLUE

GLUE (Doan et al., 2003) is an approach for schema alignment. It makes extensive use of machine learning techniques.

1. Feature Engineering:

In a first step, the similarity estimator uses a multi-strategy machine learning approach based on a sample alignment set. It learns concept classifiers for instances based on the instance descriptions (their features), i.e., their naming, or the textual content of webpages. Naturally, many example instances are needed for this learning step. Finally, the subsequent step uses features such as subsumption, frequency, etc.

2. Search Step Selection:

As in the previous approaches, GLUE checks every possible candidate alignment.

3. Similarity Computation, 4. Similarity Aggregation, 5. Interpretation:

In GLUE, steps 3, 4, and 5 are tightly interconnected, which is the reason why they are presented as one step here. From the similarity estimator (the learned concept classifiers) GLUE derives whether concepts in two schemas generally correspond to each other. It works with a similar idea as we do without explicitly explaining the basis or the calculation: using certain characteristics of the structure (or ontology) individual matchers directly return matches. These matchers can be seamlessly integrated into our process model as a special similarity operator only returning 0 or 1 as a result. The similarity estimator is a learned aggregator on individual classifiers.

Concepts and relations are compared using relaxation labeling, i.e., the similarities of entities (nodes) are typically influenced by the features of the entities' neighborhoods in the ontology graph. A local optimal alignment for each entity is determined using the similarity results of neighboring entity pairs from a previous round. The individual constraint similarities are summed for the final alignment probability. This additional step, which considers the ontological structures, is again based solely on manually encoded predefined rules.

6. Iteration:

To gain meaningful results, only the relaxation labeling step and its interpretation have to be repeated several times. The other steps are just carried out once.

For the example let's assume that GLUE has learned classifiers to match car and automobile, possibly based on the textual descriptions of the two car instances which might both contain words such as maximum speed, horsepower, and torque. Through the relaxation labeling step, which uses neighborhood considerations within the graph, it is now possible to derive that the two relations pointing to speed are also the same.

The GLUE machine learning approach suits a scenario with extensive textual instance descriptions for training, but may not suit a scenario focused more on ontology structures. Further, relations or instances cannot be directly aligned with GLUE.

5.3.3 OLA

The OWL Lite Aligner (OLA) is developed by Euzenat and Valtchev (2004).

1. Feature Engineering:

OLA uses several ontology features to determine the similarity between two entities. It follows all the ontology constructs provided in OWL Lite, i.e., labels, subsumption hierarchies, and relations between objects, which makes it very similar to the features used in NOM.

2. Search Step Selection:

OLA adheres to the one standard approach of comparing all elements of the same kind with each other (concepts with concepts, relations with relations, and instances with instances).

3. Similarity Computation:

The similarity is computed slightly differently from our approach or PROMPT. In a first iteration, the element similarities are calculated based on what the authors call *individual information*, such as labels, i.e., only feature/similariy 1 in Table 5.5. Afterwards, the similarity of two entities is recalculated based on the similarity of related entity pairs, i.e., they consider the ontology structure. This may theoretically also include external instances, such as from databases. In the table the numbers are kept the same as in Table 5.1. For the comparison of sets the authors use an own averaging measure.

Table 5.5. Features and Similarity Measures in OLA

Comparing	No.	Feature	Similarity Measure
Concepts	1	(label,X_1)	syntactic(X_1, X_2)
	4	(direct relations,Y_1)	set(Y_1, Y_2)
	6	(superconcepts,Y_1)	set(Y_1, Y_2)
	7	(subconcepts,Y_1)	set(Y_1, Y_2)
	11	(instances,Y_1)	set(Y_1, Y_2)
Relations	1	(label,X_1)	syntactic(X_1, X_2)
	4	(domain,X_{d1}) and (range,X_{r1})	object(X_{d1}, X_{d2}), (X_{r1}, X_{r2})
	5	(superrelations,Y_1)	set(Y_1, Y_2)
	6	(subrelations,Y_1)	set(Y_1, Y_2)

4. Similarity Aggregation:

For the aggregation of the individual relation similarities the user sets the weights manually. If certain similarity values return null values due to missing corresponding features of the entities, their weights are automatically set to 0 whereas the remaining weights are equally increased.

6. Iteration:

Basic element similarities are injected once. These similarity values then spread over the ontologies. In contrast to most existing work, OLA features the positive behavior that it automatically determines when to stop the iterations. If the limit of similarity changes to come is lower than needed by any candidate alignment to reach the threshold, no candidate will be able to surpass this boundary at any time in the future and the process is halted.

5. Interpretation:

The final stable similarity values differ depending on the amount of initial basic element similarities and the size of the ontologies, as these initial values are spread over the ontologies. Thus finding a suitable threshold for interpretation of the similarities is difficult. This threshold has to be set manually. The authors call refer to this step as alignment extraction.

Applying OLA to the example returns very similar results to NOM. However, despite not being visible through the example, NOM relies on some additional features and has a stronger focus on generally presetting the weights and the threshold.

In sum, OLA uses the idea of fix-point computation very consequently for ontology alignment. Making use of the ontology structure this way turns out to work very well, but as the similarities are dependent on the size of the ontologies, it is difficult to determine the threshold for the alignments. Further, OLA requires a complete fix-point computation making scalability an issue.

We summarize the approaches in Table 5.6 adding our new NOM approach as well. The adherence to the general alignment process is common to all

Table 5.6. Alignment Approaches

	PROMPT	Anchor-PROMPT	GLUE	OLA	NOM
1. Feature Engineering	labels	labels and relations	instances, structure	labels and structure	labels, structure, instances
2. Search Step Selection	complete agenda	complete agenda	complete agenda	complete agenda	complete agenda
3. Similarity Computation	syntactic measures	structural measures	multiple matchers	structural measures	structural measures
4. Similarity Aggregation	not necessary	sum	learned	manual weights	manual weights
5. Interpretation	threshold, user input	threshold, user input	learned threshold	manual threshold	manual threshold
6. Iteration	not necessary	after each user input	for relaxation labeling	until no changes	until max reached

approaches. They make use of certain ontology features, compare entity pairs, calculate and aggregate the similarities, and interpret the values in the end. Some steps are repeated iteratively. For each of the approaches we show their implementation of each process step in the table. When looking at other existing approaches for alignment, the reader will realize that they also fit this process to different extents. Any new method from our work addressing one of the process steps in general will therefore be of direct value for enhancing existing related approaches.

5.4 Evaluation of Alignment Approach

Evaluation is an important and central issue when proposing new methods. We here present the evaluation fundamentals including the evaluation scenario, individual measures, and test data sets. After having defined the general setting for evaluation we continue with the concrete evaluation of our alignment approach.

5.4.1 Evaluation Scenario

The evaluation scenario is given by the general goal definition of ontology alignment as presented in the introduction. For each evaluation run we have two ontologies at a time. No additional input, i.e., no predefined alignments are available. The alignments are now created based on some given alignment strategy, i.e., a fixed setting of parameters for the alignment process. The system only returns those alignments that have been clearly identified. Similarity values and doubtable alignments are not considered for evaluation, as it is difficult to lay down their value for an overall evaluation measure. The generated alignments are then validated against the correct alignments, which have been manually created beforehand. The manually created alignments are treated as gold standard. This is a strong claim because humans will normally not completely agree on this standard. Additional evaluation measures focusing, e.g., on time or almost correct alignments extend the analysis. As the absolute quality of alignments is highly dependent of the ontologies, we will focus on the relative performance of different strategies, rather than the absolute values of the evaluation measures.

5.4.2 Evaluation Measures

Selecting measures to evaluate a new approach is always a difficult task, especially as one is easily accused of having chosen those measures that perform favorable for the own approach. To avoid this situation we use standard measures, even though they might not completely suit the goal of evaluating ontology alignments. The standard measures have been cited and used in different literature (Do et al., 2002), have been applied in evaluation contests (Hughes, 2004; Sure et al., 2004; Ashpole et al., 2005), and have a long tradition in closely related fields, namely in information retrieval (van Rijsbergen, 1975; Harman, 1992). Nevertheless, in addition, we will present advanced measures that provide new interesting results, which are more focused toward ontology alignment.

As we need to evaluate ontology alignment from the perspective of different requirements, we need different kinds of measures (Euzenat et al., 2005):

- *Compliance measures* provide insights on the quality of identified alignments.
- *Performance measures* show how well the approach is in terms of computational resources.
- *User-related measures* help to determine the overall subjective user satisfaction, partially measured, e.g., through user effort needed.
- There are *task-related measures*, which measure how good the alignment was for a certain use case or application.

Finally, we will evaluate the evaluation itself through *statistical significance*.

Compliance Measures

We present two values measuring quality of the alignment process: precision and recall. Due to the small ratio of actual alignments among possible entity pairs, the focus will be on true positives (correct alignments), false positives (pairs that were mistakenly identified as alignments), and false negatives (missed alignments). True negatives are trivial (non alignments). These facts need to be considered when choosing the evaluation metric. We therefore use information retrieval metrics (van Rijsbergen, 1975) to assess the quality of the different approaches in this work. They have also been used before for evaluation of integration approaches for other structures such as database schemas (Do et al., 2002). For most approaches, they will be the core evaluation measures.

Definition 5.8 (Precision). *Given a reference alignment R, the precision of some alignment A is given by*

$$P(A, R) = \frac{|R \cap A|}{|A|}$$

Precision measures the ratio of found alignments that are actually correct. This corresponds to accuracy and is inverse to the error rate. A precision of 1 means that all found alignments are correct, but it does not imply that all alignments have been found. Typically, precision is balanced against another measure from information retrieval called recall.

Definition 5.9 (Recall). *Given a reference alignment R, the recall of some alignment A is given by*

$$R(A, R) = \frac{|R \cap A|}{|R|}$$

Recall measures the ratio of correct alignments found in comparison to the total number of correct existing alignments. This can also be referred to as completeness. A high recall means that many of the alignments have actually been found, but no information about the number of additionally falsely identified alignments is given. A high recall will entail also many false alignments (a lower precision) and vice versa. Therefore, often precision and recall are balanced against each other with the so-called f-measure (van Rijsbergen, 1975).

Definition 5.10 (F-Measure). *Given a reference alignment R, precision, and recall, the f-measure of some alignment A is given by*

$$F(A, R) = \frac{(b^2 + 1) \cdot P(A, R) \cdot R(A, R)}{b^2 \cdot P(A, R) + R(A, R)}$$

with $b = 1$ being the standard weight factor: $F_1(A, R) = \frac{2 \cdot P(A,R) \cdot R(A,R)}{P(A,R) + R(A,R)}$

The f-measure represents the harmonic mean of precision and recall. It will be the main measure to evaluate quality.

Due to the balancing effect, it makes sense to plot precision and recall against each other. By doing so, one sees for which precision and/or recall which method works best. The problem of these graphs is that they cannot show the threshold needed to classify into alignments and non-alignments, as the similarity is neither bounded to precision nor to recall. Thus, it does not show which method actually classifies alignments best (for which threshold). Defining the threshold is one of the core problems for alignment approaches, which lets us refrain from this type of precision/recall graphs.

Performance Measures

Time is a critical factor for many use cases. The requirements range from instantaneous response to overnight batch processing. Most existing tools do not deal with this factor explicitly. For our purposes, it will be measured in seconds, respectively milliseconds. Closely related to time is the issue of scalability. Scalability determines whether execution of an approach is also realistic for bigger scales. This is normally determined on a theoretical level in advance. Finally, memory usage is another performance measure, but due to difficulties in measurement, it will not be considered in our evaluations. Nevertheless, memory also plays an indirect role in processing time and is therefore also partially expressed through this measure.

User-related Measures

Most algorithms require interaction of the human knowledge engineer or end user to varying degrees. However, for some applications user interaction is not wished or even possible. Different levels of automation range from fully manual alignment, possibly GUI-backed, over proposal generation, minimal input in case of conflicts only, to fully automatic. We do not only distinguish between automatic or manual, but we also measure the level of user interaction required, e.g., by counting the number of interaction steps. In the end, user-related measures also include the subjective satisfaction of users.

Task-related Measures

Task-related measures focus on the suitability of an approach for a certain task or use case. These have an immanent high level of subjectivity. Due to this problem, we use this measure only for one specific approach, where the approach is optimized for different use cases. In the end, this measure only returns convincing results in combination with real applications.

In the upcoming evaluations, the so far mentioned evaluation measures will be often not only presented solely, but will be measured against each other. For efficiency, this will be f-measure over time, for a user-active alignment f-measure over the amount of user input. For use case focused alignment, either precision or recall are assigned a stronger weight.

Other Compliance Measures

There are many more compliance measures, which need to be discussed, useful for evaluating ontology alignment.

Definition 5.11 (Overall). *Given a reference alignment R, precision, and recall, the overall-measure of some alignment A is given by*

$$O(A, R) = R(A, R) \cdot (2 - \frac{1}{P(A, R)})$$

The *overall-measure* was used by Do and Rahm (2002) and balances correct alignments against wrong alignments. Even though this measure is very common, it seems inadequate for the ontology alignment case. A false positive is rated with the same penalty as a false negative. This is problematic, as it is normally much easier to simply discard a wrong found alignment, than to find another still unknown alignment. For this reason, this measure will not be applied for our evaluation.

Receiver-Operator-Curves:

In Receiver Operating Characteristic curves (ROC curves) (Egan, 1975) the true positive rate (also called sensitivity) is plotted over the false positive rate (1 - specificity). The closer the curve follows the left-hand border and then the top border of the ROC space the more accurate the results are. ROC curves are widely used in the medical domain (Hanley and McNeil, 1982). Whereas this type of evaluation is of value where both true positives and true negatives are important (e.g., medicine tests), it is insufficient when the focus lies on positives. As pointed out before, this is the case for ontology alignment. Further, different data set results cannot be directly compared. The closeness to the upper left corner is dependent on the ontology size.

Relaxed Quality Measures:

The above precision and recall measures may be criticized for two reasons: (1) They do not discriminate between a very bad and a less bad alignment; and (2) they do not measure user effort to adjust the alignment. Indeed, it often makes sense to not only have a decision whether a particular correspondence has been found or not, but measure the proximity of the found alignments. This implies that near misses should also be taken into consideration. The natural extension of precision and recall consists of replacing the expression $|R \cap A|$ in the standard definition by an overlap proximity. This should be a true generalization, thus leaving precision and recall untouched for the best case and increasing its value, if not far from target alignments are in the set of found alignments.

Definition 5.12 (Generalized Precision and Recall). *Given a reference alignment R and an overlap function ω between alignments, the precision of some alignment A is given by*

$$P_\omega(A, R) = \frac{\omega(A, R)}{|A|}$$

and recall is given by

$$R_\omega(A, R) = \frac{\omega(A, R)}{|R|}$$

Definition 5.13 (Overlap Proximity). *A proximity measure that generalizes precision and recall is*

$$\omega(A, R) = \sum_{\langle a, r\rangle \in M(A,R)} \sigma_{pair}(a, r) \cdot \sigma_{rel}(a, r) \cdot \sigma_{conf}(a, r)$$

in which $M(A, R) \subseteq A \times R$ is a matching between the correspondences of A and R and $\sigma(a, r)$ a proximity function between two correspondences.

The proximity function σ is split into three individual elements. For ontology alignment these are $\sigma_{pair}, \sigma_{rel}$, and σ_{conf}. They express the overlap in terms of the actual alignment pairs, whether the found relation is the same (normally identity, but also subsumption is possible), and whether the confidence values are the same. For M we rely on the best existing matches. These are the matches that maximize the overlap proximity. We do not elaborate how this maximum is found at this point.

We have developed three possible concrete instantiations of σ_{pair}: symmetric proximity, correction effort, and precision- and recall-oriented measures. As an example of a symmetric similarity, we use a simple one in which a concept is similar to a degree of 1 with itself (i.e., the correct alignment has been identified), of 0.5 with its direct subconcepts and direct superconcepts and of 0 with any other concept. This similarity is likely applied to relations and instances (through part-of relationships). Correction effort measures the number of actions necessary to reach the correct alignments. And finally the oriented measures, e.g., when one wants to retrieve instances of some concept, a subconcept of the expected one is correct but not complete, it thus affects recall but not precision.

The relaxed quality measures have been discussed in detail in Ehrig and Euzenat (2005). Even though the relaxed quality measures seem promising for the future we will focus on the standard and well-known precision and recall measures.

Significance

The so-far-introduced values are used to compare the different ontology alignment approaches based on test ontologies. However, being better on few data sets does not imply any general statement. In this section we will therefore briefly introduce statistical significance and its usage for evaluation of ontology alignment. To the best of our knowledge, this has not been done in any evaluation of approaches in existing literature.

Significance tests are performed to the degree of sample results supporting a certain hypothesis. This is done by rejecting the contrary null hypothesis. If the null hypothesis is rejected, then the effect found in the sample is said to be statistically significant. If the null hypothesis is not rejected, then the effect is not significant. The experimenter chooses a significance level before conducting the statistical analysis. The selected significance level represents the probability of a type I error, i.e, the probability that despite the null hypothesis being true, it is rejected.

For ontology alignment, we evaluate whether ontology alignment strategy 2 has a generally higher f-measure than strategy 1. Our null hypothesis, which has to be rejected, is that quality actually decreases using a more advanced strategy. A problem for calculating the significance is which underlying distribution to assume for the increase/decrease. F-measure itself is bound by [0,1]. We see that some data sets tend to have very high improvements in contrast with hardly any improvements for other data sets. Nevertheless, we assume that they follow the normal distribution, which is the case if several independent effects overlay. Also note, that we do not check for a symmetric interval, but only whether the f-measure is better, i.e., the lower interval bound needs to be positive; the upper interval bound is set to infinite.

In sum: For our significance we assume, that the goal variable is spread according to a normal distribution. We want to prove that the values of one set are significantly higher than the values of another set. As the standard deviation is not known, we rely on estimates for this.

Definition 5.14 (Significance). *Test of whether the average value μ of one strategy is better than μ_0 of another strategy:*

$$H_0 : \mu \leq \mu_0 \text{ versus } H_1 : \mu > \mu_0$$

$$\delta_\alpha = \begin{cases} \delta_1, \frac{1}{n}\sum_{i=1}^{n} x_i > \mu_0 + \frac{S^*(x)}{\sqrt{n}}t(n-1)_{1-\alpha} \\ \delta_0, \frac{1}{n}\sum_{i=1}^{n} x_i \leq \mu_0 + \frac{S^*(x)}{\sqrt{n}}t(n-1)_{1-\alpha} \end{cases}$$

with

- *the number of evaluations n,*
- *a significance level α,*
- *the estimator $S^*(x) = \sqrt{\frac{1}{n-1}\sum_{i=1}^{n}(x_i - \bar{x})^2}$, as the standard deviation σ is unknown,*
- *and the student's t-distribution $t(n-1)_{1-\alpha}$ to take account of the normal distribution of the results.*

Typical significance levels are 5% or 1%, which we also adhere to in our setting. Unfortunately, the number of test examples is a major issue when talking about significance of ontology alignment algorithms. Whereas there are many ontologies that could be potentially aligned in the world, there is only a minimal fraction where this alignment has been performed and recognized gold standard alignments exist. This makes it challenging to meet the significance levels envisioned.

The significance explanation was mainly focused on f-measure, as it is our main measure. In several chapters, we will also refer to the significance of other evaluation measures such as time.

5.4.3 Absolute Quality

A short comment about the absolute quality of alignments needs to be made at this point.

One should be aware that the *correct* alignments are subjective to a certain degree. Tests on manual alignments have sometimes shown an overlap of only 60% between two humans assigning them (Sheth, 1991). In another study performed by Bernstein et al. (2005a) the authors investigate how humans correlate when deciding on the similarity of two objects. Again, the results were discouraging, as humans also here tend to have different opinions. Finally, some of the alignments are simply not identifiable, not even by humans. This is the reason why some alignment strategies seem to only reach a low level of recall. The real challenge is to find alignments which match a certain application task, which is less dependent on subjective human perception.

In any case, for our purposes we treat the benchmark as a gold standard. However, following the comments of the last paragraph, the goal of reaching 100% correct alignments would not be an indicator of an especially good approach. Our considerations are therefore based on relative performance of the different measures instead of the absolute value.

5.4.4 Data Sets

Our test basis consists of 14 ontology pairs, which differ in size (30 to 500 entities), modeling primitives (RDF(S) vs. OWL), and complexity (taxonomies vs. restrictions etc.), resulting therein that some are more suitable for certain alignment approaches than others. The data set ontologies have been created by hand, which is also the case for the correct alignments. These ontologies or slight adaptations thereof have been used at the ontology alignment evaluation events I3CON, EON-OAC, and OAEI (Hughes, 2004; Sure et al., 2004; Ashpole et al., 2005). Evaluation of new ontology alignment approaches will be presented along four pairs of them, namely Russia 1, Animals, Bibliography 1, and Sports, which are very different in their nature and thus allow a critical examination of the ontology alignment approaches in the next chapter.[4] The other ten ontology pairs (Russia 2 and 3, Tourism, Networks, Computer Science, Hotels, People and Pets, Bibliography 2 to 4, and Bibliography Bibser) and their evaluation results are found in the appendix (Chapters A and B). They do not provide any completely new aspects compared to the four selected ones. Even though, they will not be presented directly, they are used for average calculation and the significance considerations. Thus, they increase our test basis. Due to the wide ranges these ontologies cover, we expect to gain an equally broad evaluation, being as objective as possible.

Russia 1:

In this first set, we have two ontologies describing the country of Russia. Students created these ontologies with the objective of representing the content of two independent travel websites about Russia. The students were familiar with the ontology constructs, but not experts. The ontologies include concepts (region, river,...), relations (has_capital, has_mouth,...), and instances (Moscow, Black_Sea,...). The ontologies were additionally altered with randomized labels and extra or removed structural elements to make them more interesting for ontology alignment. They differ substantially. Each ontology has 290 entities with an overlap of 215 possible alignments, which have already been captured during generation. Often not even humans are capable of identifying these alignments correctly.

Animals:

The two animal ontologies (see also Figure 5.4[5] for one of them) are different versions of one another. They contain 39 and 26 entities, thus being small examples. This might make it even more difficult to align them. They both make use of complex OWL constructs such as value restrictions and cardinality constraints. The 25 alignments were originally provided for the I3CON contest.

Bibliography 1:

This pair contains two ontologies from one of the ontology alignment contests: EON-OAC. The basis for the contest was a bibliographic ontology provided by INRIA Rhône-Alpes with 180 entities. INRIA provided a second ontology designed from the BibTeX in OWL ontology and a local Bibliographic XML DTD with 98 entities. The goal was to easily gather a number of RDF items. Generally, terminology is very consistent when staying within the BibTeX domain. 74 alignments have been identified for the ontologies.

---

[4] The data sets are available through http://www.aifb.uni-karlsruhe.de/WBS/ meh/foam/.

[5] The ontology is depicted with RDF Gravity (http://semweb.salzburgresearch. at/apps/rdf-gravity/). Concepts are marked by a C, relations by P (property), instances by I, and data value instances by L (literals).

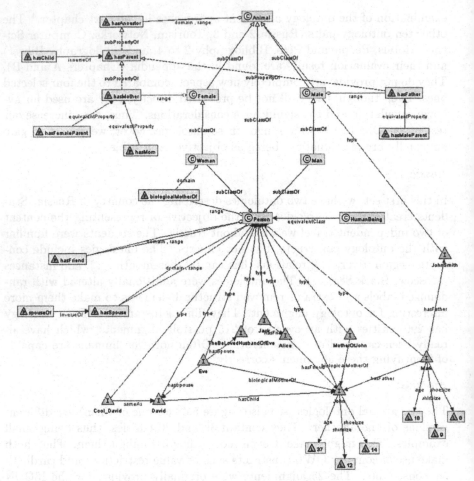

Fig. 5.4. Excerpt of the Animals Ontology

Sports:

The two sports ontologies describing the soccer domain (234 entities) and the sports event domain (395 entities) were originally created for the DAML project.[6] They were downloaded from the ontology library of the project. Typical entities of these ontologies are referee, goal, club president, and team substitute. The 150 correct alignments were created manually. The ontologies are especially interesting as they both refer to the upper-level ontologies SUMO (Niles and Pease, 2001)[7] and DOLCE (Gangemi et al., 2002)[8], because some ontology alignment approaches can make use of this additional domain

---

[6] http://www.daml.org/
[7] http://suo.ieee.org/
[8] http://www.loa-cnr.it/DOLCE.html

knowledge. Whether this will positively affect the alignment creation process, will be investigated.

5.4.5 Strategies

We have introduced a generic ontology alignment process and have extended it with specific instantiations. A thorough evaluation of them is now necessary. From all the possibilities of setting the parameters, we choose to use the following three similarity strategies at this point.

Label:

This strategy is positioned as the baseline against which we evaluate the other strategies with more advanced methods. All entities of one type are added to the list of candidate alignments. Then, for this strategy, only the labels of entities are regarded and compared with a string similarity. An optimal threshold is set in advance. If no labels have been defined in the ontologies, this strategy cannot align the entities. This strategy is equivalent to the original PROMPT strategy.

NOM Weighted:

The NOM strategies have been described in detail in this chapter. All entities of one type in the two ontologies are compared. For these, the features and similarities are taken from Table 5.1 thus covering different elements and structural aspects. They are aggregated using linear weights. The weights have been assigned by an ontology engineer, who interpreted the features with respect to their meaning for alignment. Iteration and interpretation are performed as described: ten rounds with a fixed manually set threshold. Entities are only allowed to take part in one alignment.

NOM Sigmoid:

This is the actual NOM method as used in Ehrig and Sure (2004a) and Ehrig and Staab (2004b). It is equal to the previous one, with one exception: Instead of relying on linearly weighted similarities from the different features, the introduced sigmoid function is applied. The parameters for the sigmoid function are again set manually. The list of candidate pairs is complete, thus containing all possible pairs of entities. Ten iteration rounds with a fixed threshold interpretation are further decisions made for this strategy.

The original intent was to directly run competing tools against NOM. However, to circumvent the problem of having semi-automatic merging tools (PROMPT and Anchor-PROMPT) in our fully automatic alignment tests, we assumed that every proposition of the system is meaningful and correct. PROMPT is therefore replaced by the identical Label strategy. Further, as we had difficulties in running Anchor-PROMPT with the size of the given data sets, we refer to the results of the somewhat similar NOM. For GLUE, we face another general problem. The algorithm has a strong focus on example instance alignments. As we cannot provide these, we refrained from running the tests on a poorly trained estimator, which would immediately result in poor quality results.

5.4.6 Results

We now present the results we have received from the evaluation runs in detail. Table 5.7 shows the beginning of the sorted list for the Russia 1 data set and the NOM Sigmoid strategy. The alignments are arranged by their similarity value, which is correlated to the confidence in the alignment. Music is the same in both ontologies. Confidence in costmoneyeating and costmoney is slightly lower, but still high enough to be automatically aligned.

Table 5.7. Excerpt of Alignment Table from Evaluation

Ontology Russia 1	Ontology Russia 2	Similarity
music	music	1
costmoneyeating	costmoney	0.947
haseconomofact	haseconomicalfact	0.947
includecity	includetown	0.917
whitenights	whitenights	0.9167
squaremeter	sqm	0.9167
partialmaterial	materialthing	0.9091
electrounit	electromagneticunit	0.9

We explain the complete alignment results for Russia 1. The alignments for strategies Label and NOM Weighted are depicted in Figures 5.5 and 5.6. They present precision, recall, and f-measure over the similarity value. The x-axis (similarity) decreases from left to right, from 1.0 to 0.0. The y-axis shows the value of precision, recall, and f-measure respectively. The values should be read as: If all alignments with a similarity higher than the x-value are considered, we receive a precision/recall/f-measure of y-value. The vertical line represents the threshold. Precision is depicted through the dashed dark line, recall through the dotted lighter line, and f-measure through the continuous light line.

Let us first describe the Label strategy results in Figure 5.5. The returned alignments all have a very high similarity – the labels had to be equal in both ontologies.[9] The threshold is therefore also set very high (θ=0.99). All these alignments are correct, precision is 1.0. Obviously, there were no homonyms in this data set in comparison to, e.g., the sports data set. Just relying on

---

[9] For readability the precision, recall, and f-measure points are extended to short lines in the graph.

this strategy does not return many alignments. The very low recall (0.032) entails a low f-measure (0.063) as well. As no other similarities are calculated, the right part of the graph stays empty.

Figure 5.6 in turn shows the results for the NOM Weighted strategy. We follow the diagram from left to right. As we see, precision stays high for high similarity values. A high similarity returns correct alignments. It then drops gradually, as more and more false positives are found. Recall rises, so there still are correct alignments in these newly found alignments. In fact, recall compared to the Label approach recall rises much higher reaching almost 0.5. At some point, the f-measure, which is composed from precision and recall reaches a maximum (f=0.465). Ideally this is the point to set the threshold (θ=0.25). As the threshold is set in general, it does not necessarily lead to the highest f-measure for each data set, though it is quite good for Russia 1. Afterwards the fraction of false positives becomes so high, overall quality finally drops again.

The NOM Sigmoid graph is only slightly better compared to the NOM Weighted graph, and will not be depicted here. One observation was, that its threshold could be set much more exactly than for the weighted case. The highest quality was always achieved close to θ=0.25.

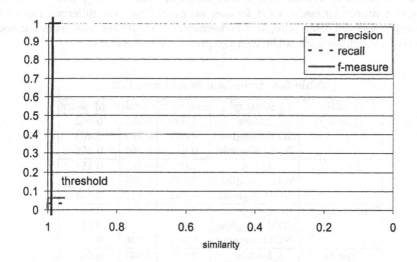

Fig. 5.5. Results of Label for Russia 1

The results of the three other data sets at the point of threshold are presented in Table 5.8 and Figure 5.7. For each of the three strategies it contains precision, recall, and f-measure for the given threshold. Further, it presents the values from the average over all data sets, i.e., all 14 data sets. Please be aware that the f-measures are averaged over the ontology pairs,

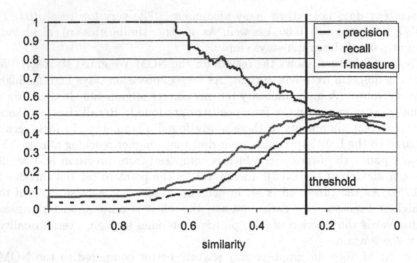

Fig. 5.6. Results of NOM Weighted for Russia 1

and not over the individual alignments found in each ontology pair. Such an average is more expressive as it focuses on averaging over different *types* of ontologies. On the other side, as a consequence the average f-measure cannot be directly calculated from the average precision and recall.

Table 5.8. Evaluation Results for NOM

Data Set	Strategy	Precision	Recall	F-Measure
Russia 1	Labels	1.000	0.032	0.063
	NOM Weighted	0.620	0.372	0.465
	NOM Sigmoid	0.612	0.367	0.459
Animals	Labels	1.000	0.083	0.154
	NOM Weighted	0.733	0.458	0.564
	NOM Sigmoid	0.769	0.417	0.541
Bibliography 1	Labels	0.941	0.865	0.901
	NOM Weighted	0.896	0.932	0.914
	NOM Sigmoid	0.909	0.946	0.927
Sports	Labels	0.875	0.047	0.089
	NOM Weighted	0.343	0.160	0.218
	NOM Sigmoid	0.438	0.140	0.212
Average	Labels	0.754	0.312	0.371
	NOM Weighted	0.657	0.471	0.499
	NOM Sigmoid	0.789	0.476	0.523

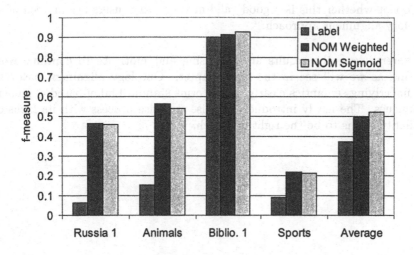

Fig. 5.7. F-Measure for Labels and NOM

5.4.7 Discussion and Lessons Learned

We will now discuss the implications of these results. As our working hypothesis, we expected better alignments from intelligent approaches making use of the semantics of ontologies. By using a similarity-based approach our hypothesis is widely fulfilled.

Please remember that our focus is to maximize the f-measure, balancing precision (accuracy) and recall (completeness). As a baseline for comparison, we used the Label strategy. The f-measure for labels alone can already be good, if the ontologies' labels have been modeled carefully. Using the advanced semantic alignment approaches results in considerably better outcomes, i.e., f-measures of 0.499 vs. 0.371 for the NOM Weighted vs. the Label strategy. Applying the evaluation results for the significance calculation, one can easily derive that the increase of the f-measure is significant at a level of 1%. Actually, f-measure as our core evaluation measure reaches the highest value for the NOM Sigmoid strategy. The semantically rich structures do help to determine sound similarities and from this better alignments, represented through NOM compared to Label. Further, the sigmoid approach is slightly better than the approach using only linear weights, unfortunately not as significantly. Overall, the average increase is 20% in precision, recall, and f-measure.

During the evaluation, we were confronted with several difficulties. In first place, it is extremely difficult to set the weights for both the linear and the sigmoid case, even for an ontology expert. Closely related is the setting of the threshold. A lot of the related work avoids this by providing general precision and recall curves and leaving the setting of weights or threshold to the user.

We doubt whether this is a good valid method when users are in need of an ontology alignment approach.

Nevertheless, the results are promising and motivate to continue work on this, as we will see in the next chapter. Ontology alignment based on the underlying semantics clearly outperforms standard label-based alignment techniques. The newly introduced concise stepwise process with its focus on similarity seems to be the right approach.

6

Advanced Methods

We have originally identified specific core requirements for different use cases. Based on our alignment approach from the previous chapter we will now stepwise address these requirements. Specific extended methods are presented in the following sections. These include efficiency increasing methods, machine learning aid, intelligent user interaction, and adaptive strategies for underlying use cases. Each section will also include an evaluation. Finally, we present a strategy combining all these individual improvements. This sophisticated approach will be the final result of all these efforts. It shall serve to practically align real world ontologies, being open for future extensions. We have motivated that such an approach is a key step towards knowledge integration in information systems.

6.1 Efficiency

This section will show that current approaches neglect efficiency. A new approach (Ehrig and Staab, 2004b) will be developed to overcome this problem.

6.1.1 Challenge

When we tried to apply existing approaches to some of the real world scenarios, we found that existing alignment methods are not suitable for the ontology integration tasks at hand, as they all neglect *efficiency*. To illustrate the requirements: We have been working in realms where ontologies are applied such as the ACM Topic hierarchy with its 10^4 concepts or folder structures of individual computers, which correspond to 10^4 to 10^5 concepts. Finally, we are working with WordNet exploiting its 10^6 concepts (Hotho et al., 2003). When aligning between such ontologies, the trade-off that one has to face is between effectiveness and efficiency, i.e., the number of correct found alignments versus the time required for it. For instance, consider the knowledge management platform built on a Semantic Web and peer-to-peer basis in SWAP (Ehrig et al., 2003b) (see Chapter 8). It is not sufficient to provide its user with the best possible alignment, but it is also necessary to answer his queries within a few seconds – even if two peers use two different ontologies and have never encountered each other before. Users will not tolerate a system that takes longer to respond to their queries.

For this purpose, we optimize the effective, but inefficient NOM approach towards this goal. The outcome is an extended version: QOM – Quick Ontology Mapping (Ehrig and Staab, 2004b, 2005). Our hypothesis is that faster alignment results can be obtained with only a negligible loss of quality. We would also like to point out that, since the efficiency gaining steps are very general, they can be applied to many other alignment approaches as well.

6.1.2 Complexity

We begin with a complexity consideration. The different algorithmic steps contributing to complexity are aligned to the canonical process. For each of the approaches, one may then determine the computational costs of each step in the process. We start with the cost for feature engineering (c_{feat}). The second step is the search step, i.e., candidate alignments selection (with a complexity of c_{sele}). For each of the selected candidate alignments ($comp$) we need to compute k different similarity functions (with a cost of c_{sim_1} to c_{sim_k}) and aggregate them (c_{agg}). The number of entities involved and the complexity of the respective similarity measure affect the runtime performance. Subsequently, the interpretation of the similarity values with respect to alignment requires c_{inter}. Finally, we have to iterate over the previous steps (c_{iter}). In this work, we assume that the retrieval of a statement involving a specific ontology entity from a database is possible in constant access time, independent of the ontology size, e.g., based on sufficient memory and a hash function. In practice, this will probably not always be the case. However, the underlying ontology management system is beyond the goal and influence of an ontology alignment approach, which is why we do not examine non-constant access times here.

Definition 6.1 (Complexity of Ontology Alignment). *The worst-case runtime complexity c is defined as*

$$c = (c_{feat} + c_{sele} + c_{comp} \cdot (\sum_{i=1..k} c_{sim_i} + c_{agg} + c_{inter})) \cdot c_{iter}$$

We refer to complexities in Big O notation, which describes the asymptotic upper bound. The individual costs of NOM and other related approaches are now described in more detail.

We determine the worst-case runtime complexity of the algorithms to propose alignments as a function of the size of two given ontologies (n is the number of entities in the ontology). Thereby, we base our analysis on realistic ontologies and not on artifacts. We avoid the consideration of large ontologies with m concepts with only one level of hierarchy or with a concept hierarchy depth of $m - 1$. Tempich and Volz (2003) have examined the structure of a large number of ontologies and found, that concept hierarchies have an average branching factor of around 2 and that the concept hierarchies are neither extremely shallow nor extremely deep. Hence, average ontologies have a tree-like structure. In the following, we base our results on their findings.

Feature engineering is only required once in the initial phase and is essentially independent of the ontology size: $c_{feat} = O(1)$.

Setting up the candidate pairs in NOM is implemented in a straightforward way with an outer iteration over all the entities of ontology 1 and an inner iteration over all entities of ontology 2. This results in a complexity of $c_{sele} = O(n^2)$. All the identified candidate pairs of individual entities $c_{comp} = O(n^2)$ will then have to be compared using features and their similarities. This is practically the same in all known approaches.

For our later considerations, we need to recapitulate the complexity levels, which occur when doing comparisons of entity sets. Retrieving single entities or fixed sets of entities is independent of the size of the ontology. As we only examine complexity in terms of the ontology size n, fixed sets of size s have a complexity of $O(s) = O(1)$. Other methods require access to a whole subtree of an ontology. The depth of a balanced tree is of $O(log(n))$. For example, to retrieve all inferred subconcepts of a concept, in average this results in $O(log(n))$ as well (Depending on the actual requested concept the actual values vary between all elements for the root concept and 1 for all leaf concepts.). Yet even other methods need access to the whole ontology. Accessing the whole ontology is naturally determined only through $O(n)$. As we assume that the costs for accessing a feature are correlated with the number of entities to retrieve, the just derived complexities correspond to the complexities of the features.

Another issue of complexity is due to specific similarity measures, some of which may be very costly. Object equality requires a fixed runtime complexity of $O(1)$, because the comparison of two individual objects (i.e., their URIs) through an equality operator is independent of the structure.[1] Checking the ontology for the explicit equality relation of an entity also results in a complexity of $O(1)$. Syntactic similarity complexity is dependent of the string size $O(length)$. Nonetheless, if we assume that the length is limited by a fixed bound, complexity also is $O(1)$, as in PROMPT. Set similarity has to compute the similarity vector for every entity with every other entity $(O(|E + F|^2) = O(setSize^2))$. Creating averages or normalizing does not change this complexity for sets.

For each feature/similarity combination, we now take the complexity of the ontology feature with its corresponding similarity measure. We give an example: To compare the subconcepts of two concepts we have to retrieve two subtrees $O(log(n))$ and use the set similarity $O(setSize^2)$. The com-

---

[1] *comp* already covers the number of candidate alignments to check.

plexity of this single similarity determination is therefore $c_{sim_i} = O(log^2(n))$. In fact, this is the highest complexity NOM or Anchor-PROMPT face for the feature/similarity combinations resulting therein that $\sum_{i=1..k} c_{sim_i} = O(log^2(n))$. If only labels are compared as in PROMPT, this maximum complexity is of $O(\sum_k sim_k) = O(1)$.

Then, for each entity pair an aggregation operation is performed once with $c_{agg} = O(1)$. The interpretation then has to check once for every new found similarity if it is higher than the threshold or an already existing alignment of the involved entities, i.e., the complexity is $c_{inter} = O(1)$. Finally, with the number of iterations fixed this results in $c_{iter} = const$.

Based on these complexity considerations the worst-case runtime behaviors of NOM and the approaches PROMPT, Anchor-PROMPT, and GLUE[2] are given in Table 6.1. The complexities are at least quadratic with respect to the ontology size. For large ontologies of several thousand entities or more this is not acceptable.

6.1.3 An Efficient Approach

One easily sees that there are two main critical elements in the complexity of NOM:

- the actual number of candidates to compare, normally n^2;
- and the costs for retrieving and comparing the features, up to $log^2(n)$.

For an efficient approach these critical elements need to be defused. We refer to this efficient approach as Quick Ontology Mapping – QOM and will explain it along the canonical process.

1. Feature Engineering:

Like NOM, QOM exploits RDF(S) features.

2. Search Step Selection:

A major element of runtime complexity is the number of candidate alignments, which have to be compared for finding the best alignments. Therefore, we use heuristics to lower the number of candidate alignments.

In particular, we use a dynamic programming approach (Boddy, 1991). In this approach, we have two main data structures. First, we have candidate alignments, which ought to be investigated. Second, an *agenda* orders the candidate alignments, discarding some of them entirely to gain efficiency. After the completion of the similarity analysis and their interpretation, new decisions have to be taken. The system has to determine which candidate alignments to add to the agenda for the next iteration. The behavior of initiative and ordering constitutes a search strategy.

---

[2] This result is based on optimistic assumptions about the learner.

Table 6.1. Complexity of Alignment Approaches

Approach	$(feat$	$+sele$	$+comp \cdot ($	$\sum_{i=1..k} sim_i$	$+agg$	$+inter))$	$\cdot iter$	Complexity
Label/PROMPT	$(1$	$+O(n^2)$	$+O(n^2) \cdot ($	$O(1)$		$)$	$\cdot 1$	$= c$
Anchor-PROMPT	$(1$	$+O(n^2)$	$+O(n^2) \cdot ($	$k \cdot O(log^2(n))$	$+O(1)$	$+O(1)))$	$\cdot 1$	$O(n^2 \cdot log^2(n))$
GLUE	$(1$	$+O(n^2)$	$+O(n^2) \cdot$	$O(1)$		$)$	$\cdot 1$	$O(n^2)$
NOM	$(1$	$+O(n^2)$	$+O(n^2) \cdot ($	$k \cdot O(log^2(n))$	$+O(1)$	$+O(1)))$	$\cdot 1$	$O(n^2 \cdot log^2(n))$
QOM	$(1$	$+O(n \cdot log(n))$	$+O(n) \cdot ($	$k \cdot O(1)$	$+O(1)$	$+O(1)))$	$\cdot 1$	$O(n \cdot log(n))$

For the integration of databases there exists a related technique called *blocking* (Hernández and Stolfo, 1998). In the blocking process, a key field is chosen. Only those data sets whose keys are already very similar are then used as candidates for integration and examined more closely. When using blocking one has to ensure that the majority of data sets later indeed need to be integrated are within the sets with a similar key. Fortunately, in our approach we do not only need to rely on a key. We can make use of ontological structures to classify the candidate alignments into promising and less promising entity pairs.

We suggest the subsequent methods to propose new candidate alignments for inspection. We use advanced blocking techniques based on the ontology structure to come up with an agenda for the similarity computation. For each method, we indicate the involved complexities.

- A simple method is to limit the number of candidate alignments by selecting for each entity a fixed number from all possible candidate alignments randomly: $c_{comp} = O(n)$.

- The closest-label method restricts candidate alignments to entity pairs whose labels are similar, represented in a sorted list. Every entity is compared to adjacent entities in the list $c_{comp} = O(n)$. Please note that the creation of the presented agendas does require processing resources. The label approach fulfills a sorting action with $c_{sele} = O(n \cdot log(n))$.

- One can compare only entities for which adjacent entities were assigned new alignments in a previous iteration. Adjacent entities are connected to the original entities by any ontology relation. This is motivated by the fact that every time a new alignment has been found, we can expect to also find similar entities adjacent to these found alignments. We call this approach change propagation. Further, to prevent very large numbers of comparisons, the number of candidate alignments per entity is restricted by an upper bound. This is necessary to exclude ontological artifacts such as ontologies with only one level of hierarchy from thwarting the efficiency efforts. We receive $c_{comp} = O(n)$ for the number of comparisons. Selecting these candidate alignments is a constant action for each entity $c_{sele} = O(n)$.

- We start comparisons at a high level of the concept and property taxonomy. An entity is compared to the root element of the other ontology and its subentities. In a next step it is only compared to the subentities of the entity it was most similar to. It is handed down until the best alignment is found. This is bounded by the depth of the tree. As we have to do this for every entity, we need $c_{comp} = O(n \cdot log(n))$ comparisons in total.

- The combined approach used in QOM follows different optimization strategies: It uses a label sub-agenda, a random sub-agenda, and a change propagation sub-agenda; i.e., $c_{comp} = O(n \cdot log(n))$. In the first iteration the label sub-agenda is pursued. Afterwards we focus on alignment change propagation. Finally, we shift to the randomness sub-agenda, if the other strategies do not identify sufficiently many correct alignment candidates.

With these multiple agenda strategies, we only have to check a bounded and restricted number of alignment candidates from ontology 2 for each original entity from ontology 1.

3. Similarity Computation:

QOM is based on a wide range of ontology feature and similarity combinations. In order to optimize QOM, we have restricted the range of costly features as specified in Table 6.2. In particular, QOM avoids the complete pair-wise comparison of (sub-)trees in favor of a(n incomplete) strategy. This affects mainly the subsumption features as well as instance sets. The accentuated feature/similarities in the table were changed from features which point to complete inferred sets to features only retrieving limited size direct sets. As pointed out in the general complexity discussion, this results in $c_{sim} = O(1)$.

4. Similarity Aggregation:

The aggregation of single methods is performed only once per candidate alignment and is therefore not critical for the overall efficiency.

5. Interpretation:

Also the interpretation step of QOM is not critical with respect to efficiency. A threshold is determined and only one alignment for each entity is maintained. The similarities of the candidate alignments have to be checked once for this.

6. Iteration:

QOM iterates to find alignments based on lexical knowledge first and based on knowledge structures later, which is equivalent to the original approach.

Assuming that ontologies have a given percentage of entities with similar lexical labels, we will easily find their correct alignments in the first iteration. We also assume that these are evenly distributed over the two ontologies. This entails that the distances between two found alignments in the ontologies are on average constant – independent of the ontology size. With the change propagation agenda, we carry on to the next adjacent alignment candidates with every iteration step. The constant distances lead to a fixed number of required iterations.

Summing up the individual elements of the new approach QOM we receive a theoretical complexity of $O(n \cdot log(n))$ (Table 6.1). The step with the highest complexity is the ordering of labels for the first agenda $O(n \cdot log(n))$. The later processing actually only requires $O(n)$.

Table 6.2. Features and Similarity Measures in QOM. Those marked with a lower case "a" have been modified for an increase in efficiency.

Comparing	No.	Feature	Similarity Measure
Concepts	1	(label,X_1)	syntactic(X_1, X_2)
	2	(identifier,X_1)	equality(X_1, X_2)
	3	(X_1,sameAs,X_2) relation	object(X_1, X_2)
	4	(direct relations,Y_1)	multi(Y_1, Y_2)
	5a	(relations of direct superconc., Y_1)	multi(Y_1, Y_2)
	6a	(direct superconcepts, Y_1)	multi(Y_1, Y_2)
	7a	(direct subconcepts, Y_1)	multi(Y_1, Y_2)
	8a	(subconc.,Y_1) / (superconc., Y_2)	multi(Y_1, Y_2)
	9a	(superconc.,Y_1) / (subconc., Y_2)	multi(Y_1, Y_2)
	10	(concept siblings,Y_1)	multi(Y_1, Y_2)
	11a	(direct instances,Y_1)	multi(Y_1, Y_2)
Relations	1	(label,X_1)	syntactic(X_1, X_2)
	2	(identifier,X_1)	equality(X_1, X_2)
	3	(X_1,sameAs,X_2) relation	object(X_1, X_2)
	4	(domain,X_{d1}) and (range,X_{r1})	object(X_{d1}, X_{d2}),(X_{r1}, X_{r2})
	5a	(direct superrelations, Y_1)	multi(Y_1, Y_2)
	6a	(direct subrelations, Y_1)	multi(Y_1, Y_2)
	7	(relation siblings,Y_1)	multi(Y_1, Y_2)
	8a	(direct relation instances,Y_1)	multi(Y_1, Y_2)
Instances	1	(label,X_1)	syntactic(X_1, X_2)
	2	(identifier,X_1)	equality(X_1, X_2)
	3	(X_1,sameAs,X_2) relation	object(X_1, X_2)
	4a	(direct parent-concepts, Y_1)	multi(Y_1, Y_2)
	5	(relation instances,Y_1)	multi(Y_1, Y_2)
Relation-Instances	1	(domain,X_{d1}) and (range,X_{r1})	object(X_{d1}, X_{d2}),(X_{r1}, X_{r2})
	2	(parent relation,Y_1)	multi(Y_1, Y_2)

6.1.4 Evaluation

In this section we show that the theoretical worst-case considerations carry over to practical experiments and that the quality of QOM is only negligibly lower than the one of other approaches.

Strategies

We evaluate the alignment strategies described in the previous sections:

- As the Label algorithm is simple and fast we use it as a baseline to evaluate the speed.
- The Naïve Ontology Alignment (NOM) was an approach making use of a wide range of features and measures. Therefore, it reaches high levels of effectiveness and represents our quality baseline. In particular, we use the NOM Sigmoid strategy.

- QOM – Quick Ontology Mapping

Evaluation measures and data sets are the same as for the general evaluation case.

Results

We exemplarily present the results of the strategies again on the Russia 1 data set (Figure 6.1). The x-axis shows the elapsed time on a logarithmic scale, the y-axis corresponds to the f-measure. The symbols represent the result after each iteration step. The rhombus represents the simple Label approach. The squares show the f-measure of NOM Sigmoid after each individual iteration. And the circles show the new QOM approach, again after each iteration round. When interpreting the time values, we should also keep in mind that they are influenced not only by the alignment approach, but also by how the underlying ontology management system performs on large ontologies.

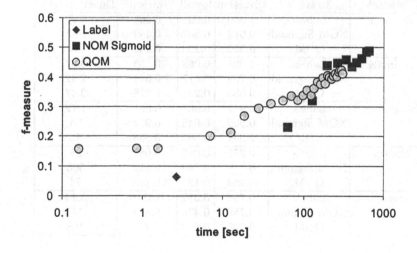

Fig. 6.1. Quality over Time for Russia 1

Depending on the data set the Labels approach may reach good results within a short period of time. Please notice that for ontologies with a small number of similar labels, such as in the Russia 1 data set, this strategy is not satisfactory (f-measure 0.06). In contrast, the f-measure value of the NOM strategy rises slowly but reaches high absolute values of up to 0.5 and above. Unfortunately, it requires much time. The plotted QOM strategy reaches high quality levels quickly, but it cannot completely reach the same levels as NOM. Nevertheless, QOM does not only achieve good quality levels, but returns first results almost instantaneously. Already the instantaneous results are better than from the Label approach, which takes considerably longer. As it is possible to stop the alignment process after every iteration, this is an important observation.

Table 6.3 shows the final results of the different approaches for more data sets. The f-measures with their corresponding times are summarized in Figure 6.2. This also includes an average measure. The quality results of QOM are in between the quality results of the Labels approach and NOM Sigmoid, most times closer to the latter (higher) one. Except for the small example of the animals ontologies the processing times are considerably lower than for the complete NOM Sigmoid approach. In fact, for this small data set the process of creating an efficient agenda takes longer than the complete alignment. With a normal number of iterations, the times of the more complex QOM are higher than by just comparing labels.

Table 6.3. Evaluation Results for QOM

Data Set	Strategy	Precision	Recall	F-Measure	Duration (sec)
Russia 1	Labels	1.000	0.033	0.063	2.70
	NOM Sigmoid	0.612	0.367	0.459	602
	QOM	0.552	0.293	0.382	146
Animals	Labels	1.000	0.083	0.153	0.07
	NOM Sigmoid	0.769	0.417	0.541	2.42
	QOM	0.538	0.291	0.378	2.47
Bibliography 1	Labels	0.941	0.865	0.901	1.72
	NOM Sigmoid	0.909	0.945	0.927	75
	QOM	0.904	0.892	0.898	42
Sports	Labels	0.875	0.046	0.089	38
	NOM Sigmoid	0.438	0.140	0.212	566
	QOM	0.463	0.127	0.199	74
Average	Labels	0.754	0.312	0.3716	5.14
	NOM Sigmoid	0.789	0.476	0.523	749
	QOM	0.705	0.433	0.477	108

6.1.5 Discussion and Lessons Learned

We had the hypothesis that faster alignment results can be obtained with only a negligible loss of quality. We here briefly present the bottom line of our considerations. In terms of quality, the Quick Ontology Mapping approach shows good results, but optimizing the alignment approach for efficiency – as QOM does – decreases the overall quality of alignments. This is not completely surprising, as the efficiency gains were reached through cutting down on search space in terms of candidate alignments and features. If ontologies are small, i.e., less than 50 entities, one should prefer to use the slower variant NOM.

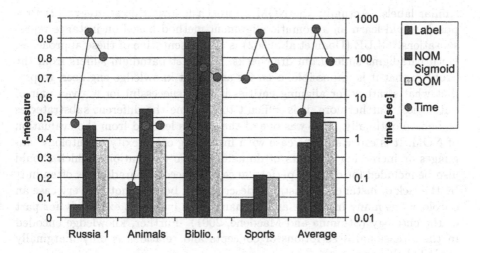

Fig. 6.2. F-Measure and Time for QOM

Still, QOM is considerably better than the Labels approach with a significance level of 5%. It is also significantly faster at 5%. However, if ontologies are small, QOM might even take longer than NOM. This is due to the more complex process of creating candidate alignments. An interesting piece of future work will be to determine after how many iterations NOM outperforms QOM and thus switch the strategy. Unfortunately, this cannot be determined for a general case as it is dependent of the ontology size. Finally, even though results from the first iterations are faster than standard Label approaches and may be directly used, if the application requires this, the normal time needed by QOM is longer than for Labels. For the presented results, QOM is processed until the presumably highest f-measure value is reached.

To sum up, QOM is not only theoretically faster than standard prominent approaches but also in practice by a factor 10 for larger ontologies.

6.2 Machine Learning

This section will show how machine learning may be used for improving the quality of ontology alignment approaches (Ehrig et al., 2005b).

6.2.1 Challenge

The so far presented approaches are constricted to one of two different paradigms: (1) Approaches would include a manually predefined method for proposing alignments, which would be used in the actual automatic alignment process. They typically consist of a number of substrategies such as finding similar labels. Actually, the NOM approach follows this strategy. (2) Proposals would learn an automatic alignment method based on instance representations. GLUE (Doan et al., 2002) is a representative of these approaches. Both paradigms suffer from drawbacks. The first paradigm suffers from the problem that it is impossible, even for an expert knowledge engineer, to predict what strategy for aligning entities is most successful for a given pair of ontologies. Furthermore, it is difficult to combine the different substrategies to behave optimally. This was one of the lessons learned from the evaluation of NOM. It is especially the case with increasing complexity of ontology languages or increasing amounts of domain specific conventions, which should also be included for optimal performance. The second paradigm is often hurt by the lack of instances or instance descriptions, because not in every case an ontology has many instances and in many cases instances exist only for part of the ontology (Stumme and Maedche, 2001). Further, knowledge encoded in the intensional descriptions of concepts and relations is only marginally exploited this way.

Hence, there remains the need to automatically combine multiple diverse and complementary alignment strategies of *all* indicators, i.e., extensional *and* intensional descriptions, in order to produce comprehensive, effective, and efficient semi-automatic alignment methods. We have developed a bootstrapping approach for acquiring the parameters that drive such an approach through machine learning techniques. In fact, the learned approach can be represented through a decision tree model (Ehrig et al., 2005b). For this approach the user does not have to worry about setting the correct parameters, e.g., for a potential confusingly large number of features and similarities, the system creates them during an initial training phase.

In Doan and Halevy (2005) schema matching approaches are split into rule-based and learning-based techniques. Rules in their sense are a logical combination of features leading to an alignment. Learning-based approaches use matched schemas for training and eventually build a model for alignment. We adopt this view for ontology alignment and claim to bridge this strict distinction with this novel approach. As in our previous approaches we continue to make extensive use of features and similarities (rule-based), but we also use learning techniques for optimization (learning-based). We will rely on machine learning.

In contrast to the previous sections, we here do not lie our focus on the actual parameters for the alignment approach, but on the way they are determined. In fact, we cannot even say which concrete features are used or which interpretation strategy is followed until the learning step has been performed with real training alignments.

6.2.2 Machine Learning for Ontology Alignment

In this section it is explained how APFEL (Alignment Process Feature Estimation and Learning) works to optimize a given parameterizable alignment method (Figure 6.3). Data structures are illustrated through white boxes and process steps through colored boxes. We will first describe the data structures, then the process steps. In the upper track, we create training alignments, the lower track actually develops reasonable features and their corresponding similarity measures, and on the right side, the weights for these measures are machine learned through the training alignments. Finally, we show how the parameterizable alignment method resulting from APFEL is applied.

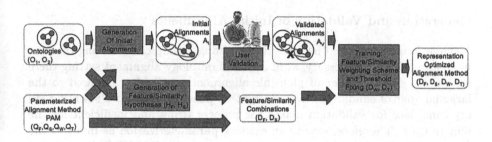

Fig. 6.3. Detailed Process of APFEL

Data Structures

APFEL requires two ontologies O_1 and O_2 as input to its processing. These are either the ontologies for which the alignment process will be optimized directly, or they are exemplary representations of a type or domain, which requires an optimized alignment method.

Core to APFEL is the process of learning the parameters. Relevant data structures for representation include: Q_F: features engineered (e.g., label, instances, domain); Q_S: similarity assessments corresponding to the features of Q_F (e.g., equality, subsumption); Q_W: weighting scheme for an aggregation of feature-similarity assessments (e.g., weighted averaging); Q_T: interpretation strategy (e.g., alignments occur if similarity is above fixed threshold).

Such a declarative representation is given to a parameterizable alignment method, PAM, for execution. PAM is a general alignment framework, which then is initialized with a representation of different strategies. Thus, an initial alignment function, $align_{init}$, may be defined by $align_{init}:=PAM(PROMPT)$ or $align_{init}:=PAM(QOM)$.

Then, APFEL uses user validations A_V of the initial proposals A_I of $align_{init}$. In general, the described input does not explicitly require an ontology engineer. The two ontologies, an arbitrary (predefined) alignment method, and the validation of the initial alignments may be processed by a typical (domain) user as well, as long as he understands the meaning of the aligned entities.

The output of APFEL is an improved alignment method defined as $align_{\text{optim}} := \text{PAM}(\text{APFEL}(O_1, O_2, Q_F, Q_S, Q_W, Q_T, A_V))$. Parameters characterizing $\text{APFEL}(O_1, O_2, Q_F, Q_S, Q_W, Q_T, A_V)$ constitute the tuple (D_F, D_S, D_W, D_T).

Through the optimization step alignment results may change: The result of $align_{\text{init}}(\text{o1:car})$ might be '$\perp$' and the result of $align_{\text{optim}}(\text{o1:car})$ might be o2:automobile.

Generation and Validation of Initial Alignments

Machine learning as used here requires training examples. Assisting the user in creating them is necessary, as in a typical ontology alignment setting there are only a small number of plausible alignments available compared to the large number of candidates, which might be possible a priori. Presenting every candidate for validation makes the process tiring and inefficient for the human user. Therefore, we use an existing parameterization as input to the Parameterizable Alignment Method, e.g., $align_{\text{init}} = \text{PAM(QOM)}$ to create the initial alignments A_I for the given ontologies O_1 and O_2. As these results are only preliminary, PAM does not have to use very sophisticated processes: Basic features and similarities (e.g., Label Similarity) combined with a naïve simple averaging and fixed threshold are sufficient in most cases. Further, the threshold should be set considerably lower, so that not only positive correct alignments, but also wrong alignments are created as training examples. Resulting proposed pairs are stored starting with the highest confidence as shown in Table 6.4. The last column still has to be filled in by the user indicating whether the proposed alignment is correct or not.

Table 6.4. Initial Alignments Returned for Validation

Ontology 1	Ontology 2	Similarity	User Grade
car	car	0.95	to be rated
auto	automobile	0.8	to be rated
wheel	tire	0.6	to be rated
speed	hasSpeed	0.6	to be rated
driver	gear	0.2	to be rated

This allows the domain expert to easily validate the initial alignments as correct or wrong (1 or 0) and thus generate training data A_V. He does not need to be an ontology engineer, but as an ontology user has to understand the meanings of the aligned entities within the ontology. Due to the assistance through the naïve alignment system, he can expect to find many more positive examples than by just randomly drawing entity pairs. If the user knows additional alignments, he can add these alignments to the validated list. Obviously, the quality of the later machine learning step depends on the quality and quantity of the validated alignments at this point. We refer to the evaluation section of Machine Learning for a discussion of this.

Generation of Feature/Similarity Hypotheses

It becomes difficult for the human user to decide which features and similarity measures make sense in indicating an alignment of two entities. Our approach therefore generates these feature/similarity combinations automatically.

The basis of the feature/similarity combinations (Q_F, Q_S) is given by a baseline alignment method such as PAM(QOM) with which we have achieved good results as presented in the previous section.

From the two given ontologies APFEL extracts additional features H_F by examining the ontologies for overlapping features. *Overlapping* means that they occur in both ontologies – with exactly the same URI or a very certain alignment. These might be additional features from the ontology model such as OWL primitives or special XML datatypes. In addition, at this point also domain-specific features are integrated into the alignment process such as auto:licensenumber from an upper-level automobile ontology. These features are added in a combinatorial way with a generic set of predefined similarity assessments including similarity measures for, e.g., equality, string similarity, or set inclusion. Thus, APFEL derives similarity assessments H_S for features H_F.

Table 6.5. Generation of Additional Hypotheses

$$\left\{ \begin{array}{l} extras \\ licensenumber \end{array} \right\} \times \left\{ \begin{array}{l} equality \\ subsumption \end{array} \right\} \Rightarrow$$

Comparing	No.	Feature H_F	Similarity H_S
Cars	FS1	(extras,X_1)	equality(X_1, X_2)
Cars	FS2	(extras,X_1)	subset(X_1, X_2)
Cars	FS3	(license no.,X_1)	equality(X_1, X_2)
Cars	FS4	(license no.,X_1)	substring(X_1, X_2)

Table 6.5 illustrates this process for generating hypotheses for feature/similarity combinations. In the given example two domain attributes H_F, extras and license number, are compared using H_S, the equality and the subsumption[3] similarity. All of the feature/similarity combinations are added for now. Some feature/similarity combinations will not be useful, e.g., FS4, checking whether one license number is a substring of another. In the subsequent training step machine learning will be used to determine those that actually improve alignment results.

---

[3] We use the term subsumption here. Depending on the compared objects this could mean substring, subset, or inclusion.

From the given feature/similarity combinations (Q_F, Q_S) and the extracted hypotheses (H_F, H_S) we derive an extended collection of feature/similarity combinations (D_F, D_S) with $D_F := Q_F \cup H_F$ and $D_S := Q_S \cup H_S$.

Training

After determining the classification of two entities (aligned or not aligned, A_V), all validated alignment pairs are processed with the automatically generated collection of features and similarities. From each feature/similarity set a numerical value is returned, which is saved together with the entity pair as shown in Table 6.6. Further, the user validation is added to the table.

Table 6.6. Training Data for Machine Learning (including value returned by the ith feature/similarity combination FS_i and user validation)

Ontology 1	Ontology 2	FS1	FS2	FS3	FS4	User Grade
car	car	1.0	1.0	0.8	0.0	1
auto	automobile	0.7	1.0	0.7	0.0	1
wheel	tire	0.0	1.0	0.8	0.0	0
speed	hasSpeed	0.7	0.0	0.0	1.0	1
driver	gear	0.2	0.0	0.0	0.0	0

We are now in the position to apply machine learning algorithms to the automatically generated feature-similarity pairs $(D_F$ and $D_S)$ using the example training alignments A_V. More specifically, the numerical values of all feature/similarity combinations are the input for the algorithm. The classification of being aligned or not represents the output. Different machine learning techniques for classification (e.g., decision tree learner, neural networks, or support vector machines) assign an optimal internal weighting D_W and threshold D_T scheme. Machine learning methods like C4.5 capture relevance values for feature/similarity combinations. Feature/similarity combinations that do not have any (or only marginal) relevance values for the alignment are given a weight of zero and can thus be omitted.

Finally, we receive the important feature/similarity combinations (features D_F and similarity D_S) and the weighting D_W and threshold D_T thereof. We now set up the final ontology alignment approach, which we call $align_{\text{optim}} := \text{PAM}(\text{APFEL}(O_1, O_2, Q_F, Q_S, Q_W, Q_T, A_V))$. Depending on the complexity of the alignment problem it might be necessary to repeat the step of test data generation (based on the improved alignment method) and training two or three times.

6.2.3 Runtime Alignment

As we do not have a fixed set of features and similarities any longer, some steps of the general alignment process have to be adjusted.

1. Feature Engineering, 3. Similarity Computation:

Features and the Similarity Computation have been learned during the training phase. Therefore, no general description of them is possible, but due to the automatic generation we now expect to also use more complex features, i.e., OWL primitives or domain-dependent information.

2. Search Step Selection:

No changes have occurred in this step. The normal procedure stays to compare all the possible alignment candidates. Of course, we may also use the more efficient methods such as QOM.

4. Similarity Aggregation:

Depending on the underlying classifier, the aggregation is performed differently. Neural networks hide the overall process of how an answer has been determined. Support vector machines have weights for different vectors consisting of the similarity values. For the decision tree approach, no aggregation is required. By following the path in the decision tree one automatically reaches the final confidence value for alignment.

5. Interpretation:

To give the reader an intuition of the results of the training we refer to Example 6.1, a decision tree. Depending on the output of each individual rule we traverse the tree and reach a leaf indicating either that two entities are aligned (1) or not (0). For example, we assume the value of feature/similarity no. 0 (here called *rule0*) to be 0.3. We then check rule 4, which is assumed to be 0. As rule 3 is 0.15, the value behind the colon is the classification: 0. A candidate alignment with the three mentioned values will not be aligned. Neural networks hide the interpretation process, whereas support vector machines determine an own threshold. To rate the quality of the decisions, most approaches provide an internal confidence value, for example in the given decision tree as returned by WEKA[4] the last two numbers in each line show the overall leaf size and the number of wrong classifications therein. (32.0/1.0) can thus be interpreted as a confidence of $1 - \frac{1}{32} = 0.9688$.

---

[4] WEKA is a free data mining and machine learning framework: http://www.cs.waikato.ac.nz/~ml/weka/

Example 6.1 (Decision Tree).

```
rule0 <= 0.5
|    rule4 <= 0
|    |    rule3 <= 0.196429: 0 (149.0/3.0)
|    |    rule3 > 0.196429
|    |    |    rule5 <= 0.967612: 1 (50.0/12.0)
|    |    |    rule5 > 0.964286
|    |    |    |    rule2 <= 0.267857: 1 (22.0)
|    |    |    |    rule2 > 0.267857: 0 (10.0)
|    rule4 > 0: 1 (10.0/4.0)
rule0 > 0.5: 1 (32.0/1.0)
```

6. Iteration:

The iteration is again independent from the specialty of this approach. Entity similarity still relies on neighboring similarities. Therefore, the iteration steps are retained as before.

6.2.4 Explanatory Component of Decision Trees

One of the requirements of the use cases was to provide the user with an explanatory component on why alignments were automatically determined this way.

Decision trees may easily be translated into natural language and presented to the user. The paths in the tree represent the argumentation scheme. Referring to the example decision tree an explanation may sound as follows:

"The labels of the two entities are similar to a very low degree, and their subconcepts do not overlap at all. The instances only have a low overlap, too. From these facts the system determined with a high confidence that the two entities are not the same and are therefore not aligned."

This corresponds to the following: The labels correspond to rule0 <= 0.5. The subconcepts correspond to rule4 <= 0. The instance overlap is expressed with rule3 <= 0.196429. The classification is expressed through 0 (149.0/3.0). If the user is interested in more details, he can easily examine the decision tree himself and the list of concrete similarity values between the two entities.

Explanation is also an issue of good user interfaces. The evaluation can only be done via a subjective user evaluation, which cannot be provided here. Still, already this simple explanatory component is more than most alignment systems supply and an important step towards fulfilling the requirement of explanations. One exception is the mentioned schema aligner S-Match of Shvaiko et al. (2005). Their argumentation presents numerous individual reasons, similarly as our approach has shown above.

6.2.5 Evaluation

Scenarios: Training and Test Data Sets

Two different scenarios have been used to evaluate the machine learning approach.

The first scenario represents a case where we align two ontologies based on *general ontology* features. We want to prove that a good algorithm for aligning very different ontologies can be learned. As training data we rely on the 14 different ontology pairs and their respective correct alignments. One of the ontology pairs was always kept back and then used for evaluation, whereas the alignments of the others were used for training. These are the ontologies previously used as test ontologies, including the ones in the appendix.

In the second scenario, we optimize the ontology alignment process for *one specific domain*. This usage scenario is directly taken from the Bibster application, a peer-to-peer system to exchange bibliographic metadata (Haase et al., 2005) (see also Section 8.2). We have only one ontology, but want to identify equal entities (duplicates) within it. In terms of the problem structure, this scenario does not differ from a scenario where we want to find equal objects in two ontologies. Thus, we do not use general training data as in the previous scenario, but data from the same ontology domain. In this scenario, the two ontologies describe bibliographical entities, such as articles, books, theses, etc. and their respective authors, editors, or involved organizations. For the 2100 entities, 275 duplicates have been manually identified by a domain expert. For the evaluation, the used training alignments are excluded.

Strategies

We pursue seven strategies for evaluating the two scenarios.

- The first strategy aligns based on the equality of labels.
- The second strategy applies a variety of general ontology alignment feature/similarity combinations and an aggregation thereof (NOM). NOM proved to be very competitive.
- The remaining strategies represent the machine learning approach. The third strategy uses a C4.5 decision tree learner. For three data sets we further vary the number of training concepts by taking 20, 50, and all possible training examples to investigate the effect of different quantities of training data. Half of the examples are positives and half are negatives, i.e., alignments resp. non-alignments. For all machine learning approaches we use the WEKA machine learning environment (Witten and Frank, 2005). The decision tree is pruned by demanding at least 30 elements in each leaf node when using all training examples.
- The next strategy uses a neural net based on all possible training examples.
- And the last strategy trains a support vector machine, again with all examples.

Results

Table 6.7. Evaluation Results for APFEL

Data Set	Strategy	Precision	Recall	F-Measure
Russia 1	Labels	1.000	0.032	0.063
	NOM Sigmoid	0.612	0.367	0.459
	Decision Tree Learner (20)	0.154	0.315	0.206
	Decision Tree Learner (50)	0.930	0.735	0.821
	Decision Tree Learner (all)	0.950	0.990	0.970
	Neural Net (all)	0.964	0.756	0.847
	Support Vector Machine (all)	0.678	0.708	0.693
Animals	Labels	1.000	0.083	0.153
	NOM Sigmoid	0.769	0.417	0.541
	Decision Tree Learner (all)	1.000	0.75	0.857
Bibliography 1	Labels	0.941	0.865	0.901
	NOM Sigmoid	0.909	0.946	0.927
	Decision Tree Learner (20)	0.933	0.565	0.704
	Decision Tree Learner (50)	0.849	0.830	0.839
	Decision Tree Learner (all)	0.885	0.932	0.908
	Neural Net (all)	0.718	0.675	0.696
	Support Vector Machine (all)	0.698	0.659	0.687
Sports	Labels	0.875	0.047	0.089
	NOM Sigmoid	0.438	0.14	0.212
	Decision Tree Learner (all)	0.806	0.773	0.789
Average	Labels	0.754	0.312	0.371
	NOM Sigmoid	0.789	0.476	0.523
	Decision Tree Learner (all)	0.858	0.727	0.767
Bibliography Extra	Labels	0.909	0.073	0.135
	NOM Sigmoid	0.279	0.397	0.328
	Decision Tree Learner (20)	0.047	0.280	0.080
	Decision Tree Learner (50)	0.456	0.246	0.318
	Decision Tree Learner (all)	0.630	0.375	0.470
	Neural Net (all)	0.542	0.359	0.432
	Support Vector Machine (all)	0.515	0.289	0.370

From several evaluation runs, we have obtained the results in Table 6.7. Although the precision of an approach based on labels only is high, the low recall level leads to a low overall f-measure, which is our key evaluation measure. Thus, our main competitor in this evaluation, NOM, receives a better f-measure with its semantically rich feature/similarity combinations. Figure 6.4 shows the f-measure for the different strategies.

To investigate the effectiveness, we first have tested the different strategies against each other (with all available training examples for the different learning methods). In both scenarios the decision tree learner returns results better than the two other machine learning approaches, i.e., neural nets and support vector machines: The decision tree learner delivers the best f-measure. In average, the f-measure improves considerably. This increase goes parallel for precision and recall. However, not always an improvement is visible: For the Bibliography 1 data set the value actually decreases slightly. For this pair of ontologies the manual set features, weights, and threshold were better than the learned general one. It is always possible to tune an algorithm until it performs optimal for one specific problem. The claim in this work is to provide a general approach suiting many ontologies, as the average f-measure shows. In the second Bibliography Extra scenario, the increase of f-measure is also good. In this bibliographic scenario, the alignment method can make extensive use of the learned domain-specific features. Finally, the lower number of feature/similarity combinations leads even to an increase in efficiency compared to NOM. Not all the features of NOM provided significant evidence for alignment.

Second, we have considered the learning rate. Quality increases with the number of training examples rising, leveling off at a good value. Unfortunately, due to the complex structures of ontologies with many possible feature/heuristics combinations, a high absolute number of training examples is required to fully capture their semantic value for alignment. In the research domain of ontology alignment with its current lack of large examples, this is a challenge. Once learned the approach can be transferred to ontology alignment problems in the same domain/ontology model without additional learning effort.

Particularly interesting are the features that were given the highest importance for alignment discrimination. Similarly as in the manual approach labels were given a high rate, but surprisingly relations with domain and range differentiate concepts better than superconcepts and subconcepts. In fact, superconcepts and subconcepts have the highest value if they are used crosswise and produce negative evidence, i.e., if superconcepts of one concept are subconcepts of the other concept; if this is the case one can infer that the two compared entities are *not* to be aligned. This removes main false alignments. Instance information is also important in classifying entity pairs. Specific OWL constructs such as inverseProperty add evidence next. For Bibliography Extra the machine learning approach identifies, e.g., the attribute last name as being highly relevant to find identical authors and rates it higher than, e.g., the middle initial.

6.2.6 Discussion and Lessons Learned

The average margin on improvement as compared to NOM (24.4 percentage points) is remarkable. Both precision and recall rise considerably. This supports our assumption that humans can only partially overview the complexity of ontology constructs for alignment much clearer than we had expected. As APFEL was run with a wide range of ontologies we do not expect this to be a random effect. The results are significantly better than NOM Sigmoid with

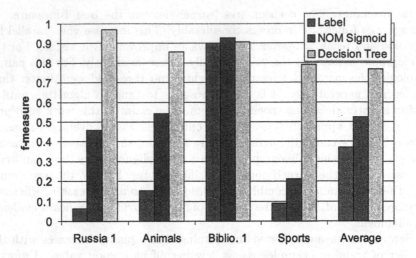

Fig. 6.4. F-Measure for APFEL Learned Approach

less than 1%. For the general ontology alignment case, the learned parameterizable alignment method clearly outperforms the existing approaches and should therefore be used.

For the domain-specific scenario the facts have to be interpreted slightly differently. Results are still considerably better than a manual approach. However, here we face the problem of training sets. Only with a fair amount of training examples an improvement can be measured. For the current ontology domain, this is a serious bottleneck. A good approach is directly linked to a high effort of creating training examples. APFEL supports this in a best possible way.

The determined importance of individual features will also be of interest for anyone creating an ontology alignment approach or setting the weights manually.

We are careful on claiming that decision trees are generally better for ontology alignment than neural networks, support vector machines, or other machine learning approaches as our evaluation has shown. Correctly tuning machine learning algorithms is very demanding. For other scenarios such as ontology learning, support vector machines showed good results in Michelson and Knoblock (2005).

To sum up, APFEL generates an alignment approach that is very competitive with the latest existing ontology alignment methods. As for setting the parameters, it is easier and better than current ontology alignment approaches. Still, it is important to apply the correct machine learner and a sufficient amount of training data.

6.3 Active Alignment

We originally argued that manual alignment is infeasible for many scenarios. In this section, we are going to show that for the other scenarios through intelligent methods manual input does make sense and improve the effectiveness of it (Ehrig and Sure, 2005a).

6.3.1 Challenge

Existing alignment approaches focus on using automatic techniques to identify alignments in an optimal way. Some approaches allow input of preknown alignments beforehand. Others present the results to the user and let him decide afterwards which ones are correct and may therefore be used in the respective application (McGuinness, 2000). A third group presents the results to the user and based on the approval or denial of the alignments restarts the process of aligning (Noy and Musen, 2000). To the best of our knowledge, none of the tools really investigates in depth the issue of human intervention. The human is mainly regarded as means to provide results in a user interface.

It is extremely difficult to create a reasonable fully automatic approach and even for the best approaches, the results are often not satisfying. We therefore want to draw attention to the problem of proper human interaction for aligning ontologies. We aim to exploit the potential of user input during runtime of an automatic alignment process in an optimal way.

In the approach of this section, we will include user input in the general process during runtime. Three core questions arise:

- At which point of the ontology alignment process is user interaction reasonable?
- What kind of input is sensible? What will the user be requested for?
- How should the input affect the process parameters, i.e., should they be adjusted?

The second question is closely related to active learning approaches in machine learning (Saar-Tsechansky and Provost, 2001). Using this analogy, two ontologies represent the input and the correct alignments are the learning goal. Through exemplary alignments, a background classifier is incrementally trained. The active learner then focuses on processing those examples first that have the highest information value for building the classifier. We present the alignment questions that have the highest information value for the alignment process to the user. In contrast to APFEL, where the user needed to enter alignments beforehand during the training phase, we now focus on user interaction *during* runtime.

6.3.2 Ontology Alignment with User Interaction

We present the novel user interaction approach along the alignment process. We assume that optimization steps that can be done before have already been performed.

1. Feature Engineering:

Active Ontology Alignment exploits RDF(S) or OWL features as the previous approaches. They are not changed during runtime.

2. Search Step Selection:

The selection of data for the comparison process is simple as before: All entities of the first ontology are compared with all entities of the second ontology. Any pair is treated as a candidate alignment. The efficient approach would also be possible, but is not performed here to only have one influence on the ontology alignment process at a time.

3. Similarity Computation:

The best strategy for similarity computation can be determined beforehand. We will therefore simply keep the methods from the NOM approach as depicted in Table 5.1. A learned strategy is the alternative.

4. Similarity Aggregation:

Again, we use a sigmoid function with manually assigned weights in this step.

5. Interpretation:

The only elements dynamically changing throughout the alignment process are the automatically identified alignments and their confidences. We therefore include the user in the interpretation step during runtime. From all the calculated similarities, we have received an aggregated similarity value. This value expresses the confidence that two compared entities are the same and can be aligned. A general threshold is set with all similarity values above the threshold leading to an alignment, all below leading to a non-alignment.

For active alignment, we involve the user in the decision on whether an entity pair should be aligned or not. For scalability reasons it is not possible to present all the found (non-)alignments to the user for validation, as shown in Example 6.2. In fact, the majority of entity pairs will not provide any information value, as they are either trivially different or obviously equal. The threshold θ represents the critical value, where the automatic classification has the highest doubt. Our hypothesis is that removing this uncertainty brings the biggest gains. Only alignments with this similarity value are presented to the user for validation. Further, similarities are heavily dependent on the graph structure of the ontology: For example, if all instances of two concepts are aligned, the concepts are probably also to be aligned. The explicit alignment of highly interlinked entities, e.g., a concept with many super- and subconcepts, affects more other entities than less interlinked entities, e.g., a leaf instance. Highly interlinked entities are therefore given priority in comparison to less interlinked ones. These two ideas are combined, i.e., the user is presented those automatically found alignments that are closest to the threshold value. If several alignments have the same similarity value, the highly interlinked ones are favored. The user input for the alignment proposal is then stored with the corresponding perfect confidence of either 1.0 (true) or 0.0 (false). In the subsequent iterations, they are used to calculate a new and better list of automatic alignments.

Example 6.2 (User Input).

```
Align o1:car with o2:automobile? (y)es/(n)o/(u)nknown)? y
Align o1:wheel with o2:tire? (y)es/(n)o/(u)nknown)? n
```

The third question was whether to adjust the process parameters reacting to the input. This is done through changing the threshold. If the majority of answers have been positive, the threshold is set too high. For the following rounds, it is decreased according to the actual ratio of positive and negative answers. The opposite applies, if negative answers exceed their positive counterparts. The threshold is too low and therefore it is increased. In practice the ratio of positives to negatives is multiplied with a fixed maximum change, which is then added or subtracted form the extant threshold.

6. Iteration:

The last iteration step again does not have the potential to gain from user interaction. We keep the NOM strategy.

These six steps make a new approach intelligently including user interaction.

6.3.3 Evaluation

For evaluation, we retain the existing data sets. However, we need to adapt the implementation for user input. For the evaluation, the input is directly taken from the gold standard alignments, thus always being correct. The test user doesn't make any mistakes. Both gold standards and infallible users do not represent the real world, but are necessary preconditions for an evaluation.

Strategies

The following concrete strategies will be applied for evaluation.

- The Label strategy is the baseline.
- The actual line of quality, which has to be surpassed, is provided through NOM.
- The third strategy applies an unfocused active approach. From all found (non-)alignments, questions are randomly presented to the user without considering the similarity value. Depending on the size of the ontologies a different amount of questions are posed to the user, 60 for larger ontologies, only 15 for smaller ones.
- And finally the fourth strategy replaces the unfocused approach through the focused approach presented in this section.

Results

We expect to improve ontology alignment through our approach. A small improvement will always occur by just adding the human classified alignments, as at least these will definitely be correct. We expect that through our method results will improve considerably beyond this. The results are presented in Table 6.8 and a summary thereof in Figure 6.5.

Table 6.8. Evaluation Results for Active Ontology Alignment

Data Set	Strategy	Precision	Recall	F-Measure	User Input
Russia 1	Labels	1.000	0.032	0.063	0
	NOM Sigmoid	0.612	0.367	0.459	0
	Active (unfocused)	0.637	0.367	0.466	60
	Active (focused)	0.866	0.391	0.538	60
Animals	Labels	1.000	0.083	0.153	0
	NOM Sigmoid	0.769	0.417	0.541	0
	Active (unfocused)	0.769	0.417	0.541	15
	Active (focused)	1.000	0.500	0.667	15
Bibliography 1	Labels	0.941	0.865	0.901	0
	NOM Sigmoid	0.909	0.946	0.927	0
	Active (unfocused)	0.912	0.951	0.931	60
	Active (focused)	0.959	0.959	0.959	60
Sports	Labels	0.875	0.047	0.089	0
	NOM Sigmoid	0.438	0.140	0.212	0
	Active (unfocused)	0.458	0.150	0.226	60
	Active (focused)	0.884	0.153	0.261	60
Average	Labels	0.754	0.312	0.371	0
	NOM Sigmoid	0.788	0.476	0.522	0
	Active (unfocused)	0.793	0.487	0.533	47
	Active (focused)	0.907	0.520	0.613	47

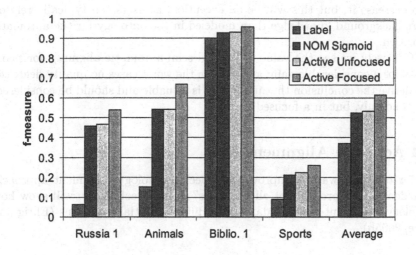

Fig. 6.5. F-Measure for Active Ontology Alignment

For each of the ontology pairs we performed the mentioned alignment strategies and determined precision, recall, and f-measure. Despite the user input, the unfocused active approach does not show any gains. For all focused runs our key evaluation measure, the f-measure, increases through user interaction. For some of the scenarios the gains are high, e.g., for Russia 1 f-measure rises by 17%. For other scenarios, especially with already high f-measure values, the gains are minimal: Bibliography 1, 3.5%. Still the average increase is significant at level 1%.

6.3.4 Discussion and Lessons Learned

The results need to be interpreted as follows: Unfocused semi-automatic alignment leads to only marginal quality increases compared to a fully automatic approach. Focused semi-automatic alignment leads to higher quality levels. Not surprisingly, more user validated alignments lead to better results as well. In some cases, fully automatic alignment alone yields good results. Hardly any additional gains are possible through user interaction in those cases. Both the absolute quality of alignment results and gains through focused semi-automatic alignment underlie a high variance. Finally, about half of the presented entity pairs were positive examples and half were negative examples, which shows that our approach finds the critical point for the highest information gain.

Nevertheless, one has to be aware that there might be complicated ontologies, where the user is not able to decide himself whether an alignment is correct or not. User input is not always capable of increasing quality, it might also decrease it, but this will be an exception, as users can typically rely on more background knowledge than modeled in the ontology for the automatic approach.

Concisely we see the value of focused semi-automatic aligning: for many scenarios a considerable gain; and even in the worst cases no quality decrease. We derive the conclusion that user input is valuable and should be considered, not randomly, but in a focused manner.

6.4 Adaptive Alignment

So far our goal was to improve one specific ontology alignment approach. But does one approach suit all use cases? In this section, we will show how ontology alignment can be adapted for different initial situations (Ehrig and Sure, 2005b).

6.4.1 Challenge

Many approaches have been brought up to align, map, integrate, and merge ontologies. For all these use cases special tools such as GLUE, PROMPT, S-Match, etc. (Doan et al., 2002; Noy and Musen, 2003; Giunchiglia et al., 2004) have been created focusing on solving exactly one of the mentioned cases, thus making it difficult to apply the tools for already slightly different use cases. In bigger projects such as SEKT we face the problem of having several use cases to address (de Bruijn and Feier, 2005) and at the same time aim for one integrated alignment framework.

In this section we will present a methodology for automatically deriving a strategy for ontology alignment so that it can be optimally applied for a wide range of alignment problems. We will give a guide on how to set the parameters of ontology alignment algorithms respectively tools based on underlying use cases, which we described in Chapter 3. This will be done by defining a function measuring the utility for the user, which we then aim to maximize. It will be possible to reuse specialized alignment approaches that have performed well in objective evaluations not only for one use case, but for a variety of them, thus increasing the impact of existing ontology alignment technology. Finally, as our methodology will focus on a general alignment process rather than a specific tool, we expect these results to be applicable to other ontology alignment approaches as well. To the best of our knowledge, there has not been any previous work on changing the parameters of an ontology alignment algorithm based on the underlying use case or the involved ontologies.

Do and Rahm (2002) generally investigated which matcher performs best, mainly for XML documents. They also mentioned that this depends on, e.g., the schema characteristics. However, they do not take the next step, which would be to include the use cases for dynamically choosing and adjusting the best matcher.

6.4.2 Overview

We present a process for adapting ontology alignment algorithms as illustrated in Figure 6.6. One required input is the use case. Further, we need

Fig. 6.6. Overview Adaptive Alignment

the specification of different side conditions such as the ontologies and the computational infrastructure. In a first step, we create a function to rate the utility of the to-be-retrieved alignments for the user. We show how to maximize this utility function. Through this second step, the optimization, we derive requirements for the core dimensions of alignments such as quality or efficiency, based on the specifics of the use case. In a third step, we derive the actual parameters based on the requirements just mentioned. Side conditions may make changes to the parameters necessary. The final output consists of the set of parameters for our parameterizable alignment method PAM. The alignment approach can now be executed leading to the best possible results for the given use case.

6.4.3 Create Utility Function

The first step of the process formally represents the utility we want to maximize.

Utility of Ontology Alignment

Ontology alignment is performed with a specific goal in mind. To which extent this goal is reached is measured through an overall utility function. Here utility represents the degree of user satisfaction. This is not trivial as the user normally has multiple objectives such as quality and time, which need to be integrated into one measure (Keeny and Raiffa, 1976).

First, an ontology alignment approach has certain parameters such as the strategy for selecting candidate alignments or the similarity strategy, which have to be set before applying it. We already referred to the alignment approach as parameterizable alignment method (PAM). Second, we calculate the result values for different dimensions such as quality or efficiency of the alignment results. Further, there are side condition constraints, such as the size or format of the involved ontologies, and processor speed or memory of computing infrastructure. Finally, there are the two actual ontologies to compare affecting the results. The result values r_i are a function f_i of all the mentioned variables.

Definition 6.2 (Result Function). *The results r_i of an alignment process can be represented through a function*

$$r_i = f_i(p_1, \ldots, p_m, s_1, \ldots, s_k, o_1, o_2)$$

with

- $p_1, \ldots, p_m$ *being the parameters of the alignment approach,*
- *the general side conditions $s_1, \ldots, s_k$,*
- *and the specific ontologies o_1 and o_2.*

The overall utility u is a function g based on preferences for each of the dimension results, and the preferences are dependent on the underlying use cases (ontology merging, query rewriting, etc.) and a subjective human notion of what *good* alignments are. The utility value u may also be expanded and written as function h.

Definition 6.3 (Utility of Ontology Alignment). *Let the utility u of ontology alignment be*

$$u = g(a, m, r_1, \ldots, r_n)$$
$$u = h(a, m, p_1, \ldots, p_m, s_1, \ldots, s_k, o_1, o_2)$$

with

- *the use case a,*
- *the subjective human notion m,*
- *and the result measures $r_1, \ldots, r_n$.*

Unfortunately, determining the exact utility based on the numerous variables is not possible, because this would require large tests with users to measure their satisfaction. Nevertheless, we can make use of this utility model for our purposes.

Maximize Utility

Goal of the adaptive approach is to maximize the utility u to find $\hat{u}$ by setting the decision variables, the algorithm parameters $\hat{p}_1, \ldots, \hat{p}_m$ correctly. We assume that the use case is given and fixed, just like the ontologies and computing equipment.

$$Max.\ u = h(p_1, \ldots, p_m)$$
$$\forall u : \hat{u} \geq u$$

with $a, s_1, \ldots, s_k$ fixed; m, o_1, o_2 removed for abstraction $\qquad$ (6.1)

As mentioned, it is not feasible to exactly calculate the utility function. However, it is possible to determine the inverse function g^{-1} and h^{-1} for an optimal utility value $\hat{u}$. The functional dependencies have been identified in various experiments with our approaches as presented in Ehrig and Sure (2004a); Ehrig and Staab (2004b); Ehrig et al. (2005b), and in the preceding sections of this work. Therefore, in the next sections, we backtrack the process of utility calculation. We rely on estimate functions for f_i and g, resp. their inverse functions, during the search in the parameter space. As we are looking for ex ante optimal results for typical ontologies and an average user, we ignore the unknown and subjective parameters o_1, o_2 and m. This will lead us to the best possible general approach. We will now derive first the requirements for each result dimension and then second the actual parameters.

6.4.4 Derive Requirements for Result Dimensions

We have identified four main *result dimensions* $r_1, \dots, r_4$ influencing the utility value u: quality, measured in terms of precision r_1 and recall r_2; time r_3; and the level of automation r_4. These four dimensions are the evaluation measures, which the user will apply in the end to determine his satisfaction. They can have values of low, medium, and high or their correspondences for time and automation-level. For a maximum utility value and a fixed use case, we invert the utility function and determine the corresponding requirements.

$$(\hat{r_1}, \dots, \hat{r_n}) = g^{-1}(\hat{u}, a) \tag{6.2}$$

This is depicted in Table 6.9. The table is read as follows: To reach a maxi-

Table 6.9. Requirements Based on a Maximum Utility and Fixed Use Cases $g^{-1}(\hat{u}, a)$

Use Case a	Precision $\hat{r_1}$ / Recall $\hat{r_2}$	Time $\hat{r_3}$	Automation $\hat{r_4}$
Alignment Discovery	medium/medium	medium	semi-automatic
Agent Negotiation	high/high	fast	fully automatic
Data Integration	medium/medium	slow	semi-automatic
Ontology Evolution	high/high	slow	semi-automatic
Ontology Merging	high/high	slow	semi-automatic
Query Rewriting	medium/high	fast	fully automatic
Reasoning	high/medium	slow	fully automatic

mum utility for the alignment discovery use case we require medium precision and medium recall rates, time should generally be in a medium range as well, and the user can be included for a semi-automatic process. The requirements have been directly copied from the textual description of the use cases in Chapter 3.

6.4.5 Derive Parameters

Once we have identified the requirements we continue with the actual parameters of the approach.

Ontology Alignment Process with Parameters

We will briefly present the general alignment process and point out those parameters that are adjusted.

1. Feature Engineering selects the excerpts of the overall ontology definition to describe a specific entity.
2. Search Step Selection chooses the entity pairs from the two ontologies to compare. Two possible parameter instantiations would be a complete comparison of ontology entities or an efficient proceeding.
3. Similarity Assessment indicates a similarity for a given description of two entities.
4. Similarity Aggregation aggregates multiple similarity assessment for one pair of entities into a single measure. The feature and similarity selection, together with the weighting scheme represents the underlying general alignment strategy. This can be done in an simple way, e.g., only the comparison of labels or complex way, e.g., all OWL primitives or even domain-specific input.
5. Interpretation uses all aggregated numbers, a threshold, and interpretation strategy to propose the alignment. In case of semi-automation, the user can interpret the numbers himself and enter whether two entities are aligned or not.
6. Iteration, as the similarity of one entity pair influences the similarity of neighboring entity pairs; the equality is propagated through the ontologies. For this the number of iterations need to be fixed.

Parameters Based on Requirements

Setting the algorithm parameters affects the results of the algorithms. The dependencies have been identified from extensive test runs. Most of the dependencies are also intuitive. To give an example: Semantically more complex features lead to higher quality, just as higher iterations of the alignment approach do. For this work, we again invert the function, i.e., identify the optimal parameters based on the n requirements.

$$(\hat{p_1}, \ldots, \hat{p_m}) = \frac{1}{n} \sum_{i=1}^{n} f^{-1}(\hat{r_i}) \qquad (6.3)$$

Each requirement implies a certain decision for the algorithm parameters. The inverted function is represented in Table 6.10. High precision and high recall represents the highest quality requirement. For this, we have to focus on using semantically complex features and heuristics. In addition, it is necessary to take a complete look at the alignment candidates. To increase quality the user is included in the loop and may provide feedback during runtime, as introduced in the previous section. Finally, we have to ensure that alignments have flooded the ontology graphs in a complete way, which only is achieved through many iteration steps.

To determine the overall parameters for the alignment algorithm we have to combine the found individual parameters from each result dimension, i.e., the parameters for precision and recall, for time, and for the automation level. By averaging, the approach can finally propose an optimal strategy for alignment.

Parameters based on Side Condition Constraints

The next step is to examine whether side conditions restrict these parameters. Side conditions are related to two fields: the ontologies to be aligned; and the computational infrastructure. We do not claim this list is complete, but cover the most important aspects.

- One key factor is the size of the involved ontologies with larger ontologies requiring more time for alignment or vice versa demanding a more efficient algorithm.
- Ontologies have different complexity – ranging from simple taxonomies to full description logics. Lower complexity might make the algorithm faster, but less semantic information makes results less reliable.
- Whether the ontologies have more schema or more instance information has an effect on whether the system needs additional input from the user. The same holds true, if only very little overlap of the involved ontologies can be expected.
- Small hand-held devices will currently not be able to properly process complex alignment algorithms in reasonable amounts of time; large servers will typically not have a problem with this.

Not every value of a side condition influences the parameters. Only the constraining ones are listed in Table 6.11. They can again be represented as an inverse function. For instance, for large ontologies we will need to rely on simple features and similarities, the search steps have to be efficient, user interaction is simply unpractical, and only a few iterations can be performed. Otherwise, the process will take too long.

$$(\hat{p_1}, \ldots, \hat{p_m}) = \sum_{i=1}^{k} f^{-1}(s_i) \tag{6.4}$$

If the parameters from the constraining side conditions are more restricting than the original ones found, the original ones are overridden. We have determined the final parameters $\hat{p_1}, \ldots, \hat{p_m}$ for a maximum utility $\hat{u}$.

Table 6.10. Optimal Parameters Based on Requirements $f^{-1}(\hat{r}_i)$

Result $\hat{r}_i$ Dimension	Feature/Similarity $\hat{p}_1$	Search Steps $\hat{p}_2$	Threshold $\hat{p}_3$	User Interaction action $\hat{p}_4$	Iterations $\hat{p}_5$
Precision/ Recall high/high	complex	many/complete	medium	yes	many
high/med.	medium	few/efficient	high	no	medium
med./high	simple	few/efficient	low	no	few
med./med.	medium	few/efficient	medium	no	medium
Time fast	simple	few/efficient		no	few
medium	complex	few/efficient		no	medium
slow	complex	many/complete		yes	medium
Automation automatic		many/complete		no	medium
semi-auto.				yes	many

Table 6.11. Parameters Based on Side Condition Constraints $f^{-1}(s_i)$

Side Condition s_i	Feature/Similarity $\hat{p}_1$	Search Steps $\hat{p}_2$	Threshold $\hat{p}_3$	User Interaction action $\hat{p}_4$	Iterations $\hat{p}_5$
large ontology size	simple	few/efficient	medium	no	few
low ontology complexity	complex	many/complete	medium	yes	many
high ontology complexity	simple	few/efficient	high	no	few
more schema	medium		high	yes	medium
more instances	medium		low	no	few
low overlap	complex	many/complete	low	no	medium
low comp. resources	simple	few/efficient	medium	yes	few

With our methodology, we have found the algorithm parameters leading to the required dimensions and thus maximizing the utility value for a certain use case. This can be easily implemented, thus the user himself does not have to worry about optimizing the parameters. The system determines them on the fly from the input use case and the side conditions.

6.4.6 Example

We will illustrate the adaptive methodology with an example. Let us assume we have two ontologies given in OWL with about 300 entities each describing the biological domain of animals. These ontologies have been developed separately by two institutes. The user wants to merge the two ontologies to receive one integrated view of the animal world. He wants to receive the highest machine support for this action. For this he has a powerful tool for ontology alignment at hand, but he is not an ontology technology expert himself. He wants to use an optimal strategy given the ontologies and his use case, but does not know how to set the individual parameters of the algorithm. In the end he wants to maximize his overall *utility*, so he is reluctant in just relying on the default parameters.

We will now look at the use case: Ontology merging is a common use case in business applications. Ontologies of individual persons or departments may be merged to create a larger potentially company wide understanding. To ensure a good final ontology quality requirements are high, whereas time resources tend to be less critical, as it is possible to execute the merging process in the background, normally only once. Ontology merging will include a human in the loop who finally checks the merged ontologies for correctness. From the description of ontology merging, we derived the *requirements* for the result dimensions from Table 6.9 as follows: precision and recall have to be high; time may be of longer duration; and semi-automation is the ideal level of user interaction.

We now *assign the parameters* according to the requirements as represented in Table 6.10. High precision and high recall represents the highest quality requirement. For this, we have to focus on using semantically complex features and heuristics. Further, it is necessary to take a complete look at the alignment candidates. A medium threshold is applied. Again to increase quality, the user is included in the loop and provides feedback during runtime. Finally, we have to ensure that alignments have flooded the ontology graphs in a complete way, which only is achieved through many iteration steps. With the allowed longer processing time, we can in the same way rely on complex features and heuristics, the user's input, and many iterations. Finally, the required level of automation is directly translated into the corresponding parameter. Semi-automation requirements trigger semi-automation of the approach.

To ensure that the utility still reaches a maximum despite the *side conditions* certain constraints are imposed on the parameters. In the running example, we face the following critical side conditions with the corresponding effects on the parameters (see Table 6.11): The ontologies do not contain many instances, only as many as needed to illustrate the most important features. Besides this, the ontologies have a small overlap. Sparse alignments require a more thorough search. This is based on the assumption that identified alignments lead the path to nearby alignments. Fortunately, these critical side conditions do not constrain the already identified parameters for ontology merging.

We summarize the final parameters: use of complex features and similarities as strategy; a complete search step selection; application of a medium threshold value; a semi-automatic approach with user interaction; and a high number of iterations.

6.4.7 Evaluation

Evaluation is difficult, as only humans are in the position to finally decide whether the maximum utility has been reached and furthermore will potentially disagree. Apart from this, it is impossible to try every combination of parameters.

Scenario

We therefore create a selection of five scenarios with different use cases, ontologies, and computing equipment.

- The first use case is ontology evolution. It is applied to the Russia 1 ontologies.
- Next, the use case is data integration. The two ontologies of Russia 2 were used. We assume a slow system.
- Third, we perform ontology merging. In specific, the two animal ontologies need to be merged. The used computer is powerful.
- In this scenario, we reason across two ontologies describing the sports domain. We assume to have a less powerful machine.
- For the final scenario, query rewriting is the required task. We want to semantically search in two distributed bibliographic ontologies (Bibliography 1) mainly based on RDF(S). The computer system is fast.

Strategies

For each scenario, we evaluate four sets of parameters:

- We automatically derive the optimal algorithm parameters according to our new methodology. For each scenario, the individual parameters will be different.

- Further, we use a presumably generally optimal parameter assignment QOM: this means broad features, efficient candidate selection, medium (0.85) threshold, 20 iterations, and fully automatic.
- A first arbitrary parameter set (Other 1): only labels are used for comparison, again efficient, a medium (0.85) threshold, only one iteration, and fully automatic.
- Finally, a second arbitrary parameter set (Other 2): broad features, complete candidate checks, low (0.7) threshold, ten iterations,[5] and semi-automatic.

Ten users were asked to carry out the five scenarios each with all the parameter sets. Urged to keep the use case in mind the users afterwards had to decide which runs were best, effectively ranking the four strategies with 1 indicating the best and 4 indicating the worst one.

Results

Table 6.12 shows the objective results of the different evaluation runs. The last column presents how users ranked the respective strategy for the given ontologies and the use case. For example, the scenario of ontologies Russia 1 and ontology evolution as use case users gave the adaptive strategy an average rating of 1.67, which indicates that some considered it the best strategy, whereas others thought it to be the second-best strategy. The Other 2 strategy was almost unanimous ranked worst. After having averaged over the different users' opinions and normalized the results we gained the subjective user results as depicted in Figure 6.7.

6.4.8 Discussion and Lessons Learned

The users confirmed that the adaptively chosen strategy in average yielded the best results according to the scenario. They are better than any fixed strategy. This is a clear indicator, that dynamically parameterizing alignment methods as proposed in this work are valuable.

Unfortunately, the adaptive parameterized approach did not always appear to be the absolute best one. To understand the reason for this we had a closer look at the Sports/Reasoning scenario. These ontologies have a controlled vocabulary and and their structure was modeled very exact. Consequently, even though the adaptive approach took considerably longer in its search for alignments, it didn't identify any additional correct ones. Due to this, the test users preferred the fast, only label-based approach. We conclude that there are conditions that affect the outcome of the ontology alignment process but cannot be explicitly detected *beforehand* and thus used for tuning our approach. Further, users tend to shift their preferences. For a different user

---

[5] Ten iterations was the default number for the naïve approach NOM.

Table 6.12. Evaluation Results for Adaptive Alignment

Data Set Use Case	Strategy	Precision	Recall	F-Measure	Duration (sec)	User Input	User Rating
Russia 1	Adaptive	0.824	0.726	0.772	178	60	1.67
Evolution	QOM	0.734	0.720	0.727	51	0	2.78
	Other 1	1.000	0.696	0.821	1	0	1.78
	Other 2	0.680	0.739	0.708	523	60	3.78
Russia 2	Adaptive	0.917	0.767	0.835	158	60	1.67
Data	QOM	0.863	0.676	0.758	52	0	2.33
Integration	Other 1	0.765	0.063	0.116	1.000	0	3.33
	Other 2	0.844	0.879	0.861	196	60	2.67
Animals	Adaptive	1.000	0.813	0.897	28	15	2.11
Ontology	QOM	1.000	0.500	0.667	1	0	2.56
Merging	Other 1	0.000	0.000	0.000	1	0	4.00
	Other 2	1.000	0.833	0.909	35	15	1.33
Sports	Adaptive	0.936	0.487	0.640	183	60	2.89
Reasoning	QOM	0.894	0.85	0.871	42	0	2.38
	Other 1	0.975	0.523	0.681	1	0	1.06
	Other 2	0.893	0.893	0.893	364	60	3.67
Bibliography 1	Adaptive	0.826	0.476	0.603	1	0	1.89
Query	QOM	0.852	0.561	0.676	8	0	2.67
Rewriting	Other 1	0.863	0.463	0.603	1	0	1.67
	Other 2	0.821	0.561	0.667	59	60	3.78
Average	Adaptive						2.05
	QOM						2.54
	Other 1						2.37
	Other 2						3.04

or a different pair of ontologies the preferences might shift again. In the end, these are the subjective parameters (m, o_1, o_2) which cannot be measured ex ante and we therefore needed to ignore for our methodology. Therefore, one should rather evaluate on an overall average basis, than claiming an optimal output for every individual case.

Surprisingly, the presumably generally best strategy only was ranked third, which shows how difficult it is to actually determine a best strategy from user perspective.

In general the results still support the assumption that ontology alignment in average (not in every single case) is much more effective when the use case is considered as a parameter. It is possible to actually reuse existing algorithms for different scenarios after adjusting the parameters automatically. Finally, it showed that our theoretic considerations were brought to a practical implementation, despite the often only inexactly defined coherences of parameters, goal dimensions, and the overall utility.

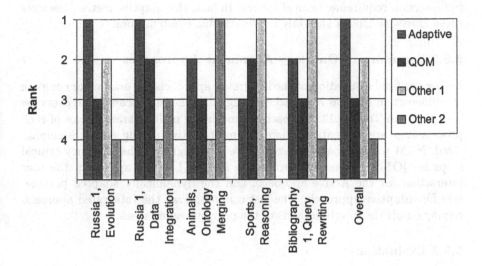

Fig. 6.7. Ranking of Different Strategies

6.5 Integrated Approach

In this Part II we have developed different approaches for ontology alignment. Each of these approaches had a specific focus, thus allowing comparing the effects of novel methods against standard approaches. The goal of this section is to integrate the numerous improvements on ontology alignment from the previous sections.

6.5.1 Integrating the Individual Approaches

The integrated approach consists of:

- Usage of features with OWL primitives and a wide range of similarity measures;
- An efficient alignment candidate selection strategy;
- A learned aggregation and interpretation strategy;
- User interaction during the process;
- And an adaptive method, which automatically sets parameters optimally for the alignment approach.

As the different methods focus on individual aspects in the alignment process there are only few dependencies between them. Nevertheless, certain combinations are not reasonable: A highly efficient approach which then needs to wait for user input does not make any sense; In case of of an efficient approach, the potentially learned features and similarities definitely need to fulfill certain requirements on efficiency. In fact, the adaptive method respects these crosswise effects and only allows sensible combinations.

6.5.2 Summary of Ontology Alignment Approaches

Before our final evaluation of the integrated approach, we once more compare the different individual approaches along the general process. The overview is depicted in Table 6.13. For each approach the main characteristics of each process step are presented, where the most distinguishing ones are emphasized. NOM was our basic approach. We then highlight the efficiency critical steps in QOM, the learned parameters for the Learned approach, the user interaction for the Active approach, and the dynamically adapted parameters for Adaptive approach. The last column shows the Integrated approach relying on all the novel methods of the previous approaches.

6.5.3 Evaluation

This final evaluation will measure the strengths and weaknesses of the different approaches against each other. Our final integrated approach will also be examined for the evaluation.

Strategies

We evaluate the alignment strategies described in the previous sections:

- As the Label algorithm is simple and fast we use it as a baseline to evaluate the other approaches against. It is equivalent to PROMPT (Noy and Musen, 2000). In addition, it already provides good results.
- Naïve Ontology Alignment (NOM) is an approach making use of a wide range of features based on RDF(S) and similarity measures. In this version we use the weighting scheme based on the sigmoid function. In terms of structural information used and complexity incurred, it is similar to Anchor-PROMPT (Noy and Musen, 2001).
- Quick Ontology Mapping (QOM) is our novel approach focusing on efficiency. Only selected candidate alignments are compared. Costly similarity measures have also been removed.
- We further presented an approach where both the similarity aggregation and the interpretation are left to a machine learning algorithm. We used pruning for the decision tree, in particular, we required a minimum number of 30 objects in each leaf. Training alignments are provided by all the ontologies at hand. The results will be evaluated with separately kept test alignments.
- Active Ontology Alignment: For the focused semi-automatic alignment, the most uncertain alignments are presented to the user for validation. In total, the user has to validate 60 entity pairs. For the smaller ontologies such as the animals ontologies only 15 entity pairs are provided.

Table 6.13. Novel Approaches

	NOM	QOM	Learned	Active	Adaptive	Integrated
1. Feature Engineering	labels and structure	labels and structure	learned, OWL domain-specific	labels and structure	labels and structure	learned, OWL and domain-specific
2. Search Step Selection	complete agenda	efficient agenda	complete agenda	complete agenda	dynamic: complete or efficient	dynamic: complete or efficient
3. Similarity Computation	all measures	efficient measures	learned measures	all measures	dynamic: all or efficient	dynamic and learned: all or efficient
4. Similarity Aggregation	manual (sigmoid)	manual (sigmoid)	learned	manual (sigmoid)	manual (sigmoid)	learned
5. Interpretation	manual threshold	manual threshold	learned threshold	user; threshold adjusted	dynamic: manual or user-adapted	dynamic: learned and user-adapted
6. Iteration	many iterations	few iterations	many iterations	many iterations	dynamic: many or few	dynamic: many or few

- We make use of the Adaptive Strategy, in specific for a Query Rewriting use case. The algorithm will then determine the best strategy for the use case. As a second case for the Adaptive Strategy we show Ontology Merging.
- Finally, we use the integrated approach from this section.

Results

On the following pages, we present the results of the different strategies. They are listed in Tables 6.14 and 6.15. The first column mentions the used data set, the second column the used strategy. We then provide the quality measures precision, recall, and f-measure. Finally, we also point out the required time and the number of user actions. The averaged results are additionally depicted in Figures 6.8 and 6.9. Further, it shows whether user interaction was possible or not. The average refers to the four individually listed ontology pairs plus the ten in the appendix of this work.

Our core evaluation measure remains the f-measure. This implies that even though precision and/or recall may be lower for the best approach, this is only the case at the threshold point. By shifting this focus, results for precision and recall may also shift considerably. Please note that the strategies QOM, Active Ontology Alignment, and Learned, are set on top of the NOM strategy, our default. This allows us to compare them. F-measures are again averaged over ontology pairs, resulting therein that it is not the harmonic mean of average precisions and recalls, but is more suitable for a discussion and interpretation.

The integrated strategy returns the best results as expected. In comparison with the up to now best individual approach, the learned approach, precision rises by another 12%, recall by 10%, and f-measure by 12%.[6] As already the individual approaches significantly outperform the simple alignment approaches, the best one is also significantly better at less than 1%. In fact, significance is ensured for an increase of 24% points between the baseline label and the integrated strategy.

6.5.4 Discussion and Lessons Learned

We now would like to draw the reader's attention to selected overall results.

Labels:

For all data sets, labels yield a high precision, but at a considerably lower recall than all the other approaches. It seems that labels provide nearly perfect alignments. At the same time many structural alignments are missed. As we do not require multiple iterations, time is low. Only for simple requirements on alignment, this approach might be already sufficient.

---

[6] In absolute percent points this translates to an increase of 10% in precision, 7% in recall, and 9% in f-measure.

Table 6.14. Integrated Evaluation Results for Individual Data Sets

Data Set	Strategy	Precision	Recall	F-Measure	Duration (sec)	User Input
Russia 1	Labels	1.000	0.033	0.063	2.70	0
	NOM Sigmoid	0.612	0.367	0.459	602	0
	QOM	0.552	0.293	0.383	146	0
	Decision Tree Learner	0.951	0.991	0.970	299	0
	Active (focused)	0.866	0.391	0.538	542	60
	Adaptive Rewriting	1.000	0.116	0.208	3.82	0
	Adaptive Merging	0.969	0.874	0.919	208	60
	Integrated	0.926	0.986	0.955	310	60
Animals	Labels	1.000	0.083	0.154	70.0	0
	NOM Sigmoid	0.769	0.417	0.541	2.42	0
	QOM	0.538	0.292	0.378	2.47	0
	Decision Tree Learner	1.000	0.750	0.857	3.01	0
	Active (focused)	1.000	0.500	0.667	6.69	15
	Adaptive Rewriting	1.000	0.083	0.153	2.48	0
	Adaptive Merging	1.000	0.750	0.857	21.0	15
	Integrated	1.000	0.750	0.857	6.73	15
Bibliography	Labels	0.941	0.865	0.901	1.72	0
	NOM Sigmoid	0.909	0.946	0.927	75.6	0
	QOM	0.904	0.892	0.898	42.8	0
	Decision Tree Learner	0.885	0.932	0.908	60.0	0
	Active (focused)	0.959	0.959	0.959	83.7	60
	Adaptive Rewriting	0.940	0.851	0.894	5.34	0
	Adaptive Merging	0.957	0.905	0.930	792	60
	Integrated	0.947	0.972	0.960	59.6	60
Sports	Labels	0.875	0.0467	0.089	37.8	0
	NOM Sigmoid	0.438	0.140	0.212	566	0
	QOM	0.463	0.127	0.199	74.0	0
	Decision Tree Learner	0.806	0.773	0.789	739	0
	Active (focused)	0.885	0.153	0.261	873	60
	Adaptive Rewriting	0.947	0.120	0.213	3.40	0
	Adaptive Merging	0.971	0.673	0.795	598	60
	Integrated	0.878	0.767	0.819	741	60

Table 6.15. Integrated Evaluation Results, Average

Data Set	Strategy	Precision	Recall	F-Measure	Duration (sec)	User Input
Average	Labels	0.754	0.312	0.370	5.14	0
	NOM Sigmoid	0.789	0.476	0.523	749	0
	QOM	0.705	0.433	0.477	108	0
	Decision Tree Learner	0.858	0.727	0.767	353	0
	Active (focused)	0.907	0.520	0.613	673	47
	Adaptive Rewriting	0.755	0.347	0.426	4.19	0
	Adaptive Merging	0.943	0.715	0.804	422	47
	Integrated	0.953	0.796	0.859	356	47

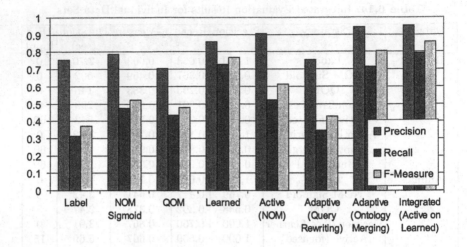

Fig. 6.8. F-Measure, Precision, and Recall for Different Strategies

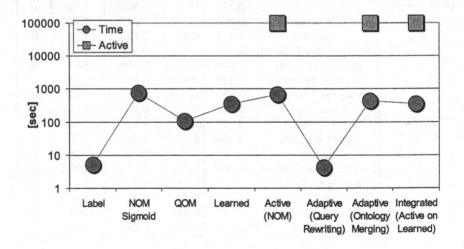

Fig. 6.9. Time and User Interaction for Different Strategies

Semantics:

The ontology semantics exploited by NOM raises recall and f-measure considerably by 50%. For some data sets, this rise is little, whereas others cannot align hardly anything without these structural components resulting in a strong rise when they are present. However, it is particularly difficult to weight the individual semantic features for the overall similarity. Semantics significantly contributes to ontology alignment.

Efficiency:

QOM lowers time considerably. QOM is faster than standard prominent approaches by a factor of 10 to 100 times. This is achieved at the cost of lowering quality to a certain degree – always compared to our baseline NOM. Nevertheless, this drop might be neglected for certain use cases.

Machine Learning:

For the optimized decision tree, we again focus on the f-measure. The learned strategy is better than the standard manually trimmed NOM approach by another 40%, effectively doubling recall and f-measure compared to labels only. This supports our assumption that humans cannot overview the complete complexity of ontological structures, but their knowledge in form of training data can considerably increase the performance of an alignment algorithm. Additionally, as the decision tree only requires the calculation of a subset of individual similarities, it is often faster than the other approaches. The drawback here was the amount of training data. As ontologies are complex structures, they require more than just a few training data. Especially if the alignment algorithm has to be trained for a domain-specific environment, creating this data could be difficult. Decision trees also have the advantageous feature of implicitly explaining the decision process on why two entities have been aligned.

User Interactivity:

By adding user input during the alignment process, according to our goal in a least intrusive way, quality increases. Focused semi-automatic alignment leads to better quality (+17%). Due to the large search space an only unfocused semi-automatic alignment does not have any effect.

Adaptive Alignment:

Finally, by applying an algorithm that takes the use case into account the results are automatically tuned in a way meeting the specific requirements of the use case. The overall evaluation with user feedback for the adaptive approach was very positive.

Ontology alignment has different facets, which can all be influenced differently. One general result of the evaluation is that there is no absolutely best ontology alignment approach. However, one sees that there is much more than just comparing labels. We have provided an overview of approaches based on semantic features of the ontologies and anchored in a very flexible parameterizable framework. In the end one has to decide which characteristics are most important: quality, efficiency, or user interaction. This task needs to be decided upon by the user. It is only possible to solve, when we understand what the ontology alignment is needed for in practice.

The major building blocks for ontology alignment have been presented in this work: the general ontology alignment process and additional original extensions thereof. Many small improvements may still be added to these approaches. Due to the ontologies being non-complete abstractions of the real world and the subjective generally diverging notion of humans on what entities to align, it will never be possible to reach *perfect* alignments. The unfortunately blurry border line seems within reach.

Part III

Implementation and Application

7

Tools

After the creation of the new approaches, we now need to deploy them. Therefore, we will first show how these are implemented. This chapter is split into three implementations of the alignment approach: a basic infrastructure for ontology alignment and mapping (FOAM), Ontology Mapping based on Axioms (OMA), and the OntoStudio plug-in OntoMap. All of them have specific strengths, though the most important implementation undoubtedly is FOAM. We will refer to it in the subsequent practical applications.

7.1 Basic Infrastructure for Ontology Alignment and Mapping – FOAM

Many methods and approaches for ontology alignment have been presented in this work, but a theoretical framework alone is not sufficient. One needs a proof of concept. In the beginning of this work we made another claim: In fact, we want a system suiting practical applications. Therefore, the goal of our Framework for Ontology Alignment and Mapping (FOAM) is twofold: first, an environment for testing of our new methods for alignment; and second, a stable ontology alignment system. The infrastructure fulfilling the two goals will now be described in detail.

7.1.1 User Example

To give an example, our user wants to align the two ontologies *animalsA.owl* and *animalsB.owl*. The goal is to find the alignments. They are supposed to be general enough for any usage afterwards. Therefore, she starts the FOAM tool from command line (Figure 7.1) with the corresponding parameters (Example 7.1), i.e., the two ontologies and the alignment discovery scenario. The whole process takes time, but this is not a critical factor for this use case. After finishing, FOAM saves the results in a file. The results are of high quality with interesting nontrivial alignments, e.g., a two-legged person in one ontology is equivalent to a bipedal person in the other one.

7.1.2 Process Implementation

We will first generally present FOAM with its parameters and the actual implementation of the process.

FOAM provides three modes for execution. It may be accessed through the command line using a simple parameter file. Further, as it has been implemented in Java,[1] it may be run through a Java API making it easy to connect to other applications. It has been run successfully on PCs under the Windows and Linux operating systems. And finally, for lightweight testing purposes, it can be run on our server as a web service which can easily be accessed via a web interface.[2] According to the twofold goal of FOAM the user can either specify all parameters himself (strategy, number of iterations, semi-automatic or not, etc.) or let the system set the optimal parameters based on the ontologies to align and the desired use case. A NOSCENARIO-option is available, if the use case is unspecified. The parameters are either set in a separate parameter file or directly handed over to the alignment class within the Java application. Example 7.1 contains two ontologies to align, the scenario, and the filename for the results.

The process of ontology alignment has been implemented as follows. FOAM requires two ontologies as input, in particular ontologies in OWL-DL. Besides, preknown alignments may be entered into the system. Figure 7.1 shows the command line call, the output information of FOAM on the used strategy, the process with several iterations, and the location where the results are saved. Alignments are provided either in the RDF-representation format or as a comma-separated list. The search step selection is implemented with different kinds of agendas. FOAM includes flexible classes for feature selection (RDF(S) and OWL), as well as a library of similarity measures (also using external information such as dictionaries). Afterwards, there are different combination strategies ranging from simple averaging to machine learned decision trees or neural nets. Whereas the iteration step is trivially implemented through a loop, the interpretation allows for human interaction, where the user has to confirm or reject questionable alignments. If required, the one alignment link strategy is enforced during the interpretation step. The final results are, according to the different implementation goals, either a file of alignments above the threshold and doubtable alignments (for human interaction), or a complete file of alignments ranked by their confidence value. If a gold standard is provided, the alignments are automatically evaluated and the evaluation results are stored as well. All methods of the previous chapters have been implemented. Sometimes, they have been extended with additional features, if this made the framework more flexible for future extensions.

---

[1] http://java.sun.com/

[2] http://www.aifb.uni-karlsruhe.de/WBS/meh/foam/

Example 7.1 (Parameter File).

```
PARAMETERS FILE FOR THE ONTOLOGY ALIGNMENT PROCESS
ontology1 = C:/FOAM/animalsA.owl;
ontology2 = C:/FOAM/animalsB.owl;
scenario = ALIGNMENTDISCOVERY;
resultFile = C:/FOAM/results.txt;
```

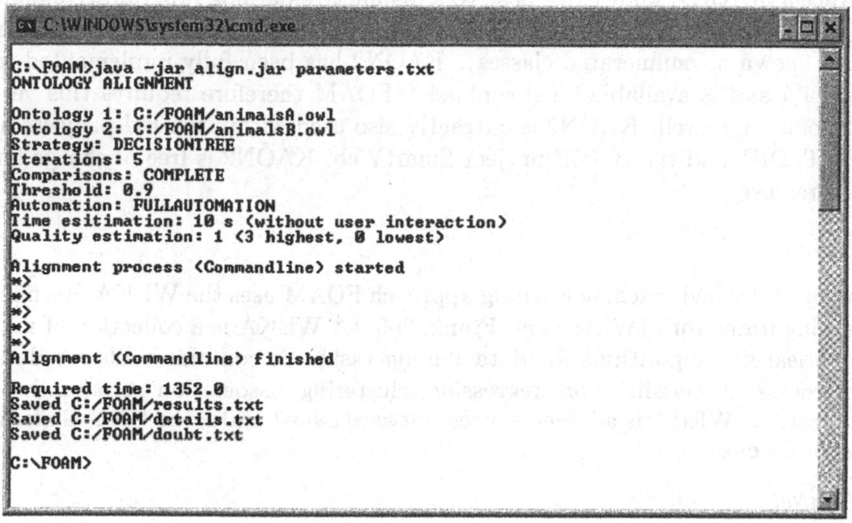

```
C:\WINDOWS\system32\cmd.exe

C:\FOAM>java -jar align.jar parameters.txt
ONTOLOGY ALIGNMENT

Ontology 1: C:/FOAM/animalsA.owl
Ontology 2: C:/FOAM/animalsB.owl
Strategy: DECISIONTREE
Iterations: 5
Comparisons: COMPLETE
Threshold: 0.9
Automation: FULLAUTOMATION
Time esitimation: 10 s (without user interaction)
Quality estimation: 1 (3 highest, 0 lowest)

Alignment process (Commandline) started
*>
*>
*>
*>
Alignment (Commandline) finished

Required time: 1352.0
Saved C:/FOAM/results.txt
Saved C:/FOAM/details.txt
Saved C:/FOAM/doubt.txt

C:\FOAM>
```

Fig. 7.1. Commandline Output

FOAM has a number of helpful extensions such as a module for translating between different alignment representations. An implementation for learning a decision tree, neural network, or support vector machine for alignment is provided as well. Two additional interface classes are also supported: one to allow running FOAM as a web service; and one to embed FOAM into the OntoStudio environment (see Section 7.3 for more details). One restriction applies to the implementation: To keep memory within tolerable ranges, we do not store every single similarity, which has been calculated. If the similarity drops below the value of 0.01, it is simply assumed zero.

The Java source code of FOAM can easily be extended. Currently the implementation contains about 200 classes with a total of 10,000 lines of code. Documentation is included in the appendix of this work.

7.1.3 Underlying Software

Fortunately, FOAM can rely on existing software for ontology management, machine learning, and dictionary look-up.

KAON2:

FOAM is built upon the KAON2 ontology environment. KAON2 is an infrastructure for managing OWL-DL ontologies and DL-safe rules, a subset of the SWRL language. It provides an API for programmatic management of OWL-DL ontologies, of which we heavily make use of. An inference engine is available, which allows us to exploit the logical relations encoded in the semantics. Reasoning in KAON2 is implemented by novel algorithms that reduce a SHIQ(D) knowledge base to a disjunctive datalog program (Hustadt et al., 2004a,b). This includes all features of OWL-DL apart from nominals (also known as enumerated classes). KAON2 has been fully implemented in Java 1.5 and is available for download.[3] FOAM therefore requires this version of Java as well. KAON2 is currently also used within the EU-projects of SEKT, DIP, and the BMBF project SmartWeb. KAON2 is free of charge for research use.

WEKA:

For the described machine learning approach FOAM uses the WEKA machine learning framework (Witten and Frank, 2005).[4] WEKA is a collection of machine learning algorithms for data mining tasks. It contains tools for data preprocessing, classification, regression, clustering, association rules, and visualization. WEKA is an open source software issued under the GNU General Public License.

WordNet:

We have seen that labels of entities are very valuable for determining similarity. WordNet allows to exploit the information encoded in the labels to a deeper extent, by looking up synonyms, translating, or extending the original terms with additional information. WordNet (Fellbaum, 1998)[5] is an online lexical reference system whose design is inspired by current psycholinguistic theories of human lexical memory. English nouns, verbs, adjectives, and adverbs are organized into synonym sets, each representing one underlying concept. Different relations link the synonym sets. Especially these synonym sets make WordNet an interesting candidate to increase quality of the alignment results.

7.1.4 Availability and Open Usage

The Framework for Ontology Alignment and Mapping is available from its webpage.[6] The page contains links to relevant publications, a download section of binaries and source code, installation guidelines and the documentation

---

[3] http://kaon2.semanticweb.org/
[4] http://www.cs.waikato.ac.nz/~ml/weka/
[5] http://wordnet.princeton.edu/
[6] http://www.aifb.uni-karlsruhe.de/WBS/meh/foam/

of FOAM, and ontologies to test the tool. There is a web interface for internet users for testing. For extensive use we recommend downloading it.

7.1.5 Summary

FOAM and its predecessors meet the two goals mentioned at the beginning of this section. It has been excessively used for testing and evaluating the different ontology alignment approaches. In fact, all the evaluation results in previous chapters have been ascertained based on this implementation. The second goal was the real world application. This will be elaborated in more detail in the chapters to come (Chapters 8 and 9). Within the SWAP project, FOAM is used to align and merge identical entities that the Bibster application returns for a bibliographic query. Additionally it provides alignments to the ontology design board for the distributed ontology creation process as required by Xarop (see Section 8.3). FOAM is also a substantial part of the mediation component in the SEKT project. The three use cases of an intelligent question answering system for judges, a semantically enabled digital library, and a collaboration tool for consulting teams use this component for different actions ranging from query rewriting to ontology merging. Due to its easy interface the partners in the independent MODALE project[7] could make use of it without any further support from the developer's side (Abecker et al., 2004). MODALE tries to integrate the different views of the different companies participating in one larger production process. Finally, the methods implemented in FOAM were objectively tested in three ontology alignment contests of the last years: I3CON, EON-OAC, and OAEI (Hughes, 2004; Sure et al., 2004; Ashpole et al., 2005). In all these cases, the results returned by FOAM were very favorable. After removing effects due to errors in the stored representation format, FOAM was among the best rated, despite the contests only allowing fully automatic tests in which time was not considered critical. FOAM's possibilities are more multilayered.

7.2 Ontology Mapping Based on Axioms

In contrast to the procedural implementation of FOAM, in this section we also expect to find alignments based on a declarative approach, more specifically based on logical rules (Ehrig and Sure, 2005d). Processing these rules by inference engines allows similar to the procedural implementation for detection, creation, and execution of alignments on the fly without human intervention. The rules can be easily reused for alignments of arbitrary ontologies, no additional modeling effort is required. Secondly and only for Ontology Mapping based on Axioms (OMA), a suitable inference engine is the only mandatory technological infrastructure, which means that no additional implementation

---

[7] http://www.modale.de/

effort is needed. Thus, OMA is an application of ontology infrastructure for ontology alignment.

For evaluation of our approach, we compare the values for precision, recall, and f-measure of the derived alignments by using our logics approach with the equivalent values of the procedural approach.

7.2.1 Logics and Inferencing

In our approach we rely on:

- F-Logic as representation language for our alignment model (Kifer et al., 1995), "F" stands for "Frames", and
- OntoBroker[8] as the inference engine to process F-Logic (Decker et al., 1999). See also Sure (2003).

F-Logic combines deductive and object-oriented aspects: *"F-logic ... is a deductive, object-oriented database language that combines the declarative semantics of deductive databases with the rich data modeling capabilities supported by the object oriented data model."* (Frohn et al., 1996) F-Logic allows for definitions with primitives known from object-oriented languages (classes, attributes, object-oriented style relations, instances). Further, it also has Predicate Logic primitives (predicates, function symbols). By using axioms the model interpretation my be further constrained. The axioms also allow defining connections between relations. F-Logic axioms have the expressive power of Horn-Logic with negation and may be transformed into Horn-Logic rules. The semantics of a set of F-Logic statements is defined by the well-founded semantics (van Gelder et al., 1991). In contrast to First-Order semantics, not all possible models are considered but one *most obvious* model is selected as the semantics of a set of axioms and facts. The model of the three-valued logic consists of a set of true, unknown, known to be false facts. Unlike Description Logics (DL), F-Logic does not provide means for subsumption (Horrocks, 1998), but it provides for efficient reasoning with instances and for the capability to express powerful axioms. It has to be noted that efforts are being made to put a general rule layer aside to the DL-based OWL language, plus an additional common layer of DL-safe rules beneath the general rules and OWL. Thus, convergence of different representation mechanisms can be expected.

The most widely published operational semantics for F-Logic is the alternating fixed-point procedure (van Gelder, 1993). This is a forward chaining method that computes the entire model for the set of axioms, i.e., the set of true and unknown facts. For answering a query the entire model must be computed and the variable substitutions for the query are then derived. The inference engine OntoBroker performs a mixture of forward and backward chaining based on the dynamic filtering algorithm (Kifer and Lozinskii, 1986)

---

[8] http://www.ontoprise.de/content/e3/e27/index_eng.html

that is much more efficient than the simple strategy. For detailed introductions to the syntax and the object model of F-Logic, in particular with respect to the implementation of F-Logic in OntoBroker, we refer to Erdmann (2001) and Ontoprise (2004).

7.2.2 Formalization of Similarity Rules as Logical Axioms

The similarities of entities for ontology alignment initially have been defined in natural language. The goal of this section is to show how they can be declaratively represented by logical axioms, which can be processed by inference engines. More specifically, we use F-Logic as ontology language and to formalize the similarity rules as axioms, and OntoBroker as inference engine to process them. F-Logic combines features from object-oriented programming and frame-logics. : is used to represent instance of and :: to denote the subconcept of relationship. Arbitrary relationships are specified by the following syntax: `concept[relation=>>concept]`, `->>` is used for the instantiation of such a relationship. # splits an identifier into namespace and local name.

Example 7.2 (F-Logic Ontology). Two concepts auto1 and auto2, which are both a subconcept of vehicle.

```
a#auto1::c#vehicle.
a#auto1[#label->>a#car].
b#auto2::c#vehicle.
b#auto2[#label->>b#automobile].
```

Example 7.2 shows a fragment of an ontology: auto1 and auto2, both from different namespaces a and b, are subclass of vehicle. They have specific labels ("car" and "automobile"). The following F-Logic examples correspond to the rule: *if superconcepts are the same, the actual concepts are similar to each other*. In a similar manner, all other rules have been formalized. Example 7.3 calculates the similarity based on the above-mentioned rule. For all namespaces and local names a similarity of superconcepts (similaritySuper) is determined if there is one common superconcept from an arbitrary namespace of both individual classes, as it is the case here with vehicle. Applying this axiom to the example ontology we receive the predicate similaritySuper(a#auto1,b#auto2).

OntoBroker is able to distinguish between different namespaces. The variables NS1, NS2, and NS3 are bound to namespaces and LN1, LN2 and LN3 to entity labels (such as concept names or relation names). Please note that one would need to add AND NOT equals(LN1,LN2) into the rule body to define, e.g., NS1 and NS2 explicitly as disjoint namespaces.

Example 7.3 (F-Logic Alignment Approach). Two concepts NS1#LN1 and NS2#LN2 are checked for identical superconcepts.

```
FORALL NS1,LN1,NS2,LN2
 similaritySuper(NS1#LN1,NS2#LN2)
 <-
 EXISTS NS3,LN3
 NS1#LN1::NS3#LN3 AND
 NS2#LN2::NS3#LN3.
```

For the integration step, all similarity predicates are summed. If a threshold is reached, the two corresponding concepts (or other entities) are declared to be aligned with each other.

By using the same kind of axioms, also alignments themselves are expressed as F-Logic.

7.2.3 Evaluation

In this section, we evaluate the behavior of the logics-based approach OMA against the standard procedural approach FOAM. The goal is to find out whether both approaches actually perform equally well.

Strategies

We here compare two strategies.

- For the Procedural Strategy (FOAM) the presented rules have been implemented as shown in the previous section, with a focus on efficiency.
- The Logics Strategy (OMA) represents the approach shown in this section, which has a focus on intuitive modeling, greater flexibility, and easier maintainability.

Results

Table 7.1 shows that the Logics Strategy works as good as the procedural implementation. More specifically, one sees from the evaluation that finding alignments through an inference engine returns results that have a similar quality (precision, recall, and f-measure) compared to the ones provided by a procedural implementation.

Discussion and Lessons Learned

Despite the recent work on inference engines, efficiency stays a problem, especially for reasoning on schema and instance level. A general logics inference

Table 7.1. Comparison of Procedural and Logics Alignment Approach

Strategy	Measure	Value
Procedural	Precision	0.772
	Recall	0.652
	F-measure	0.707
Logical Inferencing	Precision	0.784
	Recall	0.652
	F-measure	0.711

engine cannot be as focused on alignment as a direct procedural approach. However, our experiment showed that the current implementation of Onto-Broker was able to deal with real world ontologies. Any optimization in this context is beyond the direct influence of the ontology alignment approach.

The advantages of this approach are twofold. Firstly, the modeled axioms may be easily reused for alignment of arbitrary ontologies, no additional modeling effort is required, and the maintenance of the system is performed on the knowledge level. Secondly, the inference engine is the only mandatory technological infrastructure, which means that no additional implementation effort is needed.

We have shown that the approaches presented in this work can actually be implemented modeled by using logical inferencing. To sum up, inference engines together with our second implementation OMA effectively retrieve semantic alignments as well.

7.3 Integration into Ontology Engineering Platform

Besides the two direct implementations of the ontology alignment approaches, FOAM is additionally embedded in the OntoStudio/OntoMap tool, which will be explained in this section. As OntoMap is a commercial tool, we can make use of its stable infrastructure and graphical user interface. In return, OntoMap can directly be enhanced through new methods for ontology alignment. The usage of FOAM within OntoMap is an example of successful transfer of research into industrial practice.

7.3.1 OntoStudio

OntoStudio is an engineering environment for ontologies and for the development of semantic applications. It is the successor of OntoEdit (Sure et al., 2002, 2003), which has been distributed worldwide more than 5000 times. Both systems have been developed by Ontoprise,[9] a Karlsruhe based software and consulting company focusing on semantic technologies. Tight cooperation

---

[9] http://www.ontoprise.de/content/index_eng.html

exists between Ontoprise, the Institute AIFB at the University of Karlsruhe, and the FZI Research Center for Information Technologies. This allows for short times from research to application.

OntoStudio is based on IBM's development environment Eclipse,[10] which is regarded as a standard for editor frameworks. OntoStudio supports not only OWL and RDF(S) but also F-Logic and OXML. Whereas OWL is designed by the World Wide Web Consortium for the description of ontologies, F-Logic (see also Section 7.2.1) and OXML are optimized for the logic-based processing of ontologies. Different database schemas from Oracle, MS SQL, and DB2 can be imported into OntoStudio, thus lifting existing schemata to an ontology level. OntoStudio is convincing through its handling: The intuitive graphical user interface allows the user to carry out the different ontology management activities. The plug-in structure of the underlying Eclipse makes it easy to extend for various applications such as the OntoStudio Evaluator. The Evaluator is used for the implementation of rules during modeling. OntoStudio is connected to OntoBroker, a powerful and scalable reasoning engine running in the background. OntoStudio is available with a main memory- or database-based model. It is scalable and thus suitable for modeling large ontologies. The basic version as main memory option is offered free of charge for non-commercial use and may be downloaded from Ontoprise's webpage.

OntoStudio is an environment for engineering of ontologies, supports the main standards, and offers good usability and scalability. It is therefore one promising implementation platform for our ontology alignment approach.

7.3.2 OntoMap

OntoMap (Maier et al., 2003) is a plug-in for OntoStudio that supports the creation and management of ontology alignments via a graphical interface.

It comes with an alignment view (see Figure 7.2) in which alignments may be defined between several source ontologies (on the left) and one target ontology (on the right). An alignment is visualized by an arrow and is created by a single drag&drop operation from the source to the target (e.g., from automobile to car). Users just need to understand the graphical representation (e.g., an arrow connecting two concepts); they do not have to worry about the logical representation alignments. The user of OntoMap is supported by simple consistency checks on relation-alignments (automatic suggestion of necessary concept-alignments). For concept alignments, constraints may be specified on the available attributes, based on a form.

OntoStudio has its own representation of alignments, based on F-Logic rules. OntoMap supports simple types of alignments. If more complex alignments are needed (possibly using complex logical expressions or built-ins), they have to be encoded manually. OntoMap still covers a great number of use-cases. The rules that are currently supported include: concept to concept

---

[10] http://www.eclipse.org/

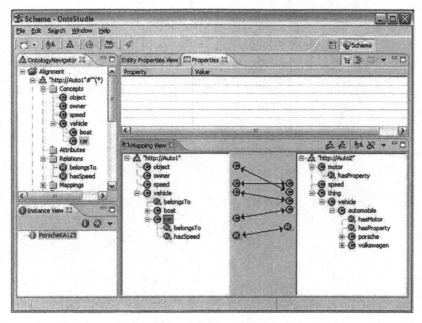

Fig. 7.2. OntoMap

alignments; attribute to attribute alignments; relation to relation alignments; and attribute to concept alignments. In OntoStudio queries on stored ontologies can be written and executed instantly, which gives users the possibility to test the consequence of alignments they have created (or imported). Any later usage of alignments, e.g., for mapping, is also easily executed through queries.

7.3.3 FOAM in OntoMap

The manual creation of alignments is a time-consuming task, even with an intuitive graphical user interface as provided by OntoMap. It is a potential bottleneck for integration. Therefore, FOAM provides an important complement to the set of tools for ontology mediation.

FOAM is tightly integrated into OntoMap. When the user presses the button *Align*, OntoMap delivers the two ontologies to the FOAM application. As soon as FOAM finishes the alignment process, it returns the results, which are then displayed within OntoMap. Users may then extend the found alignments or delete potential errors within them.

OntoMap makes the application of ontology alignment much easier and more intuitive for the users. The alignment process becomes transparent. This is exactly the role automatic ontology alignment should have: a background service supporting the user when dealing with heterogeneous ontologies.

Fig. 7.2. A 2LOncoDoc

performing as inline data-base alignments, relate to revelation augmenting
attributes to connect alignments. In OncoDoc alignments are one-time temporary
plus can be written and executed inactual, which gives users the possibility
to use the conjuncation of alignments. Since have created (on instanced) by a
cluster usage of alignments, e.g. for mapping, are also easily executed through
queries.

7.3.4 TOAM in OncoDoc

The manual creation of alignments is a time consuming task, even without
alternative mapping, user interface are provided by OncoDoc. Thus, we would
enthusiast for its service over TOAM. TOAM provides an important angle-
ment in the set of tools concerning mapping.

TOAM is therby integrated into OncoDoc ... When the user selects the
between three methods delivers the two ontologies to the TOAM application. Session a TOAM finalizes the alignment process. It returns the results
will it are then displayed within OncoDoc. Users may then extend the found
intermediate between proposed patterns within them.

TOAM enables the combination of ontology alignment much easier and
more intuitive for the user. The alignment process becomes almost transparent.
Meanwhile the automatic ontology alignments should have a specification
service suited to the above mentioned during tools with appropriate ontologies.

Semantic Web and Peer-to-Peer – SWAP

This chapter will show the application of the developed alignment techniques within the project SWAP. After a short general description of the project, its two case studies will be presented each with respective sections on ontology alignment (Haase et al., 2004a; Tempich et al., 2004). These show that the developed ideas actually do carry over to practice.

8.1 Project Description

Semantic Web and Peer-to-Peer (SWAP) is an EU-funded project with the goal to develop highly innovative technology in the area of knowledge management and peer-to-peer. The benefit is facilitation of knowledge sharing between individuals. Users can easily provide information from their own personal computer, and search and retrieve information from other PCs, e.g., within the department. The information exchange is realized via an open source peer-to-peer network, which has the advantage of not requiring any central server and administration. The second benefit is the individualization of work views. SWAP focuses on the use of Semantic Web technology, which allows computers to actually comprehend the meaning of its processed data by using the model of ontologies. As a result, SWAP can translate between the different individual users and they no longer have to adapt their information to a given fixed structure. SWAP tackles the challenges brought up by this novel combination of the Semantic Web and peer-to-peer such that knowledge finding and sharing is effectively possible. More information about the project can be found at its webpage.[1]

---

[1] http://swap.semanticweb.org/

Fig. 8.1. Semantic Web and Peer-to-Peer (SWAP)

8.1.1 Core Technologies

Peer-to-Peer technology:

The basic architecture of computer systems has evolved from the mainframe architecture to the currently widely accepted client server architecture. Peer-to-peer network architecture is the natural successor in this development (Oram, 2001). The main point in peer-to-peer networks is, that each peer has the same rights and capabilities as any other peer, which reflects more the actual situation of knowledge workers. Existing peer-to-peer systems enable the user to send messages instantly (ICQ, MSN messenger), to share files (gnutella, Kan (2001)) or to share computing power (SETI@home, Korpela et al. (2001)). However, query possibilities are restricted. The SWAP system builds upon the JXTA protocol (Gong, 2001), which is an open protocol proposed by Sun Microsystems as a standard to exchange information in a peer-to-peer environment. To enable the user to ask meaningful queries SWAP uses techniques from the Semantic Web community.

The advantages of peer-to-peer architectures over centralized approaches have been well advertised, and to some extent realized in existing applications: no centralized server (thus avoiding a bottleneck for both computational performance and information update); robustness against failure of any single component; scalability in both data volumes and the number of connected parties. Besides being the solution to many problems, the large degree of distribution of peer-to-peer systems is also the cause of a number of new problems: The lack of a single coherent schema for organizing information sources across the peer-to-peer network hinders the formulation of search queries, duplication of information across the network results in many duplicate answers to a single query, and answers to a single query often require the integration of information residing at different, independent and uncoordinated peers. Finally, query routing and network topology (which peers to connect to, and which peers to send/forward queries to) are significant problems.

The Semantic Web Approach:

The unavailability of existing ontologies is currently a bottleneck for the wide application of them. Major innovations of the project are techniques that enable the automatic generation of ontologies from existing structures. Through their interaction with the computer, humans attach meaning to the documents they are working with. This information remained unused until now. For example, the information of receiver and subject of an email is not assigned to the attached document. This information and knowledge that was previously gathered in other circumstances might help to characterize the document in a better way. This was just one example of the unused resources that we exploit to create ontologies and increase the machine understanding about what we mean. The combination of information within the peer network will further augment the process.

The research community has recently turned to the use of semantics in peer-to-peer networks to alleviate the problem of unused resources (Nejdl et al., 2002; Broekstra et al., 2003; Castano et al., 2003). The use of semantic descriptions of data sources stored by peers and the use of semantic descriptions of peers helps in formulating queries such that they can be understood by other peers, in merging the answers received from other peers, and in routing queries across the network. In particular, the use of ontologies and of Semantic Web technologies has been identified as promising for peer-to-peer systems.

8.1.2 Case Studies

The ideas and the technologies of SWAP have been applied in two case studies, which will be presented in the next two sections:

- Bibster: Sharing bibliographic metadata in a distributed environment (Section 8.2);
- Xarop: A virtual enterprise (Section 8.3).

The descriptions are widely based on Haase et al. (2004a) and Tempich et al. (2004). In one section each, we will then refer to the concrete usage of the ontology alignment approach in the applications.

8.2 Bibster

Bibster (Haase et al., 2004a,b, 2005) is a peer-to-peer software system built for the exchange of bibliographic entries. This pioneer role of Bibster was emphasized through the doIT-award 2004 of the state of Baden-Württemberg for innovative software.[2] We will describe its main properties on the following pages.

---

[2] http://www.doit-online.de/

8.2.1 Scenario

Bibster addresses a typical problem in the daily life of a researcher, where one regularly has to search for publications or their correct bibliographic metadata. Currently, people do these searches with search engines like Google and CiteSeer,[3] via university libraries or by simply asking other people that are likely to know how to obtain the desired information. The scenario that we envision here is that researchers in a community share bibliographic metadata in a peer-to-peer fashion.

As one may easily recognize, this scenario exhibits two characteristics that strongly require a semantics-based peer-to-peer system. First, a centralized solution does not exist and cannot exist, because of the multitude of informal workshops that researchers refer to, but that do not show up in centralized resources such as DBLP.[4] Any such centralized resource will only cover a limited scientific community. For example, DBLP covers many publications in the area of artificial intelligence, but only little of knowledge management, whereas much work is being done in the overlap of these two fields. At the same time, many individual researchers are willing to share their resources, provided they do not have to invest work in doing so. Second, the use of Semantic Web technology is crucial in this setting. Although a small common-core ontology of bibliographic information exists (title, author/editor, etc.), much of this information is volatile, and users define arbitrary add-ons, for example to include URLs or abstracts of publications.

Bibster is aimed at researchers that share bibliographic metadata. Requirements for Bibster must include capabilities that support their daily work. Researchers may want to do the following:

- Query a single specific peer (e.g., their own computer, because it is sometimes hard to find the right entry even there), a specific set of peers (e.g., all colleagues in an institute) or the entire network of peers (to obtain the maximal recall at the price of low precision);
- Search for bibliographic entries using simple keyword searches, but also more advanced, semantic searches, e.g., for publications of a special type, with specific attribute values, or about a certain topic;
- And integrate results of a query into a local knowledge base for future use. Such data may in turn be used to answer queries by other peers. They may also be interested in updating items that are already locally stored with additional information about these items obtained from other peers.

8.2.2 Design

The Bibster peer-to-peer system is based on the SWAP architecture, which will follow in this section. The data may have been obtained from local Bib-TeX files. Bibster allows to easily integrate, share and search bibliographic

---

[3] http://citeseer.ist.psu.edu/
[4] http://www.informatik.uni-trier.de/~ley/db/

metadata. Semantic technologies are applied throughout the system: Ontologies are used for the representation and classification of the metadata. Semantic descriptions of the peers' expertise allow to effectively routing queries. And semantic similarity measures allow to visualize and integrate the heterogeneous search results form the peers. The approaches described in the previous chapters have been used for the task mentioned last.

The Role of Ontologies

Ontologies are crucial throughout the usage of Bibster, for importing data, formulating queries, routing queries, and processing answers.

Firstly, the system enables users to import their own bibliographic metadata into a local repository. Bibliographic entries made available to Bibster by a user are automatically aligned to two common ontologies: The first ontology (Semantic Web Research Community SWRC) (Sure et al., 2005) is closely related to the bibliographic ontologies used for evaluation of our approaches. It describes different generic aspects of bibliographic metadata (and would be valid across many different research domains). The second ontology (ACM Topic Hierarchy) describes specific categories of literature for the Computer Science domain.

Secondly, queries are formulated in terms of the two ontologies: Queries may concern fields like author, publication type, etc. (using terms from the SWRC ontology) or queries may concern specific Computer Science terms (using the ACM Topic Hierarchy).

Thirdly, queries are routed through the network depending on the expertise models of the peers describing which concepts from the ACM ontology a peer can answer queries on. A matching function determines how closely the semantic content of a query matches the expertise model of a peer. Routing is then done based on this semantic ranking.

Finally, answers are returned for a query. Due to the distributed nature and potentially large size of the peer-to-peer network, this answer set might be very large, and contain many duplicate answers. Because of the semi-structured nature of bibliographic metadata, such duplicates are often not exactly identical copies. Ontologies help to measure the semantic similarity between the different answers and to remove apparent duplicates as identified by the similarity function in the alignment approach.

Architecture and Modules

The Bibster system has been implemented as an instance of the SWAP System architecture as introduced in Broekstra et al. (2003). Figure 8.2 recapitulates a high-level design of the architecture of a single node in the peer-to-peer system. We will now briefly present the individual components as instantiated for the Bibster system.

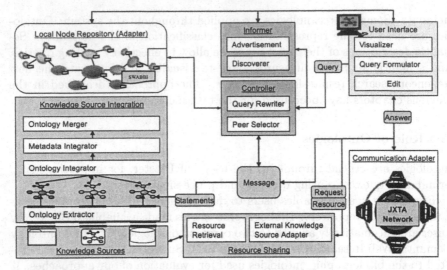

Fig. 8.2. Architecture of SWAP

Communication Adapter:

This component is responsible for the network communication between peers. It serves as a transport layer for other parts of the system, for sending and forwarding queries. It hides and encapsulates all low-level communication details from the rest of the system. In the specific implementation of the Bibster system, we use JXTA as the communication platform.

Knowledge Sources:

The knowledge sources in the Bibster system are sources of bibliographic metadata, such as BibTeX files stored locally in the file system of the user.

Knowledge Source Integrator:

The Knowledge Source Integrator is responsible for the extraction and integration of internal and external knowledge sources into the Local Node Repository, e.g., as shown in Lamparter et al. (2004). For Bibster this includes the process of semantic extraction from BibTeX files. We explain later how the knowledge of local and remote sources can be merged, i.e., how duplicate query results are detected and integrated.

Local Node Repository:

In order to manage its information models and views as well as information acquired from the network, each peer maintains a Local Node Repository providing the following functionality: mediate between views and stored information; support query formulation and processing; specify the peer's interface to the network; and provide the basis for peer ranking and selection. In the Bibster system, the Local Node Repository is based on the RDF(S) repository Sesame (Broekstra et al., 2002).[5] The query language SeRQL (Sesame RDF Query Language) (Broekstra and Kampman, 2004) is used to formulate semantic queries against the Local Node Repository.

Informer:

The task of the Informer is to pro-actively advertise the available knowledge of a peer in the peer-to-peer network and to discover peers with knowledge that may be relevant for answering the user's queries. This is realized by sending advertisements about the expertise of a peer. In the Bibster system, these expertise descriptions contain a set of topics that the peer is an expert in. Peers may accept, i.e., remember these advertisements, thus creating a semantic link to the other peer. These semantic links form a semantic topology, which is the basis for intelligent query routing.

Controller:

The Controller is the coordinating component controlling the process of distributing queries. It receives queries from the user interface or from other peers. Either way it tries to answer the query or distribute it according to the content of the query. The decision to which peers a query should be sent is based on the knowledge about the expertise of other peers. Messages are indicated as rounded boxed in the architecture diagram.

User Interface:

The user interface allows the user to import, create, and edit bibliographic metadata as well as to easily formulate queries. The screenshot in figure 8.3 shows how the use cases are realized in Bibster. The Scope widget allows for defining the targeted peers, the Search and Search Details widgets allow for keyword and semantic search; Results Table and BibTeX View widgets allow for browsing and re-using query results. The query results are visualized in a list grouped by duplicates. They may be integrated into the local repository or exported in formats such as BibTeX and HTML.

8.2.3 Ontology Alignment / Duplicate Detection

When querying the Bibster network one receives a large number of results with an often high number of duplicates. This is because we do not have one centralized but many distributed local repositories. Furthermore, the representation of the metadata is very heterogeneous and possibly even contradicting. Many entries are saved on different peers, and all these peers respond to

---

[5] http://www.openrdf.org/

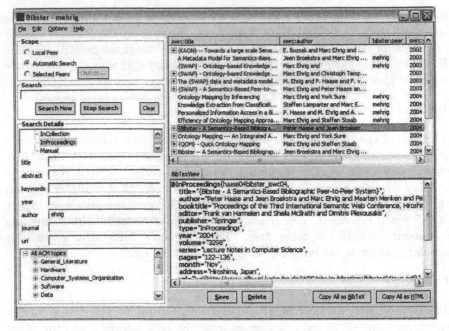

Fig. 8.3. Bibster System

the query. To enable an efficient and easily usable system it is necessary to filter out these duplicates. In specific, we do not want to confront the user with a list of all individual results. Bibster presents query results grouping duplicates together. This provides a more intuitive visualization. We check the incoming results on duplicate entries. In another step, the user can choose among the presented results what he wants to integrate into his own Local Node Repository. Now we have to check if the potential new entry is already contained in the local node repository. Again, we use duplicate detection to identify this.

Duplicates in Bibster are bibliographic entries that refer to the same publication, person, or organization in the real world, but are modeled as different resources. In terms of the problem structure, this scenario does not differ from a scenario where we want to find equal entities in two ontologies through alignment. Bibster uses the approaches presented in this work with domain-specific similarity functions to recognize two instances as being duplicates. For each resource type (person, organization, publication), we have compiled a set of specific features used to assess the similarity between two of its instances. For persons we use the first, middle, and last names. For organizations we rely solely on the organization's name. In addition, for publications we use a wide range of features such as title, publication type, authors, publisher, institute, journal with the series number, pages, year, the ACM topic the publication was classified to, etc. For each of the features we use different individual similarity functions, as presented before.

For instance, to compare the last names of persons we use the syntactic similarity. Another example: A publication resource is linked to person resources, e.g., authors. Thus, we can compare two publications based on the similarity of the sets of authors. This feature alone is not deciding, but it supports the hypothesis of having duplicate entries. To determine the similarity of two publications based on their topics we make use of the ACM topic hierarchy. We apply the hierarchical similarity function as presented earlier in this work (Rada et al., 1989). Applying background knowledge about a specific domain, we can define more appropriate similarity functions. For example, in the SWRC domain ontology there are many subconcepts of publications: articles, books, and technical reports to just name a few. Unknown publication types are often provided as Misc. We can thus define a function that returns a value of 1 if the publication type is identical, a value of, e.g., 0.75 if Misc is one of it, and 0 otherwise. The Bibster use case was heavily relying on the features and similarities that were introduced in this book as so-called domain-specific features.

The standard ontology alignment process is parameterized. For the Bibster scenario, the weights have been assigned based on experiments with sample data. More precisely, several duplicates were detected manually. From these training duplicates, the weights were adjusted to achieve a maximal f-measure value. As duplicates we consider those pairs of resources whose similarity is larger than a certain fixed threshold θ, parallel to the standard alignment approach. If we assume that the duplicate relation is transitive, we can additionally define the transitive closure as:

$$TC(D_\theta) := \{(x, z) | (x, y) \in D_\theta \land (y, z) \in D_\theta\} \tag{8.1}$$

with D_θ being the set of identified duplicates, i.e., alignments. This transitive closure essentially represents clusters of semantically similar resources. In the context of Bibster it is reasonable to calculate this transitive closure, as we do not only have entities from two ontologies, but from many peers. Through inferencing, we determine additional duplicates without explicitly having to align two additional entities. The process is fully automatic.

Instead of presenting all individual resources of the query result, duplicates are visualized as one, merged, resource. The merged resources comprise the union of statements of the individuals identified as duplicates. In the case of conflicting property values, we apply heuristics for the merging of resources (e.g., for book-titles to select the most detailed value with the least abbreviations). Again, we use domain specific knowledge for the merging of type statements. Only the most specific publication type is included.

8.2.4 Application

The reader may find additional reading material on Bibster, its underlying technologies and related material in the open available project deliverable documentation on its webpage.[6]

The Bibster system has been evaluated by means of a public field experiment. The user actions and system events have been continuously logged and analyzed to evaluate the user behavior and system performance. We have analyzed the results for a period of two months (June and July 2004) and have obtained the following interesting results: A total of 146 peers from various organizations spread mainly over Europe and North America used the Bibster system. The users shared more than 70000 bibliographic entries. While seventeen peers shared more than 1000 items each, accounting for 84% of the total content, many peers provided only little content or were "free riding". The users performed a total of 1782 queries. The SWRC ontology was used for about half of all queries, mainly for the purpose to search for special types of publications (e.g., only for articles) or for publications of a given author. In 348 queries, the users asked for topics of the ACM topic hierarchy. Thereby it is obvious that the users are accepting the ontology based searching capabilities and that there is a benefit for them in using these ontologies. With respect to query routing, with the expertise based peer selection we were able to reduce the number of query messages by about 50 percent, while retaining the same recall of documents compared with a naïve broadcasting approach. Although we have shown an improvement in the performance, the results also show that with a network of the size as in the field experiment, a naïve approach is also acceptable. On the other hand, with a growing number of peers, query routing and peer selection becomes critical: In simulation experiments with larger peer networks with thousands of peers, we have shown improvements in the order of one magnitude in terms of recall of documents and relevant peers (Haase et al., 2004c). From the perspective of ontology alignment, the results were promising. Apart from first problems in understanding the user interface, users were satisfied with the functionality. Even though occasional errors occurred in the process of duplicate detection, users appreciated this functionality. Most errors could easily be understood by the users (e.g., the same publications, which were presented at different workshops) and were therefore tolerated.

This section summarizes experiences we have gained from the development and application of Bibster. For Bibster and similar applications, the usage of Semantic Web technologies and ontologies provide a benefit – in fact, it is almost a strict requirement given its semi-structured, volatile data structures. Semantic structures serve important user concerns like high quality duplicate detection or comprehensive searching capabilities. Unsurprisingly, in small networks with small user groups, intelligent query routing is not a major issue. While it is beneficial to direct queries to specific peers known to the

---

[6] http://bibster.semanticweb.org/

user (an issue of trust), advanced routing algorithms may only be beneficial for a much larger number of users in a network. Based on our experience we now conjecture that content-based routing and trust issues will have to converge for such larger networks, too. During our experiments, the scalability of Bibster has become a major issue. First, running Bibster as an application in the background consumes much more processing resources than originally intended. Second, Bibster queries take much longer to evaluate than we originally planned for. Despite the fact that Sesame is one of the most powerful RDF architectures today, its usage in Bibster restricts the applicability of the system to small and medium size user groups. For further versions of Bibster, a manual optimization of the queries is necessary. For Semantic Web applications like Bibster to succeed in general, the Semantic Web community must investigate automatic optimization procedures for querying RDF such as have been developed for SQL.

Nevertheless, Bibster's main benefit stays its support for researchers sharing bibliographic metadata in a decentralized environment. The search and integration of data performed very well resulting in the usage of Bibster even a long time after the project consortium had ceased the development of Bibster.

8.3 Xarop

The second case study within SWAP covered the requirements of a virtual enterprise, with different peers of this enterprise having different models (Tempich et al., 2004).

8.3.1 Scenario

One of the major problems with existing knowledge management systems is, that they are IT driven and solve problems that the user did not have before. We thoroughly examined our technologies in small case studies to meet user expectations and to show the effectiveness of the SWAP approach. Majorca as one of the most popular holiday resources in Europe is currently facing increasing competition from locations in countries with lower wages. A main strategic objective of the local government is to create a better value proposition through the offer of Sustainable Tourism. Thereby the long-term success of the local tourism industry shall be guaranteed. This industry is dominated by small and medium enterprises. Information about best practices must be distributed among these highly decentralized actors. At the same time information to monitor the transition must be collected from different parties, where the only common infrastructure is the open standard of the internet.

A number of organizations participating in the case study want to collaborate on some regional issues. Therefore, they collect and share information about indicators reflecting the impact of growing population and tourist fluxes on the islands, their environment, and their infrastructures. Moreover, these indicators can be used to make predictions and help planning. For instance, organizations that require quality & hospitality management use the information to better plan, for example, their marketing campaigns. As another example, a governmental agency, the Balearic Government's co-ordination center of telematics, provides the local industry with information about new technologies that can help the tourism industry to better perform their tasks. Due to the different working areas and objectives of the collaborating organizations, it proved impossible to set up a centralized knowledge management system or even a completely centralized ontology. The case study partners asked explicitly for a system without a central server, where knowledge sharing is integrated into the normal work, but where very different kinds of information could be easily shared with others.

From a technical point of view, the different organizations can be seen as one or many independently operating nodes within a knowledge network. Nodes can join or disconnect from the network at any moment and can live and act independently of the behavior of other nodes in the system. A node may perform several tasks. The most important one is that it acts as a peer in the network, so it can communicate with other nodes to achieve its goals. Apart from that, it may act as an interface to interact with the human user of the network, or it may access knowledge sources to accomplish its tasks. One node may have one or more knowledge sources associated with it. These sources contain the information that a peer can make available to other peers. Examples are a user's file system and mail folders or a locally installed database. A node must be designed to meet the following requirements that arise from the task of sharing information from the external sources with other peers:

- Each piece of knowledge requires metadata about its origin. To retrieve external information, the metadata needs to capture information about where the piece of information was obtained from. This information will allow identifying a peer and locate resources in its repositories.
- As each peer may use its own local ontology, the distributed information is inherently heterogeneous. Alignment is required, e.g., to overcome the heterogeneous labeling of the same objects. Fortunately, in many cases some of the defined structures are very similar to each other. A general process is needed to identify commonalities and make them explicit.
- Security is a main issue. Some information may be of private nature and should not be visible to other peers. Other information may be restricted to a specific set of peers.
- In a peer-to-peer network, queries are forwarded to different peers. Due to different network latencies and resources on the answering machines, answers can come at any time. Hence, the interface must help the user to

distinguish between recent and old results, must update itself from time to time, and should visualize where results come from.

- In peer-to-peer systems a general problem is, to distribute the queries in the network. Since the number of messages increases exponentially with the number of hops a query is allowed to travel, intelligent query routing algorithms are required when the size of the network grows. This is similar to the Bibster system.

Xarop, a distributed knowledge management system, provides access to information from documents and legacy systems within a distributed infrastructure. Further, the exchange of information between different structures is enabled. Xarop enables the users to share their folder structures and other hierarchies with someone else. They can align those with a predefined shared ontology, which will evolve according to user needs. This process is supported by a set of process templates, which were defined within the project scope. Our field tests support our assumption, that user centric knowledge management does fit the user needs.

8.3.2 Design

The general SWAP architecture has already been presented in the previous section. Here we explain the methods that are most crucial to the Xarop knowledge management solution at the infrastructure, application, or community level.

Infrastructure level: A distributed security framework

Security considerations are of particular concern within a peer-to-peer framework. Users of a peer-to-peer system want to be sure that they give access to local resources only to trusted persons. Furthermore, they want to define different access control levels to their local knowledge, since they might trust different participants to various extents. While these considerations are difficult to handle, the security mechanism in a peer-to-peer system must be straightforward to define.

For authentication, we use a public-key infrastructure (PKI) with certificate authorities established within Xarop. A certain Xarop node acts as a root certificate authority for the Xarop system, all other peers will configure this node as trusted root certificate authority. In small networks, this certificate authority will issue certificates directly for users, whereas in large networks, it is possible to build a hierarchy of certificate authorities. The certificate creation will be done off-line, on the configuration level. Certificates themselves will not be transmitted within the standard SWAP user interface.

The access control model has to be based on rules, since we cannot demand from users that they will enumerate privileged users for each local resource. These rules have to be based on strict facts with proven origin (i.e., signed by the peer that generates a fact). A simple rule gives access for a single document (e.g., SWAP.doc) to a single, fixed person (e.g., Esteve). More complex rules are based on knowledge about both people and resources (All people involved in the SWAP project can download all documents from my SWAP folder.). All access control rights have to be explicit. Otherwise, we assume that access is not allowed.

The right to decide about the access properties of peers can be delegated to other peers. A person that we delegate the right to can be fixed or described by a similar pattern, forming a chain of trust (e.g., all people, about which Esteve said that they are involved in SWAP, and Mariusz said that they work for Empolis, can download all my documents about SWAP.). The access properties have to be digitally signed by the peer who assigned them.

For example, IBIT needs access control based on organization boundaries, but it is not acceptable for an average user to be forced to create and maintain organizational information by himself. Using the described security model for the IBIT case an average user has to define their administrator and access control rules for his local resources. Administrators define and maintain information about organizational structures and user membership to organizations.

Application level: Visualization

Fluit et al. (2004) have developed the Cluster Map for visualizing populated, light-weight ontologies as used for Xarop. It visualizes the instances of a number of selected classes from a hierarchy, organized by their classifications. Figure 8.4 shows an example Cluster Map, visualizing documents, classified according to topics discussed in those documents. The dark gray spheres represent ontology classes (the topics), with an attached label stating their name and cardinality.

When a subconcept relation holds between two concepts, they are connected by a directed edge. The light-colored spheres represent instances. Balloon-shaped edges connect instances to the concept(s) they belong to. Instances with the same class membership are grouped in clusters. Our example contains two clusters, one of them showing overlap between the two concepts. Cluster Maps contain a lot of information about the instantiation of the classes, specifically exploiting the overlaps between them. For example, Figure 8.4 shows that the original Lucerne folder class has a significant overlap with the swap idea. Such observations can trigger hypotheses about the available information and the domain in general. The graph layout algorithm used by the Cluster Map is a variant of the well-known family of spring embedder algorithms. Its outcome results in the geometric closeness of objects indicating their semantic closeness: Concepts that share instances are located near each other, and so are instances with the same or similar concept memberships.

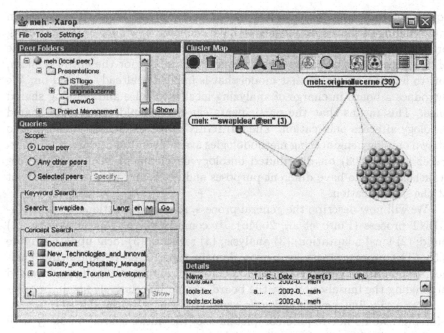

Fig. 8.4. Xarop System

The Cluster Map is embedded in a highly interactive GUI, which is designed for browsing-oriented exploration of the populated ontology. Users can subsequently create visualizations of a number of concepts by marking the check boxes in the concept tree on the left pane. The software can animate the transition from one visualization to the next, showing how the instances are regrouped in clusters. Through interaction a user can also retrieve information about the specific documents that are contained in a class or cluster. The visualization can be fine-tuned in several ways, in order to support certain tasks, or improve scalability. In the context of Xarop it was important to account for the particularities of peer-to-peer systems. Hence, the results are marked with the peer name they are coming from. Results are added to the Cluster Map incrementally, since not all peers answer at the same time. New results are highlighted. The search can be stopped when the user is satisfied. Thus, it provides the usability requirements needed for the Xarop system.

Community level: The Distributed Ontology Engineering Process

Every participant in the Xarop network is allowed to structure his knowledge according to his needs. As we found in the case study, people working on the same issue have similar ways of structuring information. Hence, a first step towards community building is to raise awareness about the existing commonalities within the group. From an ontological perspective, that is equivalent to the agreement on a shared ontology. To enable the detection and building of shared ontologies we have defined a new ontology engineering process template viz. DILIGENT. It is important to note that the purpose of this process is not to agree on a conceptual model for the entire domain, but to find the subset of that model that is implicitly already agreed on. We introduce a board in charge of analyzing local ontologies and defining shared ones. This means that the participants can and should change the shared ontology after its publication. The DILIGENT process focuses in contrast to known ontology engineering methodologies available in the literature (Gómez-Pérez et al., 2003) on distributed ontology development involving different stakeholders, who have different purposes and needs and who usually are not at the same location.

We will now describe the general process, roles and functions in the DILIGENT process (Pinto et al., 2004b). It comprises five main activities: (1) build; (2) local adaptation; (3) analysis; (4) revision; (5) local update (Figure 8.5). The process starts by having domain experts, users, knowledge engineers, and ontology engineers building an initial ontology. The team involved in building the initial ontology, the board, should be relatively small, in order to more easily find a small and consensual first version of the shared ontology. Moreover, we do not require completeness of the initial shared ontology with respect to the domain. On the first sight, it seems contradictory that the case study partners do not want to share a common infrastructure but a shared ontology. However, the existence of a shared domain, overlapping or related competencies within organizations, and the need for carrying out certain functions in cooperation suggests that it is possible to develop ontologies shared by the different sub-communities. Once the product is made available, users can start using it and locally adapting it for their own purposes. Typically, due to new business requirements, or user and organization changes, their local ontologies evolve in a similar way as folder hierarchies in a file system. In their local environment, they are free to change the reused shared ontology, but they are not allowed to directly change the ontology shared by all users. Furthermore, the control board collects change requests to the shared ontology.

The board analyzes the local ontologies and the requests and tries to identify similarities in the users' ontologies. Even though the process seems to tackle the first of two possibilities for ontology alignment, namely the common discussion and agreement on a shared ontology, at this point one can rely on ontology alignment techniques presented in this work, to support the board. Since not all of the changes introduced or requested by the users will be introduced,[7] a further crucial activity of the board is to decide which changes are going to be introduced in the next version of the shared ontology. The input from users provides the necessary arguments to underline change requests. A balanced decision that takes into account the different

---

[7] The idea in this kind of development is not to merge *all* user ontologies.

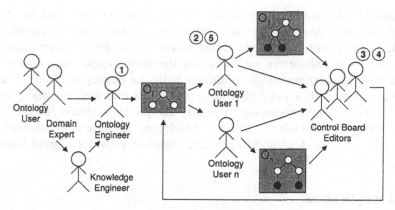

Fig. 8.5. Roles and Functions in Distributed Ontology Engineering

needs of the users and meets user's evolving requirements[8] has to be found. The board should regularly revise the shared ontology, so that local ontologies do not diverge too far from the shared ontology. Therefore, the board should have a well-balanced and representative participation of the different kinds of participants involved in the process. Once a new version of the shared ontology is released, users can update their own local ontologies to better use the knowledge represented in the new version. Even if the differences are small, users may rather reuse, e.g., the new concepts instead of using their previously locally defined concepts that correspond to the new concepts represented in the new version.

8.3.3 Ontology Alignment

For this distributed scenario to work we again need ontology alignment.

Firstly, the process of distributed ontology engineering has to regularly check the individuals' ontologies and create an updated version of the central one. Especially, if there are many individuals this task cannot be done manually. Automatic alignment supports the central board by aligning these individual ontologies automatically. The board can easily recognize entities that have been added multiple times by different individuals or how the individual ontologies all relate. A potential merging step may then rely on these proposed alignments. Unfortunately, the limited number of participants and thus only a small number of ontologies, Xarop could not gain significantly from the automatic alignment.

Secondly, it is true that individual users refer to the central ontology, but they will also have documents only applying to their extended individual ontologies. To allow querying for these documents it is necessary to do on-the-fly

---

[8] This is actually one of the trends in modern software engineering methodologies (see Rational Unified Process).

alignment. The queries are translated while passed around, and the Xarop system can find documents even if they have not been strictly modeled according to the central ontology. Most existing work for ontology alignment have laid focus exclusively on improving the effectiveness and neglected efficiency, which becomes an issue already with the ontologies required in the context of Xarop. It is not sufficient to provide its user with the best possible alignments; it is also necessary to answer his queries within a few seconds – even if the two peers use two different ontologies and have never encountered each other before. Our novel approach therefore provides a good basis for integration within Xarop.

8.3.4 Application

Xarop represents a solution for the recently recognized problem of decentralized knowledge management. We have developed a semantics based peer-to-peer knowledge-sharing platform. It was set up by the Fundació IBIT (Illes Balears Innovació Technològica),[9] a parastatal organization, whose goal is to narrow the gap between new technology and the balearic society. In this platform, we introduced an appropriate security mechanism on infrastructure level. On the application level, we introduced new alignment and visualization techniques. To foster community building we have defined a distributed ontology engineering process. Ontology alignment is one component of the process. We have described how the different methods have been applied in a concrete case study in the tourism domain.

---

[9] http://www.ibit.org/

Semantically Enabled Knowledge Technologies – SEKT

A second project relying on the developed alignment approaches is SEKT. Again the overall project will be presented first. The chapter is then going to continue with the description of the individual case studies and their need for ontology alignment.

9.1 Project Description

Semantically Enabled Knowledge Technologies (SEKT) is an Integrated Project funded by the European Union. As SEKT is still an ongoing project, it is scheduled to run from January 2004 to December 2006, the descriptions and results in this section will be extended by ongoing and future work.

Fig. 9.1. Semantically Enabled Knowledge Technologies (SEKT)

The vision of SEKT is to develop and exploit knowledge technologies that underlie next generation knowledge management. In future, knowledge workplaces integrate knowledge, document, and content management. They make knowledge management a daily activity with little effort required from the user. Appropriate knowledge is automatically delivered to the right people at the right time at the right granularity via a range of user devices. Knowledge workers are empowered to focus on their core roles and their creativity; this is the key to European competitiveness. Knowledge society is becoming reality. More information about the project can be found on its webpage.[1]

9.1.1 Core Technologies

SEKT delivers software:

- to semi-automatically learn ontologies and extract metadata;
- to maintain and evolve the ontologies and metadata over time;
- to provide knowledge access;
- to effectively integrate all the SEKT components, besides middleware;
- and developing a methodology for using semantically-based knowledge management.

9.1.2 Case Studies

The case studies in SEKT are drawn from both commercial and public sectors, each case study being built around the needs of knowledge intensive working environments.

- One case study is within the legal domain. A key aspect is to investigate the usage of SEKT technologies for decision support in complex situations, such as for legal cases.
- The second one is within the telecommunication industry. A key aspect is understanding how to minimize the overhead of metadata creation and management.
- The third is within consulting. A key aspect of this is investigating the use of semantically-enabled knowledge management amongst cooperating heterogeneous communities.

These case studies and implications on the usage of ontology alignment will be described in the following sections.

9.1.3 Ontology Alignment

Ontology Alignment within SEKT is integrated into one general work package on mediation. The mediation prototype is based on the OntoStudio/OntoMap implementation described in Section 7.3. All the mediation activities required for the use cases are executed through OntoMap. The concrete activities in SEKT such as alignment discovery, mapping, and ontology merging will be elaborated on the following pages. Ontology alignment is used as a background activity.

---

[1] http://www.sekt-project.org/

9.2 Intelligent Integrated Decision Support for Legal Professionals

Goal of this case study is to prove that semantic technologies can help to support question answering of legal professionals by combining knowledge from different knowledge sources.

9.2.1 Scenario

In many European countries, it is not unlikely to hear complaints about the slowness of legal processes. This may cause large problems for society, e.g., regarding public security and social welfare. The execution of legal processes involves a variety of different professionals, including judges, public defenders, lawyers, clerks, etc. Many of these professionals are knowledge workers in the sense that the quality of their work depends on the experience and knowledge they bear. Especially judges are few in number and their workload is extremely high in modern society. Any IT support that prevents them from spending time on non-core issues has the potential to improve the speed of legal processes. The objective of this case study is to show that SEKT results significantly improve the daily work environment of professional judges.

9.2.2 Use Cases

Several specific use cases for this case study have been identified in Casanovas et al. (2005):

- In the question-answering use case instead of calling an experienced colleague a young judge types a query into the interface of a computer system. Based on natural language processing and the background FAQ ontologies an answer is provided. The returned answer is extended by an explanation. From time to time, the question base (FAQs) has to be updated. In addition, the system provides pointers to so-called knowledge gaps, i.e., fields that have not been solved yet.
- As a second knowledge source besides the question base, existing databases are used, which the judge should be able to easily access. Therefore, the system will learn ontologies from them. After having collected ontologies from different databases, one now wants to create a general jurisprudence ontology. This step requires ontology merging. Ontology alignment as presented here is indispensable to identify the individual entities which need to be merged. The user easily browses the knowledge in the databases through the merged ontology. Along with updates of the databases, also the ontologies are updated.
- Finally, the two main knowledge sources, the expert knowledge in semantically encoded questions and answers, and the jurisprudence ontology from

databases have to be aligned. Information from one source and information from the other source shall be queried at the same time. Here again ontology alignment plays a major role. In particular, alignment is required for query and answer rewriting.

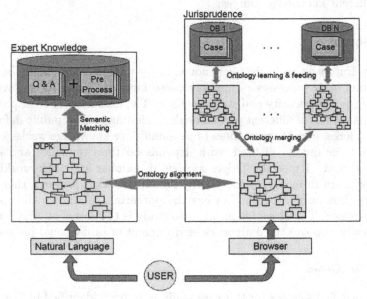

Fig. 9.2. SEKT Architecture for the Legal Case Study

9.2.3 Design

The system manages two independent kinds of knowledge, represented by two subsystems as depicted in Figure 9.2. The expert knowledge subsystem contains the expertise of experienced judges. This knowledge is represented by a repository of FAQs (frequently asked questions by novice judges) and the ontology of Legal Professional Knowledge (OLPK), which holds and structures all this knowledge. Additionally an existing body of law is given, represented by databases with existing sentences. The knowledge of each database is represented in an ontology, and all these ontologies are merged in order to get a single ontology that comprises all the knowledge in the databases. This ontology is aligned with the OLPK in order to map the concepts that are used in the two different subsystems. This allows connecting the questions and answers of the repository in the expert knowledge subsystem with the cases in the databases that are relevant in order to justify the decisions recommended in the answers. A user front-end is provided to the judges so they can easily access the system.

9.3 Retrieving and Sharing Knowledge in a Digital Library

This case study's goal is directed towards intelligent searching, browsing, and distribution of knowledge based on an existing digital library.

9.3.1 Scenario

British Telecom[2] began building a digital library in 1994 and in over ten years has developed an online system that offers its users personalization, linking to full text from abstracts, annotation tools, alerts for new content, and the foundations of profiling. The library contains journal publications, webpages, and documents for jotting. The goal for SEKT is to extend the functionality, by using an ontology-based approach. To the user this will bring a number of advantages:

- The ability to view knowledge from heterogeneous sources, using a common ontology. Accompanying, the sources of knowledge accessed by the library are further extended.
- The ability to use more sophisticated searching facilities, e.g., to filter search by author or topics from a hierarchy.
- The ability to share knowledge without overwhelming people with information, i.e., by more precisely identifying recipients for particular information.

9.3.2 Use Cases

We present the different use cases occurring in this scenario, pointing out where ontology alignment is used.

- The most important use case is information retrieval. A user may choose to enter complex semantic queries, e.g., searching for documents on a specific topic from a special journal. Based on the query the requested information is returned. As different ontological representations exist, the queries have to be translated based on the mediation component. In specific, the PROTON ontology[3] will play a central role. Different other schemas (e.g., the INSPEC digital library database schema) need to be aligned to it.
- The user's activities of searching, browsing, and reading within the digital library are monitored to discover his interests. Based on these interests queries are refined. Yet more important is the possibility to have an agent sending alerts as soon as new potentially useful information for the user has been entered into the system.

---

[2] http://www.bt.com/
[3] http://proton.semanticweb.org/

- The third use case is an expertise location tool. By analyzing documents of a user, his expertise is automatically determined. When other workers need to find somebody with a certain expertise, they can identify experts based on the profiles.

9.3.3 Design

The development of the SEKT system for this case study is still not completed. However, the need for ontology alignment has already become clear through the requirements of the use cases. As for the other case studies, mediation will be provided through the OntoMap component, which uses the ontology alignment approaches of this work to fulfill its tasks.

9.4 Heterogeneous Groups in Consulting

In this final case study, knowledge needs to be structured automatically to simplify (knowledge) business processes in the everyday work environment of a consultant.

9.4.1 Scenario

The objective of this case study is to investigate and verify how semantically enabled technologies may improve the productivity of IT and business consultants at Siemens Business Services.[4] It elaborates which added values can be created and looks for new forms of accessing, handling, and utilizing content in the IT and business services industry. Complementary to the other two case studies, it will focus on how to stipulate the emergence and creation of new knowledge and capturing it.

9.4.2 Use Cases

The main use cases of this case study are described as follows:

- Solution design for a customer proposal: The solution design describes the planned solution for a customer's problem, which an IT consultant has to face, in sufficient detail. All requirements are convincingly covered and time and effort to be spent on implementation can be reliably estimated. In his role as a proposal manager/project manager, he has to make sure the design includes only those parts necessary for demonstrating the proposed solution and for estimating expenditure. As a result, for the scenario design the sales manager has to take into account all the relevant information, such as the proposal drafts, templates, benchmark numbers, and the market position. This implies locating and sharing the relevant knowledge that can be in either external or internal sources.

---

[4] http://www.sbs.siemens.com/

- Contribution of documents/knowledge assets: Users should be able to make knowledge-asset candidates available to their colleagues. After uploading a document, the users are requested to characterize their document by means of additional attributes. Further, it can be directly sent to a community it might be of interest for. It then is checked on being a knowledge asset and if so added into the existing structures (ontologies). As entering the additional information is a bottleneck from the users' perspective the goal of this use case is to gather most of the meta information based on the semantic information coming along with the document or with the user's role or context. Equal information, but expressed differently, e.g., through use of synonyms, needs to be aligned.

- Reuse initiative: To every customer Siemens Business Services is selling primarily solutions and not reusable knowledge assets, most desirable with high quality and minimal risk. Risk reduction occurs when one can replicate project results and outstanding successes to as many customers and with as minimal effort as possible (reference selling). Basis for replication is a completed project with the proven systems architecture of an implemented solution with as many stable, reusable knowledge assets and documented modules as possible. Reusing existing knowledge allows providing competitive offerings in order to generate more business while achieving the productivity targets. The degree of reusability depends on the ability of matching the existing architectural and functional features and modules with new customer requirements.

Ontology mediation is mainly required for two actions within the use cases:

- Mediation is needed between the ontologies created based on the individual's data sources (e.g., file system) and the shared ontologies where most of the knowledge assets are stored along.

- During search, multiple repositories have to be addressed at the same time. Thus, the ontologies corresponding to the different data sources will have to be aligned and search requests mapped.

9.4.3 Design

As the partner for this last case study has joined the consortium later, concrete results could not be provided at the time this publication was finished. The interested reader is referred to the website of SEKT.[5]

This case study concludes the part on tools and applications. It showed how the theoretical considerations on ontology alignment have been transferred to tools. Further, an explanation of tool usage in two big projects has been provided. Whereas SWAP was already successfully completed, SEKT is still an ongoing project in the Semantic Web field.

---

[5] http://www.sekt-project.org/

Towards Next Generation Semantic Alignment

10

Next Steps

Due to the many facets of knowledge integration one cannot expect the goal of ontology alignment to be completed within the next years. This part, in first place, will give directions on extending the presented methodology. In specific, it will generalize the ontology alignment approach to general structure alignment. Further, it will allow more complex alignments than the current one-to-one identity alignments.

10.1 Generalization

As a first extension, we will show that our approaches are not limited to ontologies only, but may be applied to other structures as well.

10.1.1 Situation

Integration of structures and schemas has been a problem for many decades. Actually, as already pointed out, the database community has created numerous approaches addressing this topic. Practical approaches exist for database schemas or simple XML-Schemas. For other types of structures, such as object-oriented programming code (e.g., in Java), classification and relational schemes (e.g., the Unified Modeling Language, UML), or process representations (e.g., Petri Nets) the situation is different. For matching or integration only few approaches exist which go beyond basic syntactic comparisons of labels. Exceptions are the individual works of Bergmann and Stahl (1998) who investigated the notion of similarity for object-oriented programming languages. Rufai (2003) did the same for UML. Further, with the DIKE system Palopoli et al. (2000) provided an approach for alignment of entity-relationship-schemas.

To give an example for the need: companies increasingly model the workflows of business processes. In big companies, these workflows go beyond individual groups or departments, often even beyond company boundaries and include outside suppliers or distributors. For integration reasons, an immanent need for plugging these workflows together develops. We refer to Hahn et al. (2005), who present a collection of papers all addressing the topic of semantic integration for different kinds of structures, but lack automatic approaches.

To improve the current unsatisfying situation for other structures we will therefore show that it is possible to transfer the approaches presented in this work, which are ontology-based, onto many other structures. This will be done both generally in theory and in practice for one specific example from the business process world, Petri Nets.

10.1.2 Generalized Process

In this section, we refer to the standard ontology alignment process and state how it can be generalized.

Input:

Input for the standard process are two ontologies that we want to align with one another. It is often possible to add already known alignments. For generalization purposes, we relax this restriction to just having two well-defined structures. Well-defined means that the semantics of the individual constructs is defined and all implications are clear, at least the implications for alignment. Both the graph representation and the underlying logics have to be distinct. If only few semantics is defined for the structures, this will hinder the success of the alignment approach. Thus, structures with more semantics are more suited for our approach.

1. Feature Engineering:

Small excerpts of the overall structure definition are selected to describe a specific entity. In the generalized case, we select among all the features the structure has. These could be a class hierarchy, but also specific restrictions that might be defined for a relation.

2. Search Step Selection:

The derivation of alignments takes place in a search space of candidate alignments. Just as for ontologies it only makes sense to compare certain elements with each other, e.g., Java classes among each other, instead of variables with classes. These candidate types have to be identified before the actual comparison takes place.

3. Similarity Computation:

For a given description of two entities from the candidate alignments, this step indicates a similarity. Also for other structures, similarity still is the key element to retrieve alignments, but we might need different measures of similarity. For example, the similarity of Java methods might be based on the mathematical function it provides. To compare the similarity of two mathematical functions special implementations are required.

4. Similarity Aggregation:

In general, there may be several similarity values for a candidate pair of entities based on different underlying features. Like in the original approach, these similarities have to be aggregated, but again these aggregation functions are different for other kinds of structures. One can easily imagine a situation, where already one missing similarity implies that two elements are different, especially in closed world scenarios.

5. Interpretation:

Interpretation uses individual or aggregated similarity values to derive alignments between entities. Interpretation stays critical and is not trivial. Human interaction might help to defuse this point.

6. Iteration:

As the similarity of one entity pair influences the similarity of neighboring entity pairs, the equality is propagated through the ontologies. Depending on the new structure, this might or might not be an issue. Generally, we expect simple structures to be less dependent on iteration than complex interconnected graphs.

Output:

Eventually, the process returns an output. This output is a representation of alignments, in this case an alignment of elements from the two structures of whichever kind.

10.1.3 Alignment of Petri Nets

The generalization idea is now implemented for one case, which proves to be very successful: Petri Nets. Most of the process steps are kept as for ontology alignment, but we will point to specifics of the Petri Net extension of ontology alignment (Brokmans et al., 2006).

Petri Nets

Petri Nets (Peterson, 1981) are a graphical formalism for describing processes. They allow the description of sequential or parallel activities.

Definition 10.1 (Petri Nets). *A net is a triple*

$$N = (P, T, F)$$

consisting of

- *a set of places P representing static aspects of documents or resources,*
- *a set of transitions T representing events or activities,*
- *and arcs connecting P and T, which are also known as flow relations F.*

In elementary Petri Nets, tokens representing anonymous objects define the process flow. When a transition fires, tokens are moved from its input to its output places.

The graphical representation of Petri Nets uses circles for places, rectangles for transitions, and arrows for the relations between them. Figure 10.1 illustrates two Petri Nets for flight reservation processes. Each place has additional attributes and the corresponding values depicted in the tables. In business process I the token moves from the input place *sent request* to the output place *request checked*, only if the conditions of transition *check request* are fulfilled, i.e., the date and the name are specified. The details of the places are shown in the tables with the traveler's attributes and the flight information.

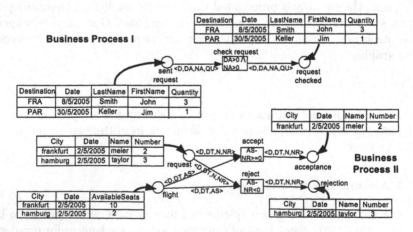

Fig. 10.1. Petri Nets for Flight Reservation

Inter-organizational business collaborations bring up synergy effects and reduce enterprise risks. Due to the introduced formal foundation of Petri

Nets, the syntactical integration problems can be solved. However, missing semantic representation hampers the exchange of business processes. The aim of this section is to provide semantic integration for distributed business processes. This allows the integration of collaborating business partners into one single value creation chain, effectively minimizing cost and reducing time currently needed for manual translation and integration efforts.

Process

Input:

Koschmider and Oberweis (2005) have shown that it can be useful to represent Petri Nets through an OWL ontology. This process reflects a translation rather than a change in representation. The semantics has been preserved during this step.

1. Feature Engineering:

With the common OWL representation, we can now focus on semantic alignment. For this we need to change the semantic basis of the already existing ontology alignment process. Still, this is the most difficult part. As a first step, we need to identify those features that may be used to compare Petri Net elements and determine whether the elements are the same. An expert interprets the meaning of the features of Petri Net elements and picked out features, such as the names, the attributes and values of a place, or the places related to a transition. We refer to Table 10.1 for a list of relevant features. They have been identified by an expert on Petri Nets. For example, to compare attributes (in Figure 10.1 the headings of the tables), one can check the name, the neighboring attributes, the concrete values the attribute can have, and the place it is linked to.

2. Search Step Selection:

Next, we need to decide which elements to compare. The standard approach is to use a complete approach, i.e., each element of the one ontology is compared with each element of the other ontology. This approach is slightly restricted by only creating candidate alignments that make sense in this scenario: place pairs, attribute pairs, value pairs, and transition pairs.

3. Similarity Computation:

The similarity computation is straightforward and in this case does not require completely new constructs. In specific, Table 10.1 also shows the similarity measures that are needed to align the two elements. Depending on the feature, these might be comparisons of strings, objects, or sets of objects. For all of these comparisons, different similarity measures already exist.

Table 10.1. Features and Similarity Measures for Petri Nets

Comparing	No.	Feature	Similarity Measure	Weight
Places	1	(name,X_1)	syntactic(X_1, X_2)	1
	2	(attribute/value, X_1)	set(X_1, X_2)	1
	3	(predecessor, X_1)	set(X_1, X_2)	0.5
	4	(succesor, X_1)	set(X_1, X_2)	0.5
Attributes	1	(name,X_1)	syntactic(X_1, X_2)	1
	2	(neighbor attribute, X_1)	set(X_1, X_2)	1
	3	(values, X_1)	set(X_1, X_2)	1
	4	(place, X_1)	object(X_1, X_2)	0.5
Values	1	(name,X_1)	syntactic(X_1, X_2)	1
	2	(attribute, X_1)	object(X_1, X_2)	1
	3	(value reference tuple, X_1)	object(X_1, X_2)	1
Transitions	1	(name,X_1)	syntactic(X_1, X_2)	1
	2	(toPlace, X_1)	set(X_1, X_2)	1
	3	(fromPlace, X_1)	set(X_1, X_2)	1

4. Similarity Aggregation:

The mentioned list of features and similarities is extended by a weight for the similarity aggregation. Only a basic linear weighting scheme has been applied at this point, which have been again determined by an expert understanding the domain of Petri Nets. Aggregations that are more complex are conceivable.

5. Interpretation:

We apply a fixed threshold to the aggregated similarities. Every similarity value above the threshold is interpreted as an alignment of the Petri Net elements, every value below does not lead to an alignment. We allow user interaction to increase the quality of these alignment results by presenting the most uncertain alignments.

6. Iteration:

Iterations are performed just as for ontology alignment. Again, the alignment of entity pairs affects the similarity of neighboring pairs. This is propagated through the Petri Net structures through iteration.

Output:

The output is a list of aligned places, attributes, values, and transitions with their corresponding confidence (aggregated similarity values).

We illustrate this process along the example of Figure 10.1. Possible candidate alignments would be the pairs of places (sent request, request), transitions (check request, accept), attributes (Quantity, Number), or values (frankfurt, FRA). Next, these candidate alignments are compared using the derived features and similarities for Petri Nets of Table 10.1. We will do this comparison for the attribute pair of Quantity and Number. The labels are obviously different, thus resulting in $sim_{name} = 0.0$. However, their neighbor attributes (Destination, Date, LastName and FirstName; and City, Date, Name) and values (3, 1 and 2, 3) are very similar resulting in $sim_{neighbors} = 0.8$ and $sim_{values} = 0.5$. Also the linked places (sent request and request) are similar with $sim_{place} = 0.5$. In fact, a background ontology helps us to determine that the Destination and City attributes actually mean the same, despite the different values (frankfurt, paris and FRA, PAR). All these similarities are aggregated and lead to $sim_{agg} = 0.443$. With a given threshold of $\theta = 0.4$, we can say $align(Quantity) = Number$; Quantity in Petri Net 1 is aligned with Number of Petri Net 2.

An excerpt of results is depicted in Table 10.2. These results have directly been taken from the implementation of the approach described in this chapter.

Table 10.2. Results of Petri Net alignment

Petri Net 1	Petri Net 2	Similarity	Alignment
Destination	City	1.0	yes
frankfurt	FRA	1.0	yes
send request	request	0.8	yes
Quantity	Number	0.5	yes
check request	accept flight	0.4	no
Smith	meier	0.2	no

Evaluation and Discussion

Meeting the current lack of semantic alignment approaches for Petri Nets, in the end, a good approach is any approach providing more alignments of entities than those that have identical labels. Our approach provides many more than these trivial propositions and thus releases the human user from manually searching the Petri Nets for alignments. The semantic alignment method presented here has been tested on several business processes (Petri Nets with more than 20 places and transitions). Despite occasional incorrect alignments such an approach might also produce, it can strongly support users in creating alignments between Petri Nets. Larger examples and real world applications are still subject future work.

10.1.4 Summary

The goal of this section was to show that ontology alignment approaches such as the one presented in this book have an impact well beyond ontologies. By slightly changing the instantiation of the alignment process, one can transfer it to any well-defined structure. This has been successfully achieved for Petri Nets.

10.2 Complex Alignments

In the beginning of this book, we have stated that simple one-to-one alignments as mainly investigated in this work might not be sufficient for real world applications. In this section, we will give first insights on how these complex alignments with other relations or composed alignments may be achieved.

10.2.1 Situation

This work focused on one-to-one identity alignments and intentionally ignored other kinds of alignments most of the time. Already creating an ontology alignment approach for one-to-one identity alignments is a demanding task. Real world however often is even more complicated. There will be many other relations that have to be identified as well.

Two ontologies that have to be aligned might show a different granularity. For instance, entities might not be completely the same, but related by subsumption or one entity might be represented by a union of two entities in the other ontology. Another example are numerical values which might be related by a function, a conversion rate. Actually, identifying the complex alignments is closely related to the task of ontology learning (Maedche and Staab, 2001; Cimiano and Völker, 2005), where one step is to bring identified concepts into relation with one another. The task is different and presumably easier for ontology alignment, as one may assume that already sufficient ontology structures exist, which we can exploit for identifying these relations.

In the work of Dhamankar et al. (2004), first steps are taken in this direction for database schemas. If a significant amount of instances exists, many relations can be identified based hereon. A whole field of research works on solving this problem: data mining and knowledge discovery (Ester and Sander, 2000; Witten and Frank, 2005). Also the Semantic Web community has become aware of this problem. Giunchiglia et al. (2004) identify subsumption relations along with identity relations, but mainly on classification schemes. de Bruijn et al. (2004) have presented a list of simple alignment types, but in their library of mapping patterns, they also allow complex composite alignments expressing union, intersection, or combinations thereof. Also Maier et al. (2003) provide basic functionality in their tool to go beyond one-to-one alignments. Complex alignment has been identified as a problem and there are first approaches to process these alignments (Haase and Motik, 2005). Actually identifying them is more difficult.

Like in the previous section, we again will show that the standard alignment process can be extended in a way that enables us to not only process identity alignments but complex alignments as well.

10.2.2 Types of Complex Alignments

Before we go into detail on identifying complex alignments, we will first provide a list of possible complex alignments. A general definition of complex alignments has already been provided in Section 2.2.

- Subsumption: objects (concepts or relations) are hierarchically related (e.g., Porsche is a subconcept of sports car).
- Instantiation: an instance is bound to a new parent concept (e.g., Marc's Porsche can be bound to sports car).
- Union or intersection: concepts are a composition of other concepts (e.g., car is a union of sports car and slow car).
- Disjointness: often it is interesting to know that two objects are actually different (e.g., sports car and slow car are disjoint).
- Inverseness: relations can be inverse to each other (e.g., drive to and come from are inverse).
- Concatenation: two or more concepts (resp. their corresponding value) need to be concatenated to yield the concept in another ontology (e.g., name is a concatenation of first name and last name). The same is true for relations.
- Simple arithmetical matches: values are transformed (e.g., price in Euro to price in Dollars).
- Complex arithmetical matches: values are mathematically composed of other values by addition, subtraction, multiplication, or division. These more complex combinations are very difficult to identify (e.g., average fuel consumption = fuel consumption / distance).
- Part / whole: one concept is an element of another concept.
- Function: specific entities may have a corresponding function.
- Time or locality: entities might be bound to a certain time from or location.

As the reader will already have noticed, many of the interesting complex alignments are taken directly from constructs of the OWL ontology model. This allows not only identifying them, but also representing and reasoning on them. Some others are related to ontology design patterns as shown in Gangemi (2005).

One important issue we have to solve before continuing, are n-ary relations or composite relations (Noy and Rector, 2004). The general ontology alignment approach only allows identifying a relation between two objects. However, for many n-ary relations it is possible to transform them into binary relations. An example of this would be splitting up the concatenation relation into the two relations firstPartOf and secondPartOf. In theory, it would also be possible to directly search for n-ary relations using n-ary comparison operators. As this requires deep changes to our methods (especially their implementations), it will not be regarded here.

10.2.3 Extended Process for Complex Alignments

Most of the process may be adopted without any changes.

Input:

Two ontologies are the input. This remains the same for discovering complex alignments.

1. Feature engineering:

Small excerpts of the overall ontology definition are selected to describe a specific entity. These features will have to be adjusted according to the alignment relation searched for. The semantics in the ontology has to be interpreted with respect to the new relation.

2. Search Step Selection:

The derivation of ontology alignments takes place in a search space of candidate alignments. This candidate selection is changed. For example, for a subsumption relation, we only need to search among the concepts and the relations, because only these can be part of a subsumption relation; instances can be not. Further, for most complex cases the relations are not symmetric any longer, i.e., we need to compare entity 1 with entity 2 *and* vice versa.

3. (Similarity) Computation:

For a given candidate alignment this step indicates a heuristic measure. Again, special measures will be required for the different alignment kinds to be identified. Exemplary, some possible features and measures to identify whether entity 1 is a superconcept of entity 2 are shown in Table 10.3. For example for feature/heuristic 1, the concept time unit is compared with the concept unit. With the labels being one feature, one can make use of the fact that the string "unit" is included as the last part in "time unit".

Table 10.3. Features and Heuristics to Identify Subsumption between Entity 1 and Entity 2

Comparing	No.	Feature of Entity 1	Feature of Entity 2	Heuristic Comparison
Concepts	1	(label, X_1)	(label, X_2)	$\text{lastPart}(X_1, X_2)$
	2	$(\text{subconcepts}, Y_1)$	(itself, Y_2)	$\text{contains}(Y_1, Y_2)$
	3	(itself, Y_1)	$(\text{subconcepts}, Y_2)$	$\text{superset}(Y_1, Y_2)$
	4	$(\text{instances}, Y_1)$	$(\text{instances}, Y_2)$	$\text{superset}(Y_1, Y_2)$
	5	$(\text{subconcepts}, Y_1)$	(equal, Y_2)	$\text{contains}(Y_1, Y_2)$
...	...	...	...	...

4. (Similarity) Aggregation:

If we have different indicators for the alignment relation, these have to be aggregated. All the methods in this work can be used for this.

5. Interpretation:

The interpretation uses individual or aggregated values to derive alignments between entities. This is a non-trivial task, but as shown machine learning helps to solve this.

6. Iteration:

As the value of one entity pair influences the values of neighboring entity pairs, the alignment relation is propagated through the ontologies. In specific, there might also be several complex alignments that influence each other as well. Identity has an effect on the confidence in subsumption, which in turn influences the confidence whether there is an "instance of" relation between a certain instance and concept.

Output:

Eventually, the process returns an output. Whereas the output normally only included the two ontologies and a corresponding confidence value, it is now necessary to also include the found relation. Possibly, a split-up n-ary relation will have to be reassembled.

10.2.4 Implementation and Discussion

This section has shown that it is theoretically possible to extend our ontology alignment approach for complex alignments as well. This has been implemented as an extension of FOAM (Ren, 2005), currently only for the subsumption relation. First experiments were conducted calculating potential subsumption alignments between concepts from the two Russia test ontologies. So far the results have shown promising behavior.

One general problem are the underlying ontologies. To identify complex alignments one has to fall back on more complex ontological structures, which most ontologies cannot provide yet. Another problem is the evaluation of such found complex alignments. Complex alignments in ontologies are a new field. Whereas it is already difficult finding a sufficiently large test set on normal equality alignments, there is practically none for complex alignments.

Developing approaches for complex alignments will be one of the most important future directions of research on ontology integration. This section could only outline basic ideas. More research still has to be performed.

11

Future

This section will focus on other generally interesting topics around ontology alignment for the near and further future. Finally, some general comments about the theoretic quality that can be achieved will be given.

11.1 Outlook

From the presented work, one can see that almost any topic around ontology alignment allows for extensions in research and practice. Numerous pointers have been given in the respective sections. This section will mention more open areas of research that will influence or will be influenced by ontology alignment. These areas have not or only superficially been addressed in this work.

Application Theory:

One open issue are the steps following ontology alignment, viz., the actual application requiring ontology alignment. More specifically, the action of ontology merging/integration seems to be very interesting for practice. The theoretical foundations for this area, however, have not been addressed in detail yet. Hitzler et al. (2005) did work on creating a theory on ontology merging. In Bouquet et al. (2004) the authors give an overview of mapping with its theoretical foundations. They distinguish between element-based and rule-based mapping. In addition, considerations around global-as-view and local-as-view concern this topic. Clarifying the notions of ontology mapping is ongoing work.

Application Practice:

Beside the theoretical foundations for the applications, practical implementations are sparse. Maedche et al. (2002) have presented MAFRA, a framework for executing mappings. The described OntoStudio uses rules to execute the mappings from OntoMap. The often-cited PROMPT system directly allows doing ontology merging. However, these efforts are still preliminary or very tightly interconnected with other systems making them difficult to utilize for external users. The question of web service composition is also related to ontology alignment. For web services, one has to identify which services match (Lara et al., 2003). Web services are an area with a lot of research going on.

Benchmarking and Evaluation:

First efforts have been made on setting up general evaluation guidelines for this important topic of ontology alignment (Euzenat et al., 2005). More work needs to be done. Especially testing has to be increased toward more complex alignments, usage evaluation, or an evaluation closer to the previously mentioned applications. Only through accurate testing and evaluation, the technology can become mature for use.

Visualization:

As for many topics visualizing coherences in an intelligent way is not an easy task. This work presented OntoMap as a tool to create alignments in a user interface. Additional work needs to be done in supporting the user in understanding how the alignments have been created by, e.g., presenting the similarity values. It is also interesting to include found alignments into existing ontology visualization tools. Here one has to provide new means to present several ontologies in an overlayed way.

Evolution:

Another issue are changes and evolution. There has been research on the evolution of ontologies (Stojanovic, 2004; Haase and Stojanovic, 2005). When ontologies change the corresponding alignments need to change too. Not only ontologies evolve, but also alignments evolve, especially in early stages of design, even if ontologies stay the same. There are various reasons why an alignment may evolve. Examples are evolving insights into the source and target ontology and their similarities, new requirements for the alignment (e.g., a new subpart of the ontologies needs to be mapped, which was not considered before), and inadequate or faulty specifications of the alignment. McCann et al. (2005) present an approach to process the alignment changes. This scenario does not only indicate the need for evolution support for ontology alignments, but also for versioning (Klein et al., 2002). Each change of alignments requires a new uniquely identifiable and accessible version of the alignments, so that applications that use a certain version continue functioning despite of changes in the mapping.

Probabilistic and Fuzzy Ontologies:

It is common agreement that there cannot be a generally shared world ontology within the Semantic Web community. On the one hand, this means that alignment is a grounding for Semantic Web research. It also means that there will be different, potentially conflicting, information on the web. Consequently, one has to come up with methods to deal with inconsistent ontologies without harming the reasoning mechanism (Huang et al., 2005). Closely related is also the notion of probabilistic ontologies and reasoning (Hitzler and Vrandecic, 2005). Fuzzy reasoning is another topic of research in this area (Straccia, 2005). In parallel to these developments in ontology engineering, it is necessary to adjust and extend ontology alignment approaches accordingly.

11.2 Limits for Alignment

With the future of ontology alignment being open it is interesting to discuss how much alignment will theoretically be possible. This requires a different view on ontologies and alignment, i.e., less technological and more sociological. We want to raise awareness that errors are an integral part of ontology alignment as also described by Doan and Halevy (2005). Both developers and users have to realize this circumstance when dealing with ontologies and their alignments.

11.2.1 Errors

Luhmann (1987) once stated that people will never be able to communicate with each other, as every person has another notion of the world and its specific entities. Nevertheless, everyday life shows that we are able to communicate, if they assume that the entities in their minds are similar to at least a certain degree. For most cases this is true. And therefore it is also possible to inference. However, in some cases, the actual entities differ and this evidently leads to inconsistencies, clashes, and mismatches. This even happens if the involved people are all experts in one single domain.

Goal of the Semantic Web is to have machines communicate and actually understand each other. Knowledge structures used for the Semantic Web are ontologies and normally much smaller than human conceptualizations. After having determined which entities can be aligned with each other, inferencing allows to derive new insights. But machines face the same general communication problem as humans do. It is not obvious whether different machines have the same notions. Or as computers are to be tools for humans, a closely related problem is whether humans using the Semantic Web actually mean the same.

11.2.2 Points of Mismatch

Despite biggest efforts in reducing errors in alignment of ontologies, mismatches always have to occur. In the following two sections, the reasons for this are explained. The first case only involves one ontology. The second case involves two or more ontologies. For both we are going to show where mismatches will occur.

Central Ontology Case

One attempt to solve the problem of interoperability is to define all entities and constructs in one ontology with a complete and exact meaning. These meanings can be explicitly defined through semantic axioms or they can be described in a lexicon of the ontology. Every entity has one own unique URI. Equality of URIs means equality per definition. Full inferencing can easily be done with the information in the shared ontology. The results will be correct and complete with respect to the representation. This method followed for shared ontology language definitions (Patel-Schneider et al., 2004) and upper level ontologies such as SUMO (Niles and Pease, 2001).

The difficulty is the standardization effort before one entity and its meaning are defined (an ontology is defined as a shared conceptualization). This is actually not just a difficulty, but it is impossible to reach a consent of 100%. Two people will always slightly differ in the understanding of one term (Figure 11.1). Because of this, even though the inferencing is consistent with respect to the model, the involved people will possibly interpret it differently. As a result, entries provided by one user will lead to results that do not represent the other user's world. One exception to this is mathematics, as it is declarative rather than based on empirical learned representations of the world. The exact logics of ontology inferencing go well up to the point between people and machines. Then a misinterpretation, an error, might occur.

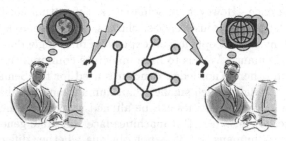

Fig. 11.1. Mismatches Occurring in Central Ontology Case

Distributed Ontology Case

The other attempt allows the creation of many entities on each individual computer or peer (just like every person has an own notion of an entity), which is a more practical approach on a large scale, e.g., for the Semantic Web. For users to communicate with each other, alignments have to be established, i.e., the entities of two computers have to be identified as being equal or at least similar, in a way we have already described for humans. This was dealt with in the previous chapters.

The key word of the last but one statement is *similar*, which is a fuzzy term and not a logical expression. One has to be aware that an alignment of this kind can never be complete in a formal way (Figure 11.2). Errors always occur in the same way they occur when two people talk to each other. Whereas the users understand their own ontologies correctly, interoperability is error prone. Even though most results are correct, one has to be aware that after several steps of inferencing, a small error may produce completely wrong results. Again, the exact logics are not applicable in general, but this time inevitable wrong alignments lead to misinterpretations.

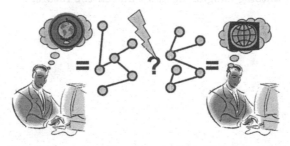

Fig. 11.2. Mismatches Occurring in Distributed Ontology Case

In fact, the ontologies we are dealing with normally only comprise a very restricted knowledge representation. Users do not model completely. Finding the correct alignments between these ontologies is even more difficult and inevitably error-prone than between two humans. This work presented many approaches for ontology alignment, but there is an inevitable border line in quality which can never be passed. We expect our approaches to be already close to this line.

11.2.3 Implications

The argumentation shows that correct inferencing is bound through the accuracy of alignments in the semantic model. However, these problems do not necessarily harm the whole idea of the Semantic Web. It is still possible to structure, share, and infer knowledge. Nevertheless, one has to be aware that no matter how carefully one models the world, eventually there will be mismatches. This does not invalidate ontology alignment as such, but new paradigms for inferencing are needed in the Semantic Web context:

- inferencing needs to be probabilistic;
- inferencing through long logical chains always breaks and returns wrong results;
- local inferencing is required.

As pointed out in the outlook section, efforts are actually already made in this direction. The application scenario finally needs to determine the effort put into the modeling and the needed level of confidence the model has to return.

As a conclusion, one can say that there is a general difficulty of aligning people's ideas. Due to this, exact alignments will also not be possible on machines, i.e., with ontologies. A weaker, but more robust, form of inferencing has to be the choice; an inferencing which can deal with good, but not perfect, alignments, as discovered in this work. On such a basis there are a lot of possibilities for ontology alignment, now and in the future.

12

Conclusion

This book extensively addressed the topic of ontology alignment. To make the contents easily memorizable for the reader we will once again summarize the main contributions in this chapter. Based hereon we will examine whether the goals defined in the beginning have been reached. Final statements conclude this work and take up any remaining loose ends.

12.1 Content Summary

The topic of this book has been ontology alignment. The general problem and the resulting goals have been presented in the introduction (Chapter 1). The goal of this research was to provide a concise methodology for aligning ontologies – and a practical implementation and application thereof. Aligning ontologies means to find those elements in two ontologies which have the same intended meaning. Aligned ontologies are crucial to overcome the heterogeneity in the Semantic Web, but also for various other structures within information systems.

Before developing an approach for ontology alignment a thorough investigation of the foundations (Part I) was indispensable. This included the definition and explanation of the main underlying structures – the ontologies. In this work, they consisted of both schema (i.e., concepts, relations) and instances plus additional information (subsumption, restrictions, etc.), which is normally encoded in axioms. Some of the axioms have a direct correspondence in OWL, which was used as ontology language in this work. Generally, an alignment meant that for two given ontologies, two corresponding entities, which have the same intended meaning, had to be identified. We also gave definitions of other related terms. This work was based on heuristics rather than logical inferencing, which made similarity considerations a central concept of this work. We have shown that similarity for ontologies may be interpreted along different layers (data, ontology, context, domain knowledge). However, goal of this work was also to create a methodology for practice. Therefore, we analyzed several use cases such as mapping or merging which rely on ontology alignment. From these scenarios, we derived specific requirements, which had to be fulfilled, such as quality and efficiency. Finally, research on integration had been numerous in the past. A thorough investigation of this related work helped us to gain an understanding of approaches and their shortcomings, and at the same time create own ideas.

We then developed a generic process for aligning ontologies (Part II). Its six main steps are: (1) feature engineering; (2) search step selection; (3) similarity computation; (4) similarity aggregation; (5) interpretation; and (6) iteration. By considering the similarity of entities one can infer alignments. All the steps were explained in detail, pointing to different instantiations thereof. One main result was the observation that exploiting the semantics of ontologies improves the quality of found alignments significantly compared to simple label-based approaches. In the sections following, different aspects of ontology alignment were addressed in specific. We have shown that it is possible to reduce the complexity of the alignment calculation, without losing much quality. Being confronted with the expressiveness of ontologies, we realized that a purely manual creation of an ontology alignment approach is not possible. We have shown that machine learning helps resolving this dilemma. Next, only a small fraction of use cases requires fully automatic ontology alignment approaches. For the others we developed a simple yet novel approach, which included the user into the loop in a best possible and least intrusive way. This again improved results. When investigating the scenarios we also realized that different use cases have very different requirements for ontology alignment, some focusing, e.g., more on quality, whereas others need results timely. These different requirements were addressed in the parameterizable process. Users were more satisfied with the ontology alignment resulting from this adaptive approach. Finally, we combined the different aspects to create a best possible integrated approach.

The methodological approach was implemented (Part III) in the procedural tool FOAM, a logics-based tool OMA, and finally integrated into the existing ontology engineering environment OntoStudio/OntoMap with a concise graphical user interface. As the practical application of our approach was one goal, these implementations were consequently used in five case studies from two projects. In Bibster entities from different ontologies were automatically merged, if they represented duplicates. For Xarop our alignment approach provided input for the ontology development board, by showing the members which identical entities have been created by independent users. For the case studies legal question answering, digital library, and heterogeneous groups in consulting, different alignment aspects were solved. Ontology alignment was needed for ontology merging, as well as on-the-fly ontology mapping with query and answer translation. The OntoStudio version of FOAM was used for this. The case studies all made use of the ontology alignment implementation (and the underlying methodology) with big success.

Next generation semantic alignment (Part IV) showed some further interesting topics. We have extended ontology alignment to an arbitrary structure alignment approach. We have illustrated this possibility for Petri Nets. Apart from this, we extended the alignment term to complex alignments not only looking for identical objects and have shown how this can be seamlessly achieved with the given ontology alignment approach. An outlook provided insights into future research on ontologies, alignment, and their overlap. Nonetheless, even with all these advanced alignment approaches one has to be aware that errors will always occur.

In this conclusion, all the results have been summarized once again.

12.2 Assessment of Contribution

Improving ontology alignment through new semantics-based technology was the core contribution of this work. It will now be assessed on different levels from the technical problems over general goals to the overall contribution. In specific, we will fall back on the requirements that have been identified for the different use cases. We will show that the problems have been solved and present the improvements compared to state-of-the-art existing approaches.

- *Quality* is a main issue when creating an ontology alignment approach. It has to be high in terms of both accuracy and completeness. More advanced methods using the semantics in different features of ontology entities and up-to-date machine learning techniques show higher quality results, both in terms of precision (plus one fourth) and recall (plus one and a half). Using the semantics for ontology alignment is indeed advantageous.

- At least for some use cases *efficiency* may not be neglected. Resources for time and memory are normally restricted. For the first time the computational complexity of ontology alignment has been explicitly addressed. In theory and practice we successfully increase efficiency by an order of magnitude. This is mainly due to the exploitation of ontology structures for an intelligent candidate alignment selection.

- Different levels of *user interaction* with the ontology alignment system ranging from semi- to fully automatic are another requirement. It is desirable to have an *explanatory component* for the proposed alignments. The human interaction component shows very favorable results, not only increasing quality. An original method favoring the presentation of alignments with highly interlinked entities for user validation maximizes the information value of user input. Each alignment is based on individual similarities, which can be well re-enacted by the user. A decision tree especially suits the explanation requirement. The whole process of ontology alignment is significantly improved from a user perspective.

- One can see that requirements differ depending on the underlying *use case*. A system should be flexible enough to react to these requirements and furthermore be easily *parameterizable*, adaptable, and extendable. FOAM is highly parameterizable. An adaptive method has been presented automatically adjusting the ontology alignment algorithm for the desired use case. For even bigger changes, the system is easily accessible via any Java development environment. For practical purposes such characteristics are indispensable for a good approach.

- Simple one-to-one alignments are only a first step and not sufficient for many applications. New approaches for *complex alignments* have to be investigated. Novel first steps towards complex ontology alignments have been broached in the last part. This work lays foundations, thus contributing to future improvements with a clear process approach. Already showing that this transfer is possible, is a significant step towards complex alignments.

- The work should not be generally restricted to ontologies. *Other structures* and schemas also need to be aligned. The transfer of our semantics- and similarity-based ontology alignment approach has been demonstrated by generalizing the process and applying it, as an example, to Petri Nets. Again, this work can serve as foundation. Especially for domains where only rudimentary approaches for alignment exist this is an improvement.

We will now examine whether our approaches have also solved the issues we had presented in the introduction of this work.

- Here we assume an IT application has to deal with a *scenario* with heterogeneous and distributed knowledge in which collaboration is required. The knowledge has to be *aligned* not only syntactically on representation format level but also semantically. Our ontology alignment approaches heavily rely on use cases and their requirements, which were overall fulfilled. In five case studies the practical validity of the approaches was examined. Ontologies are integrated on a semantic level by interpreting them. The pure syntactic translation from one format to another was not focus of this work. Moreover, the results of the semantic alignment are better than in many existing approaches.

- Knowledge is encoded in semantically rich structures: Namely, these are *ontologies*, which go beyond simple taxonomies and are based on an underlying logic. For these ontologies, the approaches successfully made use of the semantics – for different problems such as quality, efficiency, or user interaction. Indeed, our methods influence alignment techniques where semantics can be exploited, such as in ontologies.

- As the considerations of this work are thought to have practical impact, we are dealing with the *real world*. This means data is of varying size, incomplete semantic representations, and with restricted sets of axioms. Most probably the representation will not be perfect, thus have errors and mistakes in it. To solve the real world problem the method elected in this work was based on heuristical considerations; ontology alignments were identified through the similarity of individual entities. As similarity has a fuzzy notion rather than a logical exact formula, it better deals with small inconsistencies than exact logics-based alignment. The practical case studies have shown that our novel approaches based on a similarity focused process suit the real world.

- Alignment methods need to be *flexible* enough to be transferred to other applications and domains. The generality of the alignment process we have come up with allows to easily extend and adjust. This is substantiated by two presented extensions: The first extension allows for alignment of other structures than ontologies, here namely Petri Nets. The second extension pointed to complex alignments rather than simple one-to-one alignments. As the methods all have a theoretical grounding, they are open for being applied for many tasks, also within other alignment tools. We did not only create specific implementations, but in fact a concise methodology for future alignment approaches.

- Even though goal of this work was to be *theoretically* well-founded and give many pointers to existing work thereon, the focus was on solving specific problems thus addressing their *practical* difficulties with new methods and evaluating the new approaches, rather than creating a new complete theory of ontology alignment. This practical focus was also given to the work through the concrete use cases of two projects. The work therefore covered ontology alignment in a broad sense.

As a summary, the main contribution of this work has been a concise methodology and implementation for aligning ontologies. The hypothesis was that through a novel stepwise process combined with new semantic methods and the notion of similarity ontology alignment can be significantly improved. We have shown that these methods indeed amend the process of ontology alignment and the quality of the output in comparison to existing work.

Many challenges have been presented on the last two pages. For each of them we have shown how our new methods can solve problems and improve the overall task of ontology alignment. This does not imply that no research on ontology alignment is left; on the contrary, we have given indicators throughout the work where more future research is necessary. Nevertheless, this work gives a solid grounding for ontology alignment and related topics.

12.3 Final Statements

The use of semantic representations and their integration is a major improvement on handling information. Information systems transform into real knowledge systems. The importance of knowledge has increased in the last century and these days is an essential resource for any enterprise and vital component for our society. This work is one critical step on the path of building an information system infrastructure for this knowledge society.

In specific, within the last years the importance of ontologies as representations for knowledge has continuously increased. In parallel the absolute number of ontologies constantly rose. The Semantic Web community envisions a web of many ontologies rather than one world ontology. To nevertheless enable collaboration between humans and machines based on these ontologies, mechanisms for ontology alignment have to be developed (Ehrig and Studer, 2006). When we investigated existing approaches, we realized that they did not suit the practical requirements. Real world problems from numerous projects showed different requirements on ontology alignment. We therefore developed a new approach for ontology alignment. Based on the requirements it provides high quality ontology alignments, it is efficient, it allows user interaction in an intelligent way, and it suits different use cases. We then exemplarily transferred the theoretical ideas to one practical tool implementation. FOAM has proven to be very successful across the just mentioned dimensions. We further gave an outlook for future semantic alignment.

We hope the reader of this book has gained valuable insights into ontology alignment or, more generally, semantic alignment. Understanding the problems and possible solutions is an important basis. In particular, for persons interested in ontologies, the Semantic Web, or schema integration this book provided new methods for aligning. Through its practical focus, it should also have given tool developers support and insights when addressing this topic. Pointers to the future shall at the same time have inspired and raised further interest in ontology alignment.

Part V

Appendix

A

Ontologies

Four ontologies have been described in the main part of this book. The additional ontology sets, which were used for better averaging and higher significance levels, are presented now.

Russia 2:

In this set, we have two ontologies describing Russia. Like for Russia 1 students created the ontologies with the objective to represent the content of two independent travel websites about Russia. These ontologies have approximately 400 entities each, including concepts (region, river,...), relations (has_capital, has_mouth,...), and instances (Moscow, Black_Sea,...). The gold standard of 160 possible alignments was assigned by the students manually.

Russia 3:

The third set again covers Russia, but the two ontologies are more difficult to align. The gold standard of 160 possible alignments was assigned by the students manually.

Tourism:

The participants of a seminar created two ontologies which separately describe the tourism domain of Mecklenburg-Vorpommern a state in north-eastern Germany. Both ontologies have an extent of about 500 entities. No instances were modeled with this ontology, they only consist of concepts and relations. The 300 alignments have been created manually.

Networks:

Four additional ontology pairs have been provided for the I3CON contest. The computer networks ontologies are small with about 40 entities each and 30 alignments in between. They include the concepts server, cable, and hub, relations of being connect to or having a certain software.

Computer Science:

The overlap of these two ontologies is 16 alignments. The original ontologies are very different in size with 174 and 40 entities. An interesting characteristic of these two ontologies is the very low overlap.

Hotels:

The hotel ontologies are small with 18 and 24 entities. However, they include complex restrictions in OWL. Almost every entity has a correspondence in the other ontology (17 alignments). One of the ontologies is depicted in Figure A.1 through the RDF Gravity tool.[1]

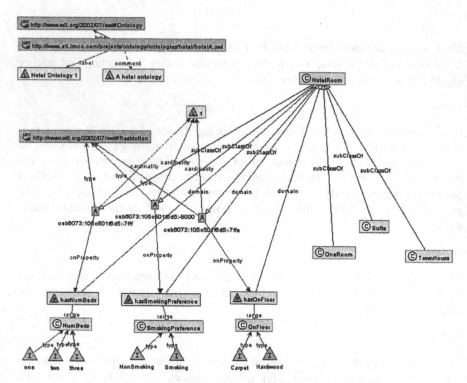

Fig. A.1. Hotel Ontology

People and Pets:

This is a larger pair of ontologies with about 120 entities of which 93 can be aligned. Again complex OWL constructs are used. Typical entities are cat_liker, animal, bicycle, elderly, etc.

---

[1] http://semweb.salzburgresearch.at/apps/rdf-gravity/

Bibliography 2:

Here we use two ontologies from the EON contest. The basis for the contest was a bibliographic ontology provided by INRIA with 180 entities (see also Figure A.2). The other one is the Karlsruhe ontology (330 entities), which is used in the OntoWeb portal. It is a refinement from other ontologies such as (KA)2. As such, it does not only define bibliographic items but many other items. 41 alignments have been identified.

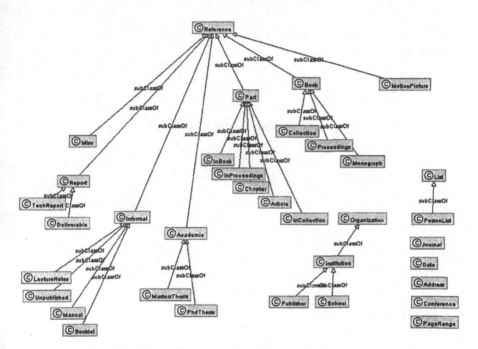

Fig. A.2. Concepts of Bibliographic Ontology

Bibliography 3:

Again, the EON contest is the starting point. This ontology with 60 entities has been provided by Massachusetts Institute of Technology (MIT). It is of wide use and relatively well thought out. This ontology is documented in BibTeX in OWL. It allows for 50 alignments.

Bibliography 4:

This ontology from the University of Maryland in Baltimore County (UMBC) is similar to the previous one and even closer to the genuine BibTeX, but with different extensions and naming conventions. It contains 50 entities and has 38 alignments.

Using as many different ontologies as in this work for evaluation has been rare. In fact, most of these ontologies haven't been available two years ago. One can expect that more ontologies will be created in the next years, so that the evaluation of future approaches can be done based on an even larger set of test ontologies.

B

Complete Evaluation Results

On the following pages, the complete evaluation results are listed (Tables B.1 to B.5). They consist of two involved ontologies and a strategy. The three quality measures precision, recall, and f-measure at the threshold point are listed thereafter. The maximum values for precision, recall, and f-measure, which could be reached follow. Please note that they are not reached together, but with different thresholds. Further statistical information on the runs are given, i.e., the number of iterations, the required time for the whole process, the number of comparisons performed over all iterations, and the number of queries posed to the users for the semi-automatic approaches.

Table B.1. Complete Evaluation Results 1

Ontology 1	Ontology 2	Strategy	Threshold Precision	Threshold Recall	Threshold F-Measure	Max Precision	Max Recall	Max F-Measure	Iter-ations	Time	Compa-risons	Ques-tions
animalsA	animalsB	Label	1.000	0.083	0.154	1.000	0.083	0.154	1	1	309	0
animalsA	animalsB	NOM (weigh)	0.733	0.458	0.564	1.000	0.542	0.634	10	3	3090	0
animalsA	animalsB	NOM (sigm)	0.769	0.417	0.541	1.000	0.542	0.650	10	2	3090	0
animalsA	animalsB	QOM	0.538	0.292	0.378	1.000	0.417	0.500	15	2	772	0
animalsA	animalsB	Learned	1.000	0.750	0.857	1.000	0.750	0.857	10	3	3090	0
animalsA	animalsB	Active	1.000	0.500	0.667	1.000	0.583	0.667	10	7	3090	15
animalsA	animalsB	Integrated	1.000	0.750	0.857	1.000	0.792	0.857	10	7	3090	15
animalsA	animalsB	Rewriting	1.000	0.083	0.154	1.000	0.083	0.154	5	2	10	0
animalsA	animalsB	Merging	1.000	0.750	0.857	1.000	0.750	0.857	25	21	9579	15
csA	csB	Label	0.000	0.000	0.000	0.000	0.000	0.000	1	2	4607	0
csA	csB	NOM (weigh)	0.400	0.125	0.190	1.000	0.250	0.231	10	76	46070	0
csA	csB	NOM (sigm)	1.000	0.063	0.118	1.000	0.188	0.316	10	69	46060	0
csA	csB	QOM	1.000	0.063	0.118	1.000	0.188	0.316	15	33	9436	0
csA	csB	Learned	0.174	0.250	0.205	0.235	0.250	0.242	10	49	46070	0
csA	csB	Active	1.000	0.250	0.400	1.000	0.250	0.400	10	76	46070	60
csA	csB	Integrated	0.889	0.500	0.640	1.000	0.500	0.667	10	49	46070	60
csA	csB	Rewriting	0.000	0.000	0.000	0.000	0.000	0.000	5	3	0	0
csA	csB	Merging	0.545	0.375	0.444	1.000	0.375	0.545	25	689	25298	15
hotelA	hotelB	Label	0.000	0.000	0.000	0.000	0.000	0.000	1	1	151	0
hotelA	hotelB	NOM (weigh)	0.000	0.000	0.000	0.250	0.118	0.148	10	7	1510	0
hotelA	hotelB	NOM (sigm)	1.000	0.176	0.300	1.000	0.235	0.381	10	1	1510	0
hotelA	hotelB	QOM	0.000	0.000	0.000	0.250	0.059	0.095	15	10	601	0
hotelA	hotelB	Learned	1.000	0.235	0.381	1.000	0.471	0.640	10	7	1510	0
hotelA	hotelB	Active	0.500	0.118	0.190	1.000	0.118	0.200	10	7	1510	15
hotelA	hotelB	Integrated	1.000	0.588	0.741	1.000	0.647	0.741	10	7	1510	15
hotelA	hotelB	Rewriting	0.000	0.000	0.000	0.000	0.000	0.000	5	3	0	0
hotelA	hotelB	Merging	1.000	0.471	0.640	1.000	0.529	0.640	25	21	4681	15

Table B.2. Complete Evaluation Results 2

Ontology 1	Ontology 2	Strategy	Threshold Precision	Threshold Recall	Threshold F-Measure	Max Precision	Max Recall	Max F-Measure	Iterations	Time	Comparisons	Questions
networkA	networkB	Label	0.000	0.000	0.000	0.000	0.000	0.000	1	1	759	0
networkA	networkB	NOM (weigh)	1.000	0.033	0.065	1.000	0.333	0.333	10	10	7590	0
networkA	networkB	NOM (sigm)	1.000	0.033	0.065	1.000	0.033	0.065	10	5	7590	0
networkA	networkB	QOM	1.000	0.033	0.065	1.000	0.400	0.465	15	11	1979	0
networkA	networkB	Learned	0.941	0.533	0.681	1.000	0.567	0.708	10	11	7590	0
networkA	networkB	Active	1.000	0.200	0.333	1.000	0.467	0.553	10	10	7590	15
networkA	networkB	Integrated	1.000	0.567	0.723	1.000	0.567	0.723	10	11	7590	15
networkA	networkB	Rewriting	0.000	0.000	0.000	0.000	0.000	0.000	5	3	0	0
networkA	networkB	Merging	1.000	0.533	0.696	1.000	0.667	0.769	25	34	23529	15
onto101	onto301	Label	1.000	0.192	0.323	1.000	0.192	0.323	1	1	3756	0
onto101	onto301	NOM (weigh)	0.824	0.269	0.406	1.000	0.500	0.559	10	37	37560	0
onto101	onto301	NOM (sigm)	0.737	0.269	0.394	1.000	0.327	0.430	10	26	37550	0
onto101	onto301	QOM	0.778	0.269	0.400	1.000	0.308	0.424	15	15	5080	0
onto101	onto301	Learned	0.919	0.654	0.764	1.000	0.750	0.788	10	41	37560	0
onto101	onto301	Active	1.000	0.327	0.493	1.000	0.327	0.493	10	37	37560	60
onto101	onto301	Integrated	1.000	0.808	0.894	1.000	0.827	0.894	10	41	37560	60
onto101	onto301	Rewriting	1.000	0.231	0.375	1.000	0.231	0.375	5	3	79	0
onto101	onto301	Merging	0.966	0.538	0.691	1.000	0.635	0.725	25	393	17784	15
onto101	onto302	Label	0.889	0.211	0.340	0.889	0.211	0.340	1	1	3201	0
onto101	onto302	NOM (weigh)	0.550	0.289	0.379	0.900	0.289	0.400	10	35	32010	0
onto101	onto302	NOM (sigm)	0.550	0.289	0.379	0.917	0.289	0.440	10	24	31980	0
onto101	onto302	QOM	0.550	0.289	0.379	0.917	0.289	0.440	15	16	6455	0
onto101	onto302	Learned	0.906	0.763	0.829	0.906	0.789	0.829	10	32	32010	0
onto101	onto302	Active	0.917	0.289	0.440	0.917	0.289	0.440	10	35	32010	60
onto101	onto302	Integrated	0.968	0.789	0.870	0.968	0.789	0.870	10	32	32010	60
onto101	onto302	Rewriting	0.889	0.211	0.340	0.889	0.211	0.340	5	3	56	0
onto101	onto302	Merging	0.962	0.658	0.781	0.962	0.684	0.781	25	561	12759	15

Table B.3. Complete Evaluation Results 3

Ontology 1	Ontology 2	Strategy	Threshold Precision	Threshold Recall	Threshold F-Measure	Max Precision	Max Recall	Max F-Measure	Iterations	Time	Comparisons	Questions
onto101	onto303	Label	0.886	0.756	0.816	0.886	0.756	0.816	1	2	7556	0
onto101	onto303	NOM (weigh)	0.586	0.829	0.687	0.895	0.829	0.861	10	71	75560	0
onto101	onto303	NOM (sigm)	0.607	0.829	0.701	0.895	0.829	0.861	10	60	75570	0
onto101	onto303	QOM	0.618	0.829	0.708	0.895	0.829	0.861	15	20	10930	0
onto101	onto303	Learned	0.822	0.902	0.860	0.886	0.927	0.860	10	66	75560	0
onto101	onto303	Active	0.854	0.854	0.854	0.897	0.854	0.875	10	72	75560	60
onto101	onto303	Integrated	0.881	0.902	0.892	0.902	0.951	0.902	10	66	75560	60
onto101	onto303	Rewriting	0.886	0.756	0.816	0.886	0.805	0.816	5	4	420	0
onto101	onto303	Merging	0.897	0.854	0.875	0.897	0.854	0.875	25	1255	25616	15
onto101	onto304	Label	0.941	0.865	0.901	0.941	0.865	0.901	1	2	5256	0
onto101	onto304	NOM (weigh)	0.896	0.932	0.914	0.932	0.959	0.932	10	83	52560	0
onto101	onto304	NOM (sigm)	0.909	0.946	0.927	0.946	0.959	0.946	10	76	52560	0
onto101	onto304	QOM	0.904	0.892	0.898	0.930	0.905	0.910	15	43	19187	0
onto101	onto304	Learned	0.885	0.932	0.908	0.940	0.959	0.916	10	60	52560	0
onto101	onto304	Active	0.959	0.959	0.959	0.959	0.959	0.959	10	84	52560	44
onto101	onto304	Integrated	0.947	0.973	0.960	0.947	0.973	0.960	10	60	52560	60
onto101	onto304	Rewriting	0.940	0.851	0.894	0.942	0.878	0.909	5	5	2458	0
onto101	onto304	Merging	0.957	0.905	0.931	0.957	0.919	0.932	25	793	34779	15
petsA	petsB	Label	0.988	0.882	0.932	0.988	0.882	0.932	1	1	4124	0
petsA	petsB	NOM (weigh)	0.967	0.935	0.951	0.989	0.935	0.961	10	34	41240	0
petsA	petsB	NOM (sigm)	0.966	0.925	0.945	0.988	0.935	0.951	10	27	41240	0
petsA	petsB	QOM	0.988	0.860	0.920	0.988	0.871	0.926	15	13	6516	0
petsA	petsB	Learned	0.988	0.914	0.950	0.989	0.968	0.978	10	37	41240	0
petsA	petsB	Active	0.989	0.946	0.967	0.989	0.957	0.973	10	34	41240	15
petsA	petsB	Integrated	0.989	0.968	0.978	0.989	0.968	0.978	10	37	41240	12
petsA	petsB	Rewriting	0.986	0.774	0.867	0.987	0.796	0.881	5	3	627	0
petsA	petsB	Merging	0.989	0.925	0.956	0.989	0.925	0.956	25	37	13469	15

Table B.4. Complete Evaluation Results 4

Ontology 1	Ontology 2	Strategy	Threshold Precision	Threshold Recall	Threshold F-Measure	Max Precision	Max Recall	Max F-Measure	Iterations	Time	Comparisons	Questions
russia1	russia2	Label	1.000	0.696	0.821	1.000	0.696	0.821	1	5	68102	0
russia1	russia2	NOM (weigh)	0.620	0.789	0.694	1.000	0.814	0.832	10	2691	681020	0
russia1	russia2	NOM (sigm)	0.674	0.807	0.734	1.000	0.820	0.858	10	2980	681000	0
russia1	russia2	QOM	0.685	0.783	0.730	1.000	0.789	0.834	15	346	65802	0
russia1	russia2	Learned	0.809	0.764	0.786	1.000	0.795	0.825	10	1205	681020	0
russia1	russia2	Active	0.850	0.807	0.828	1.000	0.826	0.874	10	2608	681020	60
russia1	russia2	Integrated	0.906	0.783	0.840	1.000	0.807	0.858	10	1218	681020	60
russia1	russia2	Rewriting	0.966	0.702	0.813	1.000	0.727	0.821	5	8	5451	0
russia1	russia2	Merging	0.984	0.783	0.872	1.000	0.807	0.875	25	391	112530	60
russiaA	russiaB	Label	1.000	0.007	0.014	1.000	0.007	0.014	1	3	39572	0
russiaA	russiaB	NOM (weigh)	0.954	0.512	0.667	1.000	0.765	0.792	10	1080	395720	0
russiaA	russiaB	NOM (sigm)	0.941	0.561	0.703	1.000	0.744	0.792	10	1143	395760	0
russiaA	russiaB	QOM	0.938	0.526	0.674	1.000	0.667	0.737	15	324	59946	0
russiaA	russiaB	Learned	0.993	0.993	0.993	1.000	0.993	0.993	10	482	395720	0
russiaA	russiaB	Active	0.959	0.649	0.774	1.000	0.835	0.865	10	1026	395720	60
russiaA	russiaB	Integrated	0.997	1.000	0.998	1.000	1.000	0.998	10	484	395720	60
russiaA	russiaB	Rewriting	1.000	0.309	0.472	1.000	0.309	0.472	5	4	4096	0
russiaA	russiaB	Merging	0.981	0.923	0.951	1.000	0.923	0.958	25	225	101196	60
russiaC	russiaD	Label	1.000	0.033	0.063	1.000	0.033	0.063	1	3	28920	0
russiaC	russiaD	NOM (weigh)	0.620	0.372	0.465	1.000	0.493	0.490	10	558	289200	0
russiaC	russiaD	NOM (sigm)	0.612	0.367	0.459	1.000	0.474	0.497	10	602	289220	0
russiaC	russiaD	QOM	0.553	0.293	0.383	1.000	0.391	0.403	15	147	38462	0
russiaC	russiaD	Learned	0.951	0.991	0.970	1.000	0.991	0.988	10	299	289200	0
russiaC	russiaD	Active	0.866	0.391	0.538	1.000	0.530	0.547	10	542	289200	60
russiaC	russiaD	Integrated	0.926	0.986	0.955	1.000	0.986	0.988	10	310	289200	60
russiaC	russiaD	Rewriting	1.000	0.116	0.208	1.000	0.116	0.208	5	4	1131	0
russiaC	russiaD	Merging	0.969	0.874	0.919	1.000	0.874	0.926	25	208	70058	60

Table B.5. Complete Evaluation Results 5

Ontology 1	Ontology 2	Strategy	Threshold Precision	Threshold Recall	Threshold F-Measure	Max Precision	Max Recall	Max F-Measure	Iterations	Time	Comparisons	Questions
event	soccer	Label	0.875	0.047	0.089	0.875	0.047	0.089	1	38	84284	0
event	soccer	NOM (weigh)	0.343	0.160	0.218	0.889	0.193	0.257	10	865	842840	0
event	soccer	NOM (sigm)	0.438	0.140	0.212	0.889	0.200	0.230	10	566	842910	0
event	soccer	QOM	0.463	0.127	0.199	0.900	0.153	0.213	15	74	62927	0
event	soccer	Learned	0.806	0.773	0.789	0.942	0.853	0.828	10	739	842840	0
event	soccer	Active	0.885	0.153	0.261	0.929	0.187	0.271	10	873	842840	60
event	soccer	Integrated	0.878	0.767	0.819	0.975	0.820	0.848	10	741	842840	60
event	soccer	Rewriting	0.947	0.120	0.213	0.952	0.133	0.234	5	3	446	0
event	soccer	Merging	0.971	0.673	0.795	0.971	0.753	0.812	25	598	110944	60
tourismA	tourismB	Label	0.978	0.597	0.742	0.978	0.597	0.742	1	12	170589	0
tourismA	tourismB	NOM (weigh)	0.699	0.885	0.781	0.982	0.885	0.887	10	4055	1705890	0
tourismA	tourismB	NOM (sigm)	0.838	0.845	0.841	0.981	0.881	0.876	10	4905	1705980	0
tourismA	tourismB	QOM	0.851	0.810	0.830	0.993	0.845	0.866	15	459	135089	0
tourismA	tourismB	Learned	0.820	0.726	0.770	0.978	0.757	0.792	10	1917	1705890	0
tourismA	tourismB	Active	0.922	0.841	0.880	0.981	0.885	0.883	10	4027	1705890	60
tourismA	tourismB	Integrated	0.966	0.765	0.854	0.981	0.810	0.854	10	1927	1705890	60
tourismA	tourismB	Rewriting	0.958	0.704	0.811	0.993	0.783	0.853	5	10	6418	0
tourismA	tourismB	Merging	0.983	0.752	0.852	0.994	0.819	0.852	25	685	247830	60

C

FOAM Tool Details

This chapter provides additional information on the ontology alignment implementation FOAM. The documentation included in the download package and provides a good overview on its usage.

C.1 Short description

The ontology alignment framework is a tool to fully or semi-automatically align two or more OWL ontologies. It is based on heuristics (similarity) of the individual entities (concepts, relations, and instances). As result we receive pairs of aligned entities. The underlying research has been presented at different events, such as ESWS04, ISWC04, PAKM04, WWW05, and ISWC05. See the publication webpage[1] for references. Please keep in mind that this is research work in progress. Parts of the tool might be programmed neither very sophisticated nor free of bugs. This is proof of concept, but still – it works.

C.2 Download and Installation

To use the alignment framework you need to download the most important files from the webpage[2] first. It is the main portal for people interested in the Framework for Ontology Alignment and Mapping (Figure C.1). The zipped file includes both the source and binary files. Further, it contains this short documentation, examples of parameter files, ontologies, and results. Unzip it to a folder of your preference. The alignment framework is based on KAON2

---

[1] http://www.aifb.uni-karlsruhe.de/Publikationen/showPublikationen?id_db=80

[2] http://www.aifb.uni-karlsruhe.de/WBS/meh/foam/

and therefore requires the installation of Java jre1.5.0. If you want to extensively use and program with the alignment tool, additional libraries (WEKA, WordNet, GoogleAPI) are required. Please refer to the respective developers for information on their use.

C.3 Usage

The alignment framework is started from command line as follows:

    `java -jar align.jar parameter_file`

An example parameter file is provided with the download. For detailed use or just understanding of the tool, we recommend using it from a programming environment. The main file is edu.unika.aifb.rules.main.Main. The code is extensively commented and only a brief overview is therefore presented here. First, the alignment class is initialized. The ontologies have to be loaded. Then the parameters are set. They can be set individually or the system can propose a plausible setup, based on the application scenario. If alignments are already known they may be used as external input. Then the alignment process is started. Afterwards four different results may be accessed: all alignment values, including very low confidences; only alignments above a sensible threshold; alignments which are very doubtful and should be validated by the user for a better run; evaluation measures (if a reference alignment is given). If the threaded approach is used, the results can already be accessed during runtime of the algorithm.

C.4 Web Service

Besides the downloadable version, there is an alignment web service. It requires the standard parameters, and, if available, the reference goal alignments for evaluation. The alignment procedure will need time to produce the alignments. The result will be directly displayed in the browser.

C.5 Parameters

The parameters are now explained along the parameter file. We will first mention the standard mandatory parameters and then add optional parameters for experienced users. The parameters from the programming environment should also be intuitive then. The parameters of the web service are restricted to the standard subset of parameters.

```
PARAMETERS FILE FOR THE ONTOLOGY ALIGNMENT PROCESS
ontology1 = C:/animalsA.owl;
ontology2 = C:/animalsB.owl;
```

```
scenario = ONTOLOGYMERGING;
cutoffFile = C:/results.txt;
```

We have to assign the two ontologies. The alignment system is based on KAON2, which can handle the DLP-fragment of OWL. Please check the ontologies with the online WonderWeb OWL Ontology Validator [3]. Already known alignments have to be saved in the explicit file as follows: uri1; uri2; confidence. The explicit file may be empty. The NOSCENARIO scenario should be fine for most cases. Further scenarios are DATAINTEGRATION, ONTOLOGYMERGING, ONTOLOGYEVOLUTION, MAPPINGDISCOVERY, QUERYREWRITING, and REASONING. Finally, the interpreted results (above the threshold) have to be stored. The output format is: uri1; uri2; confidence.

The additional parameters are used for fine-tuning of the system and will only be explained briefly. Please refer to the code for detailed use of the parameters.

```
strategy = DECISIONTREE;
```
if you want to choose the strategy directly: EQUALLABELS, ONLYLABELS, MANUALWEIGHTED, MANUALSIGMOID, MACHINE, or DECISIONTREE
```
internaltoo = EXTERNAL;
```
if you would like to look for duplicates within one namespace, this has to be set to INTERNAL
```
efficientAgenda = EFFICIENT;
```
speed the process up or do a complete comparison: COMPLETE
```
classifierFile = C:/Work/tree25a.obj;
```
only needed for MACHINE or DECISIONTREE strategy;
should contain WEKA learned classifier or decisiontree
```
rulesFile = C:/Work/generatedRules.obj;
```
only needed for MACHINE or DECISIONTREE strategy;
should contain WEKA generated/learned rules
```
semi = FULLAUTOMATIC;
```
user interaction during alignment process or not;
results can improve significantly: SEMIAUTOMATIC
```
maxError = 0.95;
```
alignments with this confidence value are presented to the user for validation first
```
numberQuestions = 5;
```
how many questions are given to the user. 5-20 are default.
multiply by 3 to receive the total number of queries
```
maxiterations = 10;
```
the process is iterative
```
cutoffvalue = 0.95;
```
where to set the threshold, this is tricky and depends on the strategy chosen and the

---

[3] http://phoebus.cs.man.ac.uk:9999/OWL/Validator/

application scenario
`removeDoubles = REMOVEDOUBLES;`
normally alignments between ontologies align two entities directly; if you want

to allow more than one alignment per entity set this to `ALLOWDOUBLES`
`resultFile = C:/Work/result.txt;`
all results are saved, also below the threshold
`questionFile = C:/Work/question.txt;`
questionable alignments are saved for manual inspection
`manualmappingFile = C:/Work/goldstandard.txt;`
for the evaluation the goldstandard is necessary

C.6 Additional features of the tool

There are a number of additional features in the download-able version of the ontology alignment framework. For detailed output of the similarities calculated during the comparison call `Save.saveCompleteEval(align.ontology,align.resultListLatest,` `manualmappingsFile,resultFile);` The manual mappings file contains the correct alignments (gold standard). The result file will then have the following format: uri1, label1, uri2, label2, overall confidence, 1...n individual confidences (normally according to the rules of ManualComplex), whether the alignment is correct or not.

The machine learning component is Train. This class contains several methods which allow the creation of the rules from the feature/similarity combinations, training examples for validation through the user, preparation of these validated examples for the training step, and the training and machine learning step using different classifiers from WEKA. Comments are included in the code to make this easier.

A translation component between different ontology alignment formats, i.e., the here used array format (uri1,uri2,confidence), the INRIA alignment API format, and the Lockheed Martin N3 format. This feature is found under util.

Feel free to contact me, if you encountered difficulties in the usage or find bugs or want to provide new ideas for the next version of it: Marc Ehrig, ehrig@aifb.uni-karlsruhe.de

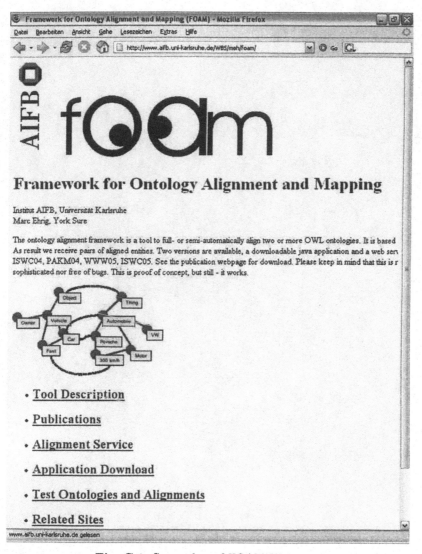

Fig. C.1. Screenshot of FOAM Webpage

References

(2002). *Proceedings of the Eleventh International World Wide Web Conference (WWW-2002)*, Honululu, HW, USA.

(2006). *The Merriam Webster Dictionary*. Merriam-Webster. http://www.m-w.com/.

Abecker, Andreas, Bauer, Michael, and Hefke, Mark (2004). MODALE – modellbasiertes Anlagen-Engineering, kundenorientierte Dienstleistungen für Anlagensteuerung und -kontrolle. In *Forschungsoffensive "Software Engineering"*, Berlin, Germany.

Aberer, Karl et al., editors (2003). *Proceedings of the Workshop Semantics in Peer-to-Peer and Grid Computing (SemPGRID) at WWW-2003*, Budapest, Hungary.

Agrawal, Rakesh and Srikant, Ramakrishnan (2001). On integrating catalogs. In *Proceedings of the Tenth International World Wide Web Conference (WWW-10)*, pages 603–612, Hong Kong, China. ACM Press.

Althoff, Klaus-Dieter, Dengel, Andreas, Bergmann, Ralph, Nick, Markus, and Roth-Berghofer, Thomas, editors (2005). *WM 2005: Professional Knowledge Management – Experiences and Visions, Contributions to the Third Conference Professional Knowledge Management – Experiences and Visions*, volume 3782 of *Lecture Notes in Artificial Intelligence*, Kaiserslautern, Germany. Springer.

Ashpole, Benjamin, Ehrig, Marc, Euzenat, Jérôme, and Stuckenschmidt, Heiner, editors (2005). *Proceedings of the Workshop on Integrating Ontologies at K-Cap 2005*, volume 156 of *CEUR Workshop Proceedings*, Banff, AB, Canada. CEUR-WS Publication.

Baader, Franz, McGuinness, Deborah L., Nardi, Daniele, and Patel-Schneider, Peter F. (2003). *The Description Logic Handbook*. Cambridge University Press.

Barwise, Jon and Seligman, Jerry (1997). *Information Flow: the logic of distributed systems*. Number 44 in Cambridge Tracts in Theoretical Computer Science. Cambridge University Press.

Bench-Capon, Trevor J. M. and Malcolm, Grant (1999). Formalising ontologies and their relations. In Bench-Capon, Trevor J. M., Soda, Giovanni, and Tjoa, A. Min, editors, *Proceedings of the Tenth International Conference and Workshop on Database and Expert Systems Applications (DEXA-99)*, volume 1677 of *Lecture Notes in Computer Science*, pages 250–259, Florence, Italy. Springer.

Benjamins, V. Richard and Gómez-Pérez, Asunción, editors (2002). *Proceedings of the 13th European Conference on Knowledge Acquisition and Management (EKAW-2002)*, volume 2473 of *Lecture Notes in Computer Science*, Siguenza, Spain. Springer.

Bergamaschi, Sonia, Castano, Silvana, Vincini, Maurizio, and Beneventano, Domenico (2001). Semantic Integration of Heterogeneous Information Sources. *Special Issue on Intelligent Information Integration, Journal of Data and Knowledge Engineering*, 36(1):215–249.

Bergmann, Ralph (2002). *Experience Management: Foundations, Development Methodology, and Internet-Based Applications*. Springer.

Bergmann, Ralph and Stahl, Armin (1998). Similarity measures for object-oriented case representations. In Smyth, Barry and Cunningham, Padraig, editors, *Proceedings of the Fourth European Workshop on Advances in Case-Based Reasoning (EWCBR-98)*, volume 1488, pages 25–36, Dublin, Ireland. Springer.

Berkovsky, Shlomo, Eytani, Yaniv, and Gal, Avigdor (2005). Measuring the relative performance of schema matchers. In Skowron, Andrzej, Agrawal, Rakesh, Luck, Mike, Yamaguchi, Takahira, Morizet-Mahoudeaux, Pierre, Liu, Jiming, and Zhong, Ning, editors, *Proceedings of the 2005 IEEE/WIC/ACM International Conference on Web Intelligence (WI 2005)*, pages 366–371, Compeigne, France. IEEE Computer Society.

Berners-Lee, Tim (2000). Semantic Web – XML 2000.

Berners-Lee, Tim (2005). The Semantic Web: An interview with Tim Berners-Lee. *Consortium Standards Bulletin*, 4(6).

Berners-Lee, Tim, Hendler, Jim, and Lassila, Ora (2001). The Semantic Web. *Scientific American*, 2001(5).

Bernstein, Abraham, Kaufmann, Esther, Bürki, Christoph, and Klein, Mark (2005a). How similar is it? Towards personalized similarity measures in ontologies. In *Wirtschaftsinformatik 2005: eEconomy, eGovernment, eSociety, Siebte Internationale Tagung Wirtschaftsinformatik 2005*, pages 1347–1366, Bamberg, Germany. Physica-Verlag.

Bernstein, Abraham, Kaufmann, Esther, Kiefer, Christoph, and Bürki, Christoph (2005b). Simpack: A generic java library for similarity measures in ontologies. Technical report, University of Zurich, Department of Informatics, Zurich, Switzerland.

Bernstein, Philip A. et al., editors (2002). *Proceedings of 28th International Conference on Very Large Data Bases (VLDB-2002)*, Hong Kong, China. Morgan Kaufmann Publishers.

Bisson, Gilles (1992). Learning in FOL with a similarity measure. In *Proceedings of the Tenth National Conference on Artificial Intelligence (AAAI-92)*, pages 82–87, San Jose, CA, USA. The AAAI Press.

Bisson, Gilles (1995). Why and how to define a similarity measure for object based representation systems. In Mars, Nicolaas J.I., editor, *Towards Very Large Knowledge Bases, Knowledge Building & Knowledge Sharing 1995*, pages 236–246, Amsterdam, The Netherlands. IOS Press.

Boddy, Mark S. (1991). Anytime problem solving using dynamic programming. In *Proceedings of the Ninth National Conference on Artificial Intelligence*, pages 738–743, Anaheim, CA, USA. Shaker Verlag.

Böhm, Klemens, Jensen, Christian S., Haas, Laura M., Kersten, Martin L., Larson, Per-Åke, and Ooi, Beng Chin, editors (2005). *Proceedings of 31st International Conference on Very Large Data Bases (VLDB-2005)*, Trondheim, Norway. ACM Press.

Bouquet, Paolo, Euzenat, Jérôme, Franconi, Enrico, Serafini, Luciano, Stamou, Giorgos, and Tessaris, Sergio (2004). Knowledge Web deliverable D2.2.1: Specification of a common framework for characterzing alignment. Technical report.

Bray, Tim, Paoli, Jean, Sperberg-McQueen, C. M., Maler, Eva, and cois Yergeau, Fran(2004). Extensible Markup Language (XML) 1.0 (Third Edition). W3C Recommendation 04 February.

Brickley, Dan and Guha, Ramanathan V. (2004). RDF Vocabulary Description Language 1.0: RDF Schema. W3C Recommendation 10 February.

Brinkhoff, Andreas (2004). Similarity measures in ontologies, taxonomies and other representation systems. Technical report, Institut AIFB, Universität Karlsruhe (TH).

Broekstra, Jeen, Ehrig, Marc, Haase, Peter, van Harmelen, Frank, Kampman, Arjohn, Sabou, Marta, Siebes, Ronny, Staab, Steffen, Stuckenschmidt, Heiner, and Tempich, Christoph (2003). A metadata model for semantics-based peer-to-peer systems. In Aberer et al. (2003).

Broekstra, Jeen and Kampman, Arjohn (2004). SeRQL: An RDF query and transformation language. Technical report, Vrije Universiteit Amsterdam.

Broekstra, Jeen, Kampman, Arjohn, and van Harmelen, Frank (2002). Sesame: A generic architecture for storing and querying RDF and RDF schema. In Horrocks and Hendler (2002), pages 54–64.

Brokmans, Saartje, Ehrig, Marc, Koschmider, Agnes, Oberweis, Andreas, and Studer, Rudi (2006). Semantic alignment of business processes. In *Eigth International Conference on Enterprise Information Systems (ICEIS-2006)*, Cyprus.

Burstein, Mark H. and McDermott, Drew V. (2005). Ontology translation for interoperability among Semantic Web services. *AI Magazine*, 26(1):71–82. Special Issue: Semantic Integration.

Bussler, Christoph, Davis, John, Fensel, Dieter, and Studer, Rudi, editors (2004). *Proceedings of the First European Semantic Web Symposium*

230   References

(ESWS-2004), volume 3053 of *Lecture Notes in Computer Science*, Heraklion, Greece. Springer.

Caplan, Priscilla (1995). You call it corn, we call it syntax-independent metadata for document-like objects (defining a standard for describing network-accessible information resources). *Public-Access Computer Systems Review*, 6(4):19–23.

Carr, Nicholas G. (2003). IT doesn't matter. *Harvard Business Review*, 81(5):41–50.

Casanovas, Pompeu, Gorronnogoitia, Jésus, Contreras, Jésus, Bázquez, Mercedes, Casellas, Nuria, Vallbé, Joan-Josep, Poblet, Marta, Ramos, Francesc, and Benjamins, V. Richard (2005). SEKT legal use case components: Ontology and architectural design. In *Proceedings of the Tenth International Conference on Artificial Intelligence and Law (ICAIL-05)*, Bologna, Italy.

Castano, Silvana, Antonellis, Valeria De, and di Vimercati, Sabrina De Capitani (2001). Global viewing of heterogeneous data sources. *IEEE Transactions on Knowledge and Data Engineering*, 13(2):277–297.

Castano, Silvana, Antonellis, Valeria De, Fugini, Maria Grazia, and Pernici, Barbara (1998). Conceptual schema analysis: Techniques and applications. *ACM Transaction Database Systems*, 23(3):286–333.

Castano, Silvana, Ferrara, Alfio, Montanelli, Stefano, Pagani, Elena, and Rossi, Gian Paolo (2003). Ontology-addressable contents in P2P networks. In Aberer et al. (2003).

Chaves, Marcirio Silveira (2003). Um estudo e apreciação sobre algoritmos de stemming para a língua portugesa. In *IX Jornadas Iberoamericanas de Informática*, Cartagena de Indias, Colombia.

Cimiano, Philipp and Völker, Johanna (2005). Text2Onto - a framework for ontology learning and data-driven change discovery. In *Natural Language Processing and Information Systems, Tenth International Conference on Applications of Natural Language to Information Systems (NLDB-05)*, volume 3513 of *Lecture Notes in Computer Science*, pages 227–238, Alicante, Spain. Springer.

Cimpian, Emilia, Drumm, Christian, Stollberg, Michael, Constantinescu, Ion, Cabral, Liliana, Domingue, John, Hakimpour, Farshad, and Kiryakov, Atanas (2004). DIP deliverable D5.1: Report on the state-of-the-art and requirements analysis (WP5 service mediation). Technical report.

Ciocoiu, Mihai, Nau, Dana S., and Gruninger, Michael (2001). Ontologies for integrating engineering applications. *Journal of Computing and Information Science in Engineering*, 1(1):12–22.

Clifton, Chris, Housman, Ed, and Rosenthal, Arnon (1997). Experience with a combined approach to attribute-matching across heterogeneous databases. In Spaccapietra, Stefano and Maryanski, Fred J., editors, *Data Mining and Reverse Engineering: Searching for Semantics, Seventh Conference on Database Semantics (DS-7)*, volume 124 of *IFIP Conference Proceedings*, pages 428–, Leysin, Switzerland. Chapman and Hall.

de Bruijn, Jos, Ehrig, Marc, Feier, Cristina, Martín-Recuerda, Francisco, Scharffe, François, and Weiten, Moritz (2006). Ontology mediation, merging, and aligning. In Davies, John and Studer, Rudi, editors, *Semantic Web Technologies*. John Wiley & Sons, Ltd.

de Bruijn, Jos, Ehrig, Marc, Martín-Recuerda, Francisco, Polleres, Axel, and Predoiu, Livia (2005). SEKT deliverable D4.4.1: Ontology mediation management v1. Technical report.

de Bruijn, Jos and Feier, Cristina (2005). SEKT deliverable D4.6.1: Report on ontology mediation for case studies. Technical report.

de Bruijn, Jos, Foxvog, Douglas, and Zimmerman, Kerstin (2004). SEKT deliverable D4.3.1: Ontology mediation patterns library v1. Technical report.

de Mántaras, Ramon López and Saitta, Lorenza, editors (2004). *Proceedings of the 16th Eureopean Conference on Artificial Intelligence (ECAI 2004)*, Valencia, Spain. IOS Press.

Decker, Stefan, Erdmann, Michael, Fensel, Dieter, and Studer, Rudi (1999). Ontobroker: Ontology based access to distributed and semi-structured information. In et al., Robert Meersman, editor, *Semantic Issues in Multimedia Systems*, pages 351–369. Kluwer Academic Publisher, Boston.

Dhamankar, Robin, Lee, Yoonkyong, Doan, AnHai, Halevy, Alon, and Domingos, Pedro (2004). iMAP: discovering complex semantic matches between database schemas. In Weikum, Gerhard, König, Arnd Christian, and Deßloch, Stefan, editors, *Proceedings of the 2004 ACM SIGMOD International Conference on Management of Data (SIGMOD-04)*, pages 383–394, Paris, France. ACM.

Ding, Ying, Fensel, Dieter, Klein, Michel C. A., and Omelayenko, Borys (2002). The Semantic Web: yet another hip? *Data Knowledge Engineering*, 41(2-3):205–227.

Do, Hong-Hai, Melnik, Sergej, and Rahm, Erhard (2002). Comparison of schema matching evaluations. In *Proceedings of the Second International Workshop on Web Databases (German Informatics Society)*.

Do, Hong-Hai and Rahm, Erhard (2002). COMA – a system for flexible combination of schema matching approaches. In Bernstein et al. (2002), pages 610–621.

Doan, AnHai, Domingos, Pedro, and Halevy, Alon (2003). Learning to match the schemas of data sources: A multistrategy approach. *VLDB Journal*, 50:279–301.

Doan, AnHai, Domingos, Pedro, and Halevy, Alon Y. (2001). Reconciling schemas of disparate data sources: A machine-learning approach. In Aref, Walid G., editor, *Proceedings of the 2001 ACM SIGMOD International Conference on Management of Data (SIGMOD-01)*, pages 509–520, Santa Barbara, CA, USA. ACM Press.

Doan, AnHai and Halevy, Alon Y. (2005). Semantic-integration research in the database community. *AI Magazine*, 26(1):83–94. Special Issue: Semantic Integration.

Doan, AnHai, Madhavan, Jayant, Domingos, Pedro, and Halevy, Alon Y. (2002). Learning to map between ontologies on the Semantic Web. In www (2002), pages 662–673.

Drucker, Peter F. (1993). *A Post Capitalist Society*. HarperCollins, New York.

Egan, James P. (1975). Signal detection theory and ROC analysis. *Psychometrika*.

Ehrig, Marc and Euzenat, Jérôme (2005). Relaxed precision and recall for ontology alignment. In Ashpole et al. (2005), pages 25–32.

Ehrig, Marc, Haase, Peter, Hefke, Mark, and Stojanovic, Nenad (2005a). Similarity for ontologies - a comprehensive framework. In Bartmann, Dieter, Rajola, Federico, Kallinikos, Jannis, Avison, David, Winter, Robert, Ein-Dor, Philip, Becker, Jörg, Bodendorf, Freimut, and Weinhardt, Christoph, editors, *Proceedings of the Thirteenth European Conference on Information Systems (ECIS)*, Regensburg, Germany.

Ehrig, Marc, Haase, Peter, Staab, Steffen, and Tempich, Christoph (2003a). SWAP – a semantics-based peer-to-peer system. In Gronau, Norbert and Benger, Alf, editors, *Proceedings of JXTA Workshop - Potenziale, Konzepte, Anwendungen*, pages 85–90, Berlin.

Ehrig, Marc, Haase, Peter, van Harmelen, Frank, Siebes, Ronny, Staab, Steffen, Stuckenschmidt, Heiner, Studer, Rudi, and Tempich, Christoph (2003b). The SWAP data and metadata model for semantics-based peer-to-peer systems. In Schillo, Michael, Klusch, Matthias, Müller, Jörg, and Tianfeld, Huaglory, editors, *Proceedings of the First German Conference on Multiagent Technologies (MATES-2003)*, volume 2831 of *Lecture Notes in Artificial Intelligence*, pages 144–155, Erfurt, Germany. Springer.

Ehrig, Marc and Staab, Steffen (2004a). Efficiency of ontology mapping approaches. In *International Workshop on Semantic Intelligent Middleware for the Web and the Grid at ECAI-04*, pages 47–61, Valencia, Spain.

Ehrig, Marc and Staab, Steffen (2004b). QOM – quick ontology mapping. In van Harmelen et al. (2004), pages 683–696.

Ehrig, Marc and Staab, Steffen (2005). Satisficing ontology mapping. In Staab and Stuckenschmidt (2005), chapter 11, pages 215–232.

Ehrig, Marc, Staab, Steffen, and Sure, York (2005b). Bootstrapping ontology alignment methods with APFEL. In Gil et al. (2005), pages 186–200.

Ehrig, Marc, Staab, Steffen, and Sure, York (2005c). Supervised learning of an ontology alignment process. In Althoff et al. (2005).

Ehrig, Marc, Staab, Steffen, Tempich, Christoph, van Harmelen, Frank, Stuckenschmidt, Heiner, Sabou, Marta, Siebes, Ronny, and Broekstra, Jeen (2003c). SWAP: Ontology-based knowledge management with peer-to-peer. In Reimer, Ulrich, Abecker, Andreas, Staab, Steffen, and Stumme, Gert, editors, *Workshop ontologiebasiertes Wissensmanagement at WM-2003*, volume P-28 of *Lecture Notes in Informatics*, pages 17–20, Lucerne, Switzerland. Gesellschaft für Informatik.

Ehrig, Marc and Studer, Rudi (2006). Wissensintegration mit Ontologien. In Blumauer, Andreas and Pellegrini, Tassilo, editors, *Semantic Web - Auf dem Weg zur vernetzten Wissensgesellschaft*. Springer.

Ehrig, Marc and Sure, York (2004a). Ontology mapping - an integrated approach. In Bussler et al. (2004), pages 76–91.

Ehrig, Marc and Sure, York (2004b). Ontology mapping - an integrated approach. Rote Reihe 427, Institut AIFB, Universität Karlsruhe (TH).

Ehrig, Marc and Sure, York (2005a). Active ontology alignment. In *Proceedings of the Collaboration Workshop for the Future Semantic Web at ESWC-2005*, Heraklion, Greece.

Ehrig, Marc and Sure, York (2005b). Adaptive semantic integration. In *Proceedings of the ODBIS workshop at the 31st VLDB Conference*, Trondheim, Norway.

Ehrig, Marc and Sure, York (2005c). FOAM - framework for ontology alignment and mapping, results of the ontology alignment evaluation initiative. In Ashpole et al. (2005), pages 72–76.

Ehrig, Marc and Sure, York (2005d). Ontology mapping by axioms (OMA). In Althoff et al. (2005).

Erdmann, Michael (2001). *Ontologien zur konzeptuellen Modellierung der Semantik von XML*. Books on Demand. PhD Thesis.

Ester, Martin and Sander, Jörg (2000). *Knowledge Discovery und Data Mining: Techniken und Andwendungen*. Springer.

Euzenat, Jérôme (2004). An API for ontology alignment. In van Harmelen et al. (2004), pages 698–712.

Euzenat, Jérôme, Ehrig, Marc, and Castro, Raúl García (2005). Knowledge Web deliverable D2.2.2: Specification of a benchmarking methodology for alignment techniques. Technical report.

Euzenat, Jérôme, Maynard, Diana, Stamou, Giorgos, Stuckenschmidt, Heiner, Zaihrayeu, Ilya, Barrasa, Jesús, Hauswirth, Manfred, Ehrig, Marc, Jarrar, Mustafa, Bouquet, Paolo, Shvaiko, Pavel, Dieng-Kuntz, Rose, Hernández, Rubén Lara, Tessaris, Sergio, Acker, Sven Van, and Bach, Thanh-Le (2004). Knowledge Web deliverable D2.2.3: State fo the art on ontology alignment. Technical report.

Euzenat, Jérôme, Scharffe, François, and Serafini, Luciano (2006). Knowledge Web deliverable D2.2.6: Specification of the delivery alignment format. Technical report.

Euzenat, Jérôme and Valtchev, Petko (2003). An integrative proximity measure for ontology alignment. In Doan, AnHai, Halevy, Alon, and Noy, Natasha F., editors, *Proceedings of the Semantic Integration Workshop at ISWC-2003*, pages 33–38, Sanibel Island, FL, USA.

Euzenat, Jérôme and Valtchev, Petko (2004). Similarity-based ontology alignment in OWL-lite. In de Mántaras and Saitta (2004), pages 333–337.

Fellbaum, Christiane (1998). *WordNet: An Electronic Lexical Database*. Bradford Books.

Fensel, Dieter and Bussler, Chris (2002). The web service modeling framework WSMF. *Electronic Commerce: Research and Applications*, 1:113–137.

Fluit, Christiaan, Sabou, Marta, and van Harmelen, Frank (2004). Supporting user tasks through visualisation of light-weight ontologies. In Staab, Steffen and Studer, Rudi, editors, *Handbook on Ontologies in Information Systems*, International Handbooks on Information Systems. Springer.

Friedman, Marc, Levy, Alon, and Millstein, Todd (1999). Navigational plans for data integration. In *Proceedings of the 16th National Conference on Artificial Intelligence*, pages 67–73. AAAI Press.

Frohn, Jürgen, Himmeröder, Rainer, Kandzia, Paul-Th., and Schlepphorst, Christian (1996). How to write F–Logic programs in FLORID. A tutorial for the database language F–Logic. Technical report, Institut für Informatik der Universität Freiburg. Version 1.0.

Fürst, Frédéric and Trichet, Francky (2005). Axiom-based ontology matching: a method and an experiment. Technical report, Laboratoire d'Informatique de Nantes Atlantique.

Gangemi, Aldo (2005). Ontology design patterns for Semantic Web content. In Gil et al. (2005), pages 262–276.

Gangemi, Aldo, Guarino, Nicola, Masolo, Claudio, Oltramari, Alessandro, and Schneider, Luc (2002). Sweetening ontologies with DOLCE. In Benjamins and Gómez-Pérez (2002), pages 166–181.

Ganter, Bernhard and Wille, Rudolph (1999). *Formal Concept Analysis: Mathematical Foundations*. Springer.

Gil, Yolanda, Motta, Enrico, and Benjamins, V. Richard, editors (2005). *Proceedings of the Fourth International Semantic Web Conference (ISWC-2005)*, volume 3729 of *Lecture Notes in Computer Science*, Galway, Ireland. Springer.

Giunchiglia, Fausto, Shvaiko, Pavel, and Yatskevich, Mikalai (2004). S-match: an algorithm and an implementation of semantic matching. In Bussler et al. (2004), pages 61–75.

Goldstone, Robert L. (2001). Similarity. In Wilson, Robert A. and Keil, Frank C., editors, *The MIT Encyclopedia of the Cognitive Sciences (MITECS)*. MIT Press, Cambridge, MA, USA.

Gómez-Pérez, Asunción and Euzenat, Jérôme, editors (2005). *Second European Semantic Web Conference (ESWC-2005)*, volume 3532 of *Lecture Notes in Computer Science*, Heraklion, Greece. Springer.

Gómez-Pérez, Asuncíon, Fernández-López, M., and Corcho, Oskar (2003). *Ontological Engineering*. Advanced Information and Knowlege Processing. Springer.

Gong, Li (2001). Project JXTA: A technology overview. Technical report, Sun Microsystems Inc.

Gruber, Tom R. (1995). Toward Principles for the Design of Ontologies Used for Knowledge Sharing. *International Journal of Human-Computer Studies*, 43(5/6):907–928.

Guarino, Nicola (1997). Understanding, building and using ontologies. *International Journal of Human and Computer Studies*, 46(2/3):293–310.

Haase, Peter, Broekstra, Jeen, Ehrig, Marc, Menken, Maarten, Mika, Peter, Plechawski, Michal, Pyszlak, Pawel, Schnizler, Björn, Siebes, Ronny, Staab, Steffen, and Tempich, Christoph (2004a). Bibster – a semantics-based bibliographic peer-to-peer system. In van Harmelen et al. (2004), pages 122–136.

Haase, Peter and Motik, Boris (2005). A mapping system for the integration of OWL-DL ontologies. In *Proceedings of the ACM-Workshop: Interoperability of Heterogeneous Information Systems (IHIS05)*, Bremen, Germany.

Haase, Peter, Schnizler, Björn, Broekstra, Jeen, Ehrig, Marc, van Harmelen, Frank, Menken, Maarten, Mika, Peter, Plechawski, Michal, Pyszlak, Pawel, Siebes, Ronny, Staab, Steffen, and Tempich, Christoph (2004b). Bibster – a semantics-based bibliographic peer-to-peer system. *Journal of Web Semantics*, 2(1):99–103.

Haase, Peter, Schnizler, Björn, Broekstra, Jeen, Ehrig, Marc, van Harmelen, Frank, Menken, Maarten, Mika, Peter, Plechawski, Michal, Pyszlak, Pawel, Siebes, Ronny, Staab, Steffen, and Tempich, Christoph (2005). Bibster – a semantics-based bibliographic peer-to-peer system. In Staab and Stuckenschmidt (2005), chapter 18, pages 347–362.

Haase, Peter, Siebes, Ronny, and van Harmelen, Frank (2004c). Peer selection in peer-to-peer networks with semantic topologies. In Bouzeghoub, Mokrane, Goble, Carole A., Kashyap, Vipul, and Spaccapietra, Stefano, editors, *Semantics for Grid Databases, First International IFIP Conference on Semantics of a Networked World (ICSNW-04)*, volume 3226 of *Lecture Notes in Computer Science*, pages 108–125, Paris, France. Springer.

Haase, Peter and Stojanovic, Ljiljana (2005). Consistent evolution of OWL ontologies. In Gómez-Pérez and Euzenat (2005), pages 182–197.

Hahn, Axel, Abels, Sven, and Haak, Liane, editors (2005). *Proceedings of the Workshop Semantic Model Integration (SMI05) at Dritte Konferenz Professionelles Wissensmanagement*, Kaiserslautern, Germany. DFKI.

Hanley, James A. and McNeil, Barbara J. (1982). The meaning and use of the area under the Receiver Operating Characteristic (ROC) curve. *Radiology*, 143(1):29–36.

Harman, Donna K., editor (1992). *NIST Special Publication 500-207: The First Text REtrieval Conference (TREC-1)*, Gaithersburg, MD, USA. Department of Commerce, National Institute of Standards and Technology.

Hernández, Mauricio A. and Stolfo, Salvatore J. (1998). Real-world data is dirty: Data cleansing and the merge/purge problem. *Data Mining and Knowledge Discovery*, 2(1):9–37.

Hitzler, Pascal, Krötzsch, Markus, Ehrig, Marc, and Sure, York (2005). What is ontology merging? A category-theoretical perspective using pushouts. In Shvaiko, Pavel, Euzenat, Jérôme, Leger, Alain, McGuinness, Deborah L., and Wache, Holger, editors, *Proceedings of the First International Work-*

shop on Contexts and Ontologies: Theory, Practice and Applications (C&O) at *AAAI-05*, pages 104–107. AAAI Press.

Hitzler, Pascal and Vrandecic, Denny (2005). Resolution-based approximate reasoning for OWL-DL. In Gil et al. (2005), pages 383–397.

Horrocks, Ian (1998). Using an Expressive Description Logic: FaCT or Fiction? In Cohn, Anthony G., Schubert, Lenhard K., and Shapiro, Stuart C., editors, *Proceedings of the Sixth International Conference on Principles of Knowledge Representation and Reasoning (KR'98)*, pages 636–647, Trento, Italy. Morgan Kaufmann Publishers.

Horrocks, Ian and Hendler, Jim, editors (2002). *Proceedings of the International Semantic Web Conference: The Semantic Web (ISWC-2002)*, volume 2342 of *Lecture Notes in Computer Science*, Sardinia, Italy. Springer.

Horrocks, Ian and Patel-Schneider, Peter F. (2004). A proposal for an OWL rules language. In Feldman, Stuart I., Uretsky, Mike, Najork, Marc, and Wills, Craig E., editors, *Proceedings of the 13th International World Wide Web Conference (WWW-2004)*, pages 723–731, New York, NY, USA. ACM Press.

Hotho, Andreas, Staab, Steffen, and Stumme, Gerd (2003). Ontologies improve text document clustering. In *Proceedings of the International Conference on Data Mining (ICDM-03)*, pages 541–544, Melbourne, FL, USA. IEEE Press.

Hu, Wei, Jian, Ningsheng, Qu, Yuzhong, and Wang, Yanbing (2005). GMO: A graph matching for ontologies. In Ashpole et al. (2005), pages 41–48.

Huang, Zhisheng, van Harmelen, Frank, and ten Teije, Annette (2005). Reasoning with inconsistent ontologies. In Saffiotti et al. (2005), pages 454–459.

Hughes, Todd, editor (2004). *Proceedings of the Information Interpretation and Integration Conference (I3CON) at PerMIS-04*, Gaithersburg, MD, USA.

Hustadt, Ullrich, Motik, Boris, and Sattler, Ulrike (2004a). Reasoning in Description Logics with a Concrete Domain in the Framework of Resolution. In de Mántaras and Saitta (2004), pages 353–357.

Hustadt, Ullrich, Motik, Boris, and Sattler, Ulrike (2004b). Reducing SHIQ-description logic to disjunctive datalog programs. In Dubois, Didier, Welty, Christopher A., and Williams, Mary-Anne, editors, *Proceedings of Ninth International Conference on Knowledge Representation and Reasoning (KR-04)*, pages 152–162, Whistler, Canada. AAAI Press.

Jannink, Jan, Pichai, Srinivasan, Verheijen, Danladi, and Wiederhold, Gio (1998). Encapsulation and composition of ontologies. In *Proceedings of th AAAI Workshop on Information Integration, AAAI Summer Conference*, Madison, WI, USA.

Kalfoglou, Yannis and Schorlemmer, Marco (2002). Information-flow-based ontology mapping. In Meersman and Tari (2002), pages 1132–1151.

Kalfoglou, Yannis and Schorlemmer, Marco (2003). Ontology mapping: the state of the art. *Knowledge Engineering Review*, 18(1):1–31.

Kan, Gene (2001). Gnutella. In Oram (2001), pages 94–122.

Kashyap, Vipul and Sheth, Amit P. (1996). Semantic and schematic similarities between database objects: A context-based approach. *VLDB Journal: Very Large Data Bases*, 5(4):276–304.

Keeny, Ralph L. and Raiffa, Howard (1976). *Decisions with multiple objectives: Preferences and value tradeoffs*. Wiley, New York.

Kent, Robert E. (2000). The information flow foundation for conceptual knowledge organization. In Beghtol, Clare, Howarth, Lynne C., and Williamson, Nancy J., editors, *Dynamism and Stability in Knowledge Organization: Proceedings of the Sixth International Conference of the International Society in Information Systems (ISKO)*, Toronto, Canada. Ergon-Verlag.

Kifer, Michael, Lausen, Georg, and Wu, James (1995). Logical foundations of object-oriented and frame-based languages. *Journal of the ACM*, 42(4):741–843.

Kifer, Michael and Lozinskii, Eliezer L. (1986). A framework for an efficient implementation of deductive databases. In *Proceedings of the 6th Advanced Database Symposium*, pages 109–116, Tokyo.

Klein, Michel (2001). Combining and relating ontologies: an analysis of problems and solutions. In Gómez-Pérez, Asuncíon, Gruninger, Michael, Stuckenschmidt, Heiner, and Uschold, Michael, editors, *Proceedings of Workshop on Ontologies and Information Sharing at IJCAI-01*, Seattle, WA, USA.

Klein, Michel C. A., Fensel, Dieter, Kiryakov, Atanas, and Ognyanov, Damyan (2002). Ontology versioning and change detection on the web. In Benjamins and Gómez-Pérez (2002), pages 197–212.

Korpela, Eric, Werthimer, Dan, Anderson, David, Cobb, Jeff, and Lebofsky, Matt (2001). SETI@home - massively distributed computing for SETI. *Computing in Science and Engineering*, 3(1):78–83.

Koschmider, Agnes and Oberweis, Andreas (2005). Ontology based business process description. In Castro, Jaelson and Teniente, Ernest, editors, *Proceedings of the CAiSE-05 Workshops*, number 2, pages 321–333, Porto, Portugal.

Lamparter, Steffen, Ehrig, Marc, and Tempich, Christoph (2004). Knowledge extraction from classifiaction schemas. In Meersman, Robert and Tari, Zahir, editors, *On the Move to Meaningful Internet Systems 2004: CoopIS, DOA, and ODBASE, OTM Confederated International Conferences, Proceedings, Part I*, volume 3290 of *Lecture Notes in Computer Science*, pages 618–636, Agia Napa, Cyprus. Springer.

Lara, Rubén, Lausen, Holger, Arroyo, Sinuhé, de Bruijn, Jos, and Fensel, Dieter (2003). Semantic Web Services: description requirements and current technologies. In *Semantic Web Services for Enterprise Application Integration and e-Commerce workshop (SWSEE-03) at ICEC-03*, Pittsburgh, PA, USA.

Levenshtein, I. Vladimir (1965). Binary codes capable of correcting deletions, insertions, and reversals. *Doklady Akademii Nauk SSSR*, 163(4):845–848.

Li, Wen-Syan and Clifton, Chris (1994). Semantic integration in heterogeneous databases using neural networks. In Bocca, Jorge B., Jarke, Matthias, and Zaniolo, Carlo, editors, *Proceedings of 20th International Conference on Very Large Data Bases (VLDB-94)*, pages 1–12, Santiago de Chile, Chile. Morgan Kaufmann Publishers.

Luhmann, Niklas (1987). *Soziale Systeme.* Suhrkamp.

Madhavan, Jayant, Bernstein, Philip A., and Rahm, Erhard (2001). Generic schema matching with Cupid. In *Proceedings of the 27th International Conference on Very Large Data Bases (VLDB-01)*, pages 49–58, San Francisco, CA, USA. Morgan Kaufmann Publishers.

Maedche, Alexander, Motik, Boris, Silva, Nuno, and Volz, Raphael (2002). MAFRA – a MApping FRamework for distributed ontologies. In Benjamins and Gómez-Pérez (2002), pages 235–250.

Maedche, Alexander and Staab, Steffen (2001). Ontology learning for the Semantic Web. *IEEE Intelligent Systems*, 16(2):72–79.

Maedche, Alexander and Staab, Steffen (2002). Measuring similarity between ontologies. In Benjamins and Gómez-Pérez (2002), pages 251–263.

Maier, Andreias, Schnurr, Hans-Peter, and Sure, York (2003). Ontology-based information integration in the automotive industry. In Fensel, Dieter, Sycara, Katia, and Mylopoulos, John, editors, *Proceedings of the Second International Semantic Web Conference: The Semantic Web (ISWC-2003)*, volume 2870 of *Lecture Notes in Computer Science*, pages 897–912, Sanibel Island, FL, USA. Springer.

McCann, Robert, AlShebli, Bedoor K., Le, Quoc, Nguyen, Hoa, Vu, Long, and Doan, AnHai (2005). Mapping maintenance for data integration systems. In Böhm et al. (2005), pages 1018–1030.

McGuinness, Deborah L. (2000). Conceptual modeling for distributed ontology environments. In Ganter, Bernhard and Mineau, Guy W., editors, *Conceptual Structures: Logical, Linguistic, and Computational Issues, Proceedings of the Eigth International Conference on Conceptual Structures (ICCS-2000)*, volume 1867 of *Lecture Notes in Computer Science*, pages 100–112. Springer.

McGuinness, Deborah L., Fikes, Richard, Rice, James, and Wilder, Steve (2000). The Chimaera ontology environment. In *Proceedings of the 17th National Conference on Artificial Intelligence and Twelfth Conference on on Innovative Applications of Artificial Intelligence*, pages 1123–1124, Austin, TX, USA. AAAI Press / The MIT Press.

Meersman, Robert and Tari, Zahir, editors (2002). *On the Move to Meaningful Internet Systems, 2002 - DOA/CoopIS/ODBASE 2002 Confederated International Conferences Proceedings*, volume 2519 of *Lecture Notes in Artificial Intelligence*, Irvine, CA, USA. Springer.

Meersman, Robert, Tari, Zahir, and Stevens, Scott, editors (1999). *Database Semantics: Semantic Issues in Multimedia Systems*. Kluwer Academic Publisher, Boston.

Melnik, Sergej, Garcia-Molina, Hector, and Rahm, Erhard (2002). Similarity flooding: A versatile graph matching algorithm and its application to schema matching. In *Proceedings of the 18th International Conference on Data Engineering (ICDE-2002)*, page 117. IEEE Computer Society.

Melnik, Sergey, Rahm, Erhard, and Bernstein, Philip A. (2003). Rondo: A programming platform for generic model management. In *Proceedings of the 2003 ACM SIGMOD International Conference on Management of Data (SIGMOD-03)*, pages 193–204, San Diego, CA, USA. ACM Press.

Michelson, Matthew and Knoblock, Craig A. (2005). Semantic annotation of unstructured and ungrammatical text. In Saffiotti et al. (2005).

Mitra, Prasenjit and Wiederhold, Gio (2001). An ontology-composition algebra. Technical report, Stanford University, Stanford, CA, USA.

Mitra, Prasenjit and Wiederhold, Gio (2002). Resolving terminological heterogeneity in ontologies. In *Proceedings of the Workshop on Ontologies and Semantic Interoperability at ECAI-02*, Lyon, France.

Mitra, Prasenjit, Wiederhold, Gio, and Kersten, Martin (2000). A graph-oriented model for articulation of ontology interdependencies. In *Proceedings of the Conference on Extending Database Technology 2000 (EDBT-00)*, volume 1777 of *Lecture Notes in Computer Science*, pages 86+, Konstanz, Germany. Springer.

Nejdl, Wolfgang, Wolf, Boris, Qu, Changtao, Decker, Stefan, Sintek, Michael, Naeve, Ambjörn, Nilsson, Mikael, Palmér, Matthias, and Risch, Tore (2002). EDUTELLA: A P2P networking infrastructure based on RDF. In www (2002), pages 604–615.

Niles, Ian and Pease, Adam (2001). Towards a standard upper ontology. In *Proceedings of the Second International Conference on Formal Ontology in Information Systems (FOIS 2001)*, pages 2–9, Ogunquit, ME, USA. ACM Press.

Noy, Natasha and Rector, Alan (2004). Defining n-ary relations on the Semantic Web: Use with individuals. W3C Working Draft 21 July.

Noy, Natasha F. and Musen, Mark A. (1999). SMART: Automated support for ontology merging and alignment. In *Proceedings of the Twelfth Workshop on Knowledge Acquisition, Modeling, and Management*, Banff, AB, Canada.

Noy, Natasha F. and Musen, Mark A. (2000). PROMPT: Algorithm and tool for automated ontology merging and alignment. In *Proceedings of the Seventeenth National Conference on Artificial Intelligence (AAAI-2000)*, pages 450–455, Austin, TX, USA. AAAI Press / The MIT Press.

Noy, Natasha F. and Musen, Mark A. (2001). Anchor-PROMPT: Using non-local context for semantic matching. In *Workshop on Ontologies and Information Sharing at the 17th International Joint Conference on Artificial Intelligence (IJCAI-2001)*, pages 63–70, Seattle, WA, USA.

Noy, Natasha F. and Musen, Mark A. (2002). PromptDiff: a fixed-point algorithm for comparing ontology versions. In *Proceedings of the 18th National Conference on Artificial Intelligence (AAAI-02)*, pages 744–750, Edmonton, AB, Canada. AAAI Press.

Noy, Natasha F. and Musen, Mark A. (2003). The PROMPT suite: interactive tools for ontology merging and mapping. *International Journal of Human-Computer Studies*, 59(6):983–1024.

Noy, Natasha F., Sintek, Michael, Decker, Stefan, Crubézy, Monica, Fergerson, Ray W., and Musen, Mark A. (2001). Creating Semantic Web contents with Protégé-2000. *IEEE Intelligent Systems*, 16(2):60–71.

Ontoprise (2004). *How to Write F-Logic Programs – A Tutorial for the Language F-Logic*. Tutorial version 1.9 that covers Ontobroker version 3.5.

Oram, Andy, editor (2001). *Peer-to-Peer: Harnessing the Benefits of a Disruptive Technology*. OReilly, Sebastopol, CA, USA.

Palopoli, Luigi, Terracina, Giorgio, and Ursino, Domenico (2000). The system DIKE: Towards the semi-automatic synthesis of cooperative information systems and data warehouses. In *Symposium on Advances in Databases and Information Systems (ADBIS-DASFAA)*, pages 108–117, Prague, Czech Republic. Matfyzpress.

Patel-Schneider, Peter F., Hayes, Patrick, and Horrocks, Ian (2004). OWL web ontology language semantics and abstract syntax. W3C Recommendation 10 February.

Peterson, James Lyle (1981). *Petri Net Theory and the Modeling of Systems*. Prentice Hall PTR, Upper Saddle River, NJ, USA.

Pinto, H. Sofia, Staab, Steffen, Tempich, Christoph, and Sure, York (2004a). DILIGENT: Towards a fine-grained methodology for DIstributed, Looselycontrolled and evolvInG Engineering of oNTologies. In de Mántaras and Saitta (2004), pages 393–397.

Pinto, Sofia, Staab, Steffen, Sure, York, and Tempich, Christoph (2004b). OntoEdit empowering SWAP: a case study in supporting DIstributed, Looselycontrolled and evolvInG Engineering of oNTologies (DILIGENT). In Bussler et al. (2004), pages 16–30.

Popa, Lucian, Velegrakis, Yannis, Miller, Renée J., Hernández, Mauricio A., and Fagin, Ronald (2002). Translating web data. In Bernstein et al. (2002), pages 598–609.

Porter, Martin F. (1980). An algorithm for suffix stripping. *Program*, 14(3):130–137.

Probst, Gilbert J. B., Raub, Steffen, and Romhardt, Kai (1998). *Wissen managen*. Gabler Verlag, Wiesbaden.

Quillan, M. Ross (1967). Word concepts: A theory and simulation of some basic capabilities. *Behavioral Science*, 12:410–430.

Rada, Roy, Mili, Hafedh, Bicknell, Ellen, and Blettner, Maria (1989). Development and application of a metric on semantic nets. *IEEE Transactions on Systems, Man and Cybernetics*, 19(1):17–30.

Rahm, Erhard and Bernstein, Philip A. (2001). A survey of approaches to automatic schema matching. *VLDB Journal: Very Large Data Bases*, 10(4):334–350.

Ren, Pengyun (2005). Complex ontology mapping. Master's thesis, Institut AIFB, Universität Karlsruhe (TH), Karlsruhe, Germany.

Rodríguez, M. Andrea and Egenhofer, Max J. (2000). Determining semantic similarity among entity classes from different ontologies. *IEEE Transactions on Knowledge and Data Engineering*.

Rufai, Raimi Ayinde (2003). Similarity metric for UML models. Master's thesis, King Fahd University of Petroleum and Minerals, Saudi-Arabia.

Saar-Tsechansky, Maytal and Provost, Foster J. (2001). Active learning for class probability estimation and ranking. In Nebel, Bernhard, editor, *Proceedings of the Seventeenth International Joint Conference on Artificial Intelligence (IJCAI 2001)*, pages 911–920, Seattle, WA, USA. Morgan Kaufmann Publishers.

Saffiotti, Alessandro, Guestrin, Carlos, and Givan, Robert, editors (2005). *Proceedings of the 19th International Joint Conference on Artificial Intelligence (IJCAI-05)*, Edinburgh, UK. Morgan Kaufmann Publishers.

Sayyadian, Mayssam, Lee, Yoonkyong, Doan, AnHai, and Rosenthal, Arnon (2005). Tuning schema matching software using synthetic scenarios. In Böhm et al. (2005), pages 994–1005.

Sheth, Amit (1991). Issues in schema integration: Perspective of an industrial researcher. Presented at the ARO-Workshop on Heterogeneous Databases.

Shvaiko, Pavel and Euzenat, Jérôme (2005). A survey of schema-based matching approaches. *Journal on Data Semantics (JoDS)*, 3730(IV):146–171.

Shvaiko, Pavel, Giunchiglia, Fausto, da Silva, Paulo Pinheiro, and McGuinness, Deborah (2005). Web explanations for semantic heterogeneity discovery. In Gómez-Pérez and Euzenat (2005), pages 303–317.

Smith, Michael K., Welty, Chris, and McGuinness, Deborah L. (2004). OWL Web Ontology Language Guide. W3C Recommendation 10 February 2004.

Staab, Steffen and Stuckenschmidt, Heiner, editors (2005). *Semantic Web and Peer-to-Peer*. Springer.

Stoilos, Giorgos, Stamou, Giorgos B., and Kollias, Stefanos D. (2005). A string metric for ontology alignment. In Gil et al. (2005), pages 624–637.

Stojanovic, Ljiljana, Maedche, Alexander, Motik, Boris, and Stojanovic, Nenad (2002). User-driven Ontology Evolution Management. In Meersman and Tari (2002), pages 285–300.

Stojanovic, Ljiljana (2004). *Methods and Tools for Ontology Evolution*. PhD thesis, Institut AIFB, Universität Karlsruhe (TH), Karlsruhe, Germany.

Stojanovic, Nenad (2005). *Semantic Query Expansion*. PhD thesis, Institut AIFB, Universität Karlsruhe (TH), Karlsruhe, Germany.

Straccia, Umberto (2005). Towards a fuzzy description logic for the Semantic Web (preliminary report). In Gómez-Pérez and Euzenat (2005), pages 167–181.

Strawson, Peter F. and Bubner, Rüdiger (1975). *Semantik und Ontologie*. Vandenhoeck & Ruprecht.

Studer, Rudi, Benjamins, V. Richard, and Fensel, Dieter (1998). Knowledge engineering principles and methods. *Data and Knowledge Engineering*, 25(1–2):161–197.

Stumme, Gerd, Ehrig, Marc, Handschuh, Siegfried, Hotho, Andreas, Maedche, Alexander, Motik, Boris, Oberle, Daniel, Schmitz, Christoph, Staab, Steffen, Stojanovic, Ljiljana, Stojanovic, Nenad, Studer, Rudi, Sure, York, Volz, Raphael, and Zacharias, Valentin (2003). The Karlsruhe view on ontologies. Technical report, Institut AIFB, Universität Karlsruhe (TH), Karlsruhe, Germany.

Stumme, Gerd and Maedche, Alexander (2001). FCA-Merge: Bottom-up merging of ontologies. In *Proceedings of the International Joint Conference on Artificial Intelligence (IJCAI 2001)*, pages 225–230, Seattle, WA, USA.

Sure, York (2003). *Methodology, Tools and Case Studies for Ontology based Knowledge Management*. PhD thesis, Institut AIFB, Universität Karlsruhe (TH), Karlsruhe, Germany.

Sure, York, Angele, Jürgen, and Staab, Steffen (2003). Ontoedit: Multifaceted inferencing for ontology engineering. *Journal on Data Semantics*, 2800:128–152.

Sure, York, Bloehdorn, Stephan, Haase, Peter, Hartmann, Jens, and Oberle, Daniel (2005). The SWRC ontology – Semantic Web for research communities. In *Workshop on Building and Applying Ontologies for the Semantic Web (BAOSW 2005) at the 12th Portuguese Conference on Artificial Intelligence (EPIA 2005)*.

Sure, York, Corcho, Oscar, Euzenat, Jérôme, and Hughes, Todd, editors (2004). *Proceedings of the Third Workshop on Evaluation of Ontology-based Tools (EON-2004) at ISWC-2004*, volume 128 of *CEUR Workshop Proceedings*, Hiroshima, Japan. CEUR-WS Publication.

Sure, York, Erdmann, Michael, Angele, Jürgen, Staab, Steffen, and Wenke, Dirk (2002). Ontoedit: Collaborative ontology engineering for the Semantic Web. In Horrocks and Hendler (2002), pages 221–235.

Tempich, Christoph, Ehrig, Marc, Fluit, Christiaan, Haase, Peter, Martí, Esteve Lladó, Plechawski, Michal, and Staab, Steffen (2004). XAROP: A midterm report in introducing a decentralized semantics-based knowledge sharing application. In Karagiannis, Dimitris and Reimer, Ulrich, editors, *Proceedings of the Fifth International Conference on Practical Aspects of Knowledge Management (PAKM 2004)*, volume 3336 of *Lecture Notes in Computer Science*, Vienna, Austria. Springer.

Tempich, Christoph, Tane, Julien, Staab, Steffen, Ehrig, Marc, and Schmitz, Christoph (2003). Towards evaluation of peer-to-peer-based distributed information management systems. In van Elst, Ludger, Dignum, Virginia, and Abecker, Andreas, editors, *Agent-mediated Knowledge Management (AMKM-2003), AAAI Spring Symposium 2003, Stanford, March 24-26*, volume 2926 of *Lecture Notes in Computer Science*, pages 73–88, Stanford, CA, USA. Springer.

Tempich, Christoph and Volz, Raphael (2003). Towards a benchmark for Semantic Web reasoners - an analysis of the DAML ontology library. In Sure, York, Angele, Jürgen, and Corcho, Oscar, editors, *Proceedings of the Second International Workshop on Evaluation of Ontology-based Tools*

(EON-2003) at ISWC-2003, volume 87 of *CEUR Workshop Proceedings*, Sanibel Island, Florida, USA. CEUR-WS Publication.

Ullman, Jeffrey D. (1997). Information integration using logical views. In Afrati, Foto N. and Kolaitis, Phokion G., editors, *Proceedings of the Sixth International Conference on Database Theory (ICDT-97)*, volume 1186 of *Lecture Notes in Computer Science*, pages 19–40, Delphi, Greece. Springer.

Valtchev, Petko (1999). *Construction automatique de taxonomies pour l'aide à la représentation de connaissances par objects*. PhD thesis, Université Joseph Fourier, Grenoble, France.

van Gelder, Allen (1993). The alternating fixpoint of logic programs with negation. *Journal of Computer and System Sciences*, 47(1):185–221.

van Gelder, Allen, Ross, Kenneth A., and Schlipf, John S. (1991). The well-founded semantics for general logic programs. *Journal of the ACM*, 38(3):620–650.

van Harmelen, Frank, McIlraith, Sheila, and Plexousakis, Dimitris, editors (2004). *Proceedings of the Third International Semantic Web Conference (ISWC-2004)*, volume 3298 of *Lecture Notes in Computer Science*, Hiroshima, Japan. Springer.

van Heijst, Gertjan, Schreiber, August Th., and Wielinga, Bob J. (1997). Using explicit ontologies in KBS development. *International Journal of Human and Computer Studies*, 46(2/3):183–292.

van Rijsbergen, Cornelis Joost (1975). *Information retrieval*. Butterworths, London (UK).

Volz, Raphael, Handschuh, Siegfried, Staab, Steffen, Stojanovic, Ljiljana, and Stojanovic, Nenad (2004). Unveiling the hidden bride: deep annotation for mapping and migrating legacy data to the Semantic Web. *Journal of Web Semantics*, 1(2):187–206.

Volz, Raphael, Oberle, Daniel, Staab, Steffen, and Studer, Rudi (2003). WonderWeb deliverable D11: OntoLiFT Prototype. Technical Report 11.

Weinstein, Peter and Birmingham, William P. (1999). Comparing concepts in differentiated ontologies. In *Proceedings of the Twelfth Workshop on Knowledge Acquisition, Modeling and Management (KAW'99)*, Banff, AB, Canada.

Wiederhold, Gio (1994). An algebra for ontology composition. In *Proceedings of 1994 Monterey Workshop on formal Methods*, pages 56–61, U.S. Naval Postgraduate School, Monterey, CA, USA.

Witten, Ian H. and Frank, Eibe (2005). *Data Mining: Practical machine learning tools and techniques*. Morgan Kaufmann Publishers, San Francisco, 2nd edition.

Index